OREGON AND WASHINGTON'S ROADSIDE ECOLOGY

OREGON AND WASHINGTON'S ROADSIDE ECOLOGY

33 EASY WALKS THROUGH THE REGION'S AMAZING NATURAL AREAS

RODDY SCHEER

TIMBER PRESS + PORTLAND, OREGON

To Thoreau, Muir, and Leopold: thanks for pointing me down the right path.

Frontispiece: A mountain hemlock tree hugs the heather- and huckleberry-strewn ridge just off the Fire and Ice Trail near Washington's northernmost Cascade peak, Mount Baker.

Published in 2022 by Timber Press, Inc.

The Haseltine Building
133 S.W. Second Avenue, Suite 450
Portland, Oregon 97204-3527
timberpress.com

Printed in China

Text design by Hillary Caudle
Cover design by Amanda Weiss

ISBN 978-1-64326-041-9

A catalog record for this book is available from the Library of Congress.

CONTENTS

7   INTRODUCTION

OREGON

10   Yaquina Head Outstanding Natural Area

18   Tahkenitch Dunes

26   Dean Creek Elk Viewing Area

34   Rough and Ready Botanical Wayside

44   Limpy Botanical Trail

54   Oregon Caves, Cliff Nature Trail

69   Rogue River Natural Bridge

77   Erratic Rock State Natural Site

84   Camassia Natural Area

92   Salt Creek Falls

100   Trail of the Molten Land

112   Rimrock Trail

122   Clarno Palisades

131   Islands in Time Trail

142   Zumwalt Prairie Preserve

WASHINGTON

152   Kalaloch Beach 4

163   Quinault Rain Forest Nature Trail

181   Hurricane Ridge

192   West Beach Sand Dunes

202   Tideland Ecology Trail

212   Touch of Nature Interpretive Trail

220   Nisqually Vista Trail

228   Magnuson Park Wetlands

239   Traditional Knowledge Trail

246   Layser Cave

252   Billy Frank Jr. Nisqually National Wildlife Refuge

264   Deception Falls Nature Trail

273   Fire and Ice Trail

282   Ginkgo Petrified Forest

290   Dry Falls

301   Pine Lakes Loop Trail

310   Steptoe Butte

317   Palouse Falls

327   LIST OF SPECIES

340   SELECTED REFERENCES

345   ACKNOWLEDGMENTS

347   PHOTOGRAPHY CREDITS

348   INDEX

INTRODUCTION

I have been blessed to live in the Pacific Northwest for the last two decades, and exploring many of the wilder and more remote sections of the region has been my great privilege. But little did I know how much fun it would be to visit all of the accessible roadside attractions covered in this guide—and to flex my ecological-interpretation and photo-documentation muscles in the process.

My only regret is not getting to spend more time exploring these 33 sites—places that represent a diverse cross-section of the different types of ecosystems found in Washington and Oregon. The trails I've highlighted here serve as great introductions to various regions, but I hope to get back and do additional hikes and get deeper into the backcountry in several of the areas I visited. And I hope that you will use the hikes in the book likewise, as jumping-off points for further explorations.

I also hope that reading about the remarkable places in this book will spark an interest in ecology and the natural world, even for those of you who may not ever visit any of the sites covered. Researching and writing this manuscript has been enlightening. I've learned so much about my home region—its bogs, butterflies, ridges, wildflowers, dunes, caves, and coastlines—that I never knew (and I thought I was already an expert). But even more, it's been heartening to see firsthand how so many people have put so much time, energy, and money into restoring and maintaining these prized landscapes. They represent the age-old natural heritage of the Pacific Northwest, now and forever the wildest corner of the Lower 48.

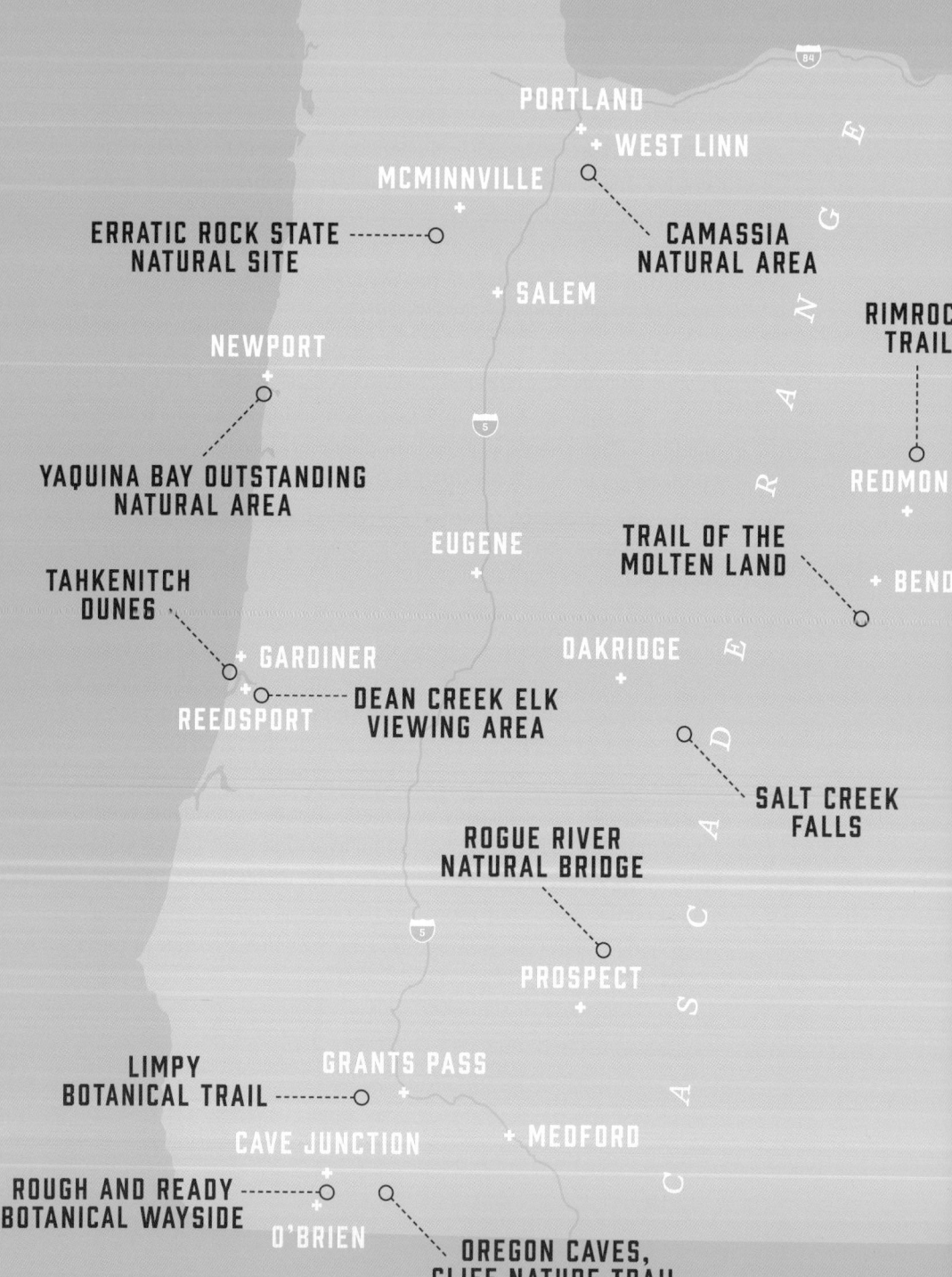

PORTLAND
+
+ WEST LINN

MCMINNVILLE
+

ERRATIC ROCK STATE ------- ○
NATURAL SITE

CAMASSIA
NATURAL AREA

+ SALEM

RIMROCK
TRAIL

NEWPORT
+
○

YAQUINA BAY OUTSTANDING
NATURAL AREA

EUGENE
+

REDMOND
+

TRAIL OF THE
MOLTEN LAND

+ BEND

TAHKENITCH
DUNES

+ GARDINER
○
+ ○ ------- DEAN CREEK ELK
VIEWING AREA

REEDSPORT

OAKRIDGE
+

○

SALT CREEK
FALLS

ROGUE RIVER
NATURAL BRIDGE

○

PROSPECT

LIMPY
BOTANICAL TRAIL -------- ○

GRANTS PASS
+

CAVE JUNCTION
+

+ MEDFORD

ROUGH AND READY -------- ○
BOTANICAL WAYSIDE

○

O'BRIEN

OREGON CAVES,
CLIFF NATURE TRAIL

C A S C A D E   R A N G E

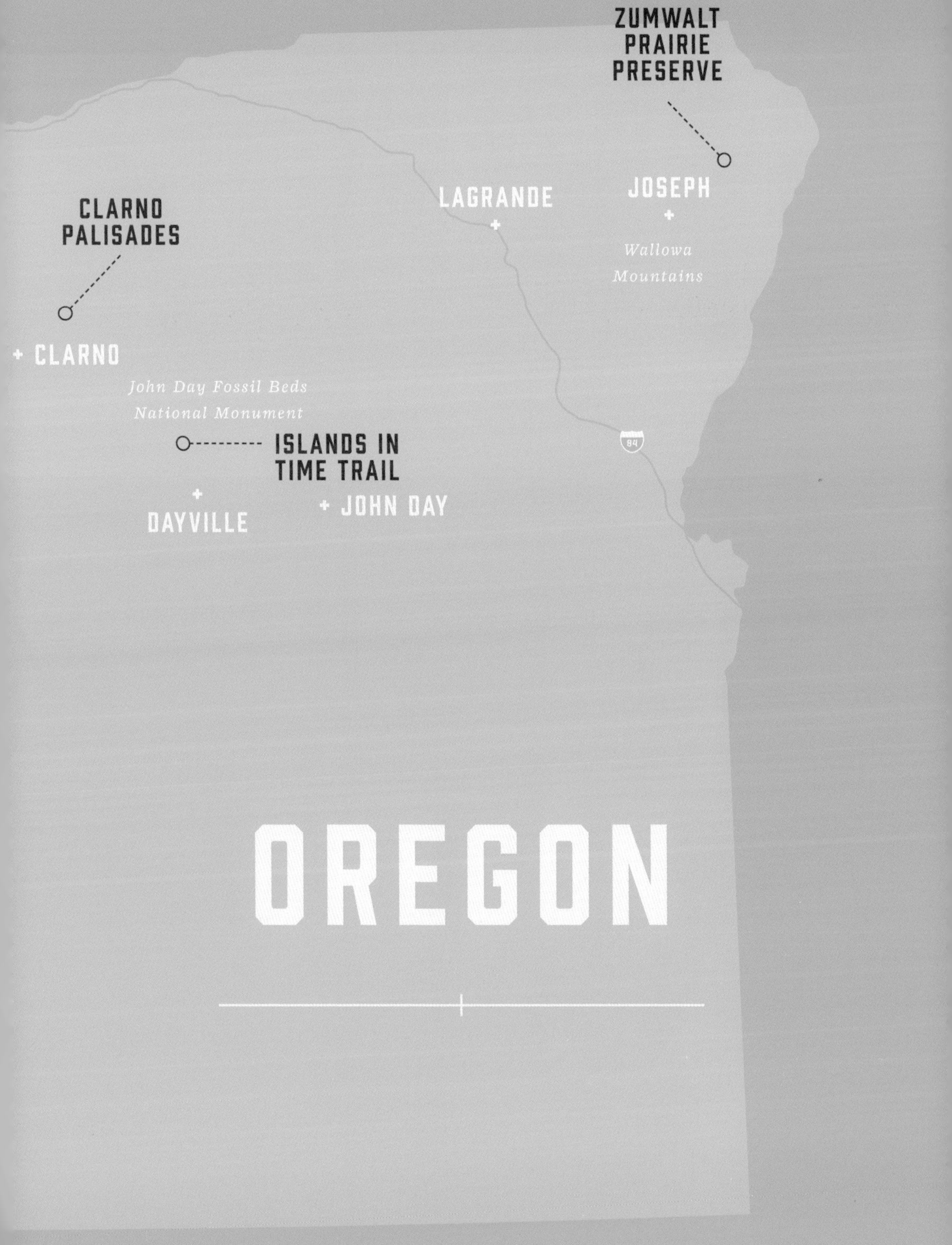

ZUMWALT
PRAIRIE
PRESERVE

CLARNO
PALISADES

LAGRANDE
+

JOSEPH
+

*Wallowa
Mountains*

+ CLARNO

*John Day Fossil Beds
National Monument*

ISLANDS IN
TIME TRAIL

+ JOHN DAY

+
DAYVILLE

84

OREGON

YAQUINA HEAD OUTSTANDING NATURAL AREA

Panoramic vistas, easy tide pool access, and an 1873 lighthouse

DIFFICULTY
Moderate

LOCATION
Newport, Oregon

LENGTH
0.25 to 1 mile

Looking south from Yaquina Head toward Agate Beach.

Jutting out a mile into the Pacific Ocean, Yaquina Head Outstanding Natural Area lies smack dab in the middle of the wild and woolly Oregon coast. This delightful portal is right off Highway 101 and well worth a stop and a leg stretch. If you time it right, you can even tour the 93-foot-tall Yaquina Head Lighthouse and gain a true bird's-eye view of the coastal ecosystems spread out before you.

You could spend a half hour or a full day exploring Yaquina Head, depending on how much ground you want to cover. Five short hiking trails crisscross the 95-acre headland, ensuring that each of the different ecosystems there is accessible. The best time of year to visit is late spring through early fall, when temperatures are mild and the notorious Pacific Northwest drizzle has subsided. That said, hearty raincoat-clad travelers can find plenty to like about visiting here any time of year.

Given the exposed nature of Yaquina Head, watch out for high winds that can yank car doors open and make walking difficult. Watch your step on high cliffsides. If you venture down to the beach or tide pools, stay away from high-surf areas and watch out for sneaker waves (sudden tidal surges that can strike at any time and knock you off your feet into the cold Pacific). Keep kids within arm's reach (and all dogs on leash) and never turn your back on the ocean.

The ground under your feet didn't exist until around 14 million years ago. That's when lava erupted out of inland cracks in Earth's crust and flowed hundreds of miles west, where it met the Pacific Ocean. There it quickly cooled and hardened into the basalt rock that makes up the natural foundation of this mile-long mini-peninsula.

Driftwood, sand, and beach grasses commingle near the shoreline of Quarry Cove.

There are several short hikes on Yaquina Head, each yielding access to surprisingly different ecosystems, given the small amount of land. Start your visit with a 0.25-mile hike down to Quarry Cove, the former site of a rock quarry that was converted back to a more natural setting in 1980, when the Bureau of Land Management took over management of Yaquina Head. While it might not seem like a former rock quarry would be much of a draw for amateur naturalists, au contraire! Shore pines, Sitka willows, Pacific wax myrtle, and salal line the trail on the way down.

Near the bottom, the trail switches back toward the inside of the cozy little cove. The sandy shoreline along the protected inner cove is teeming with a diverse selection of estuarine grasses, sedges, and shrubs. American searocket, beach morning glory, silverweed cinquefoil, smallflower melic, American beachgrass, and Henderson's angelica are just a few of the plants populating this sandy transition zone. When you've had enough peace and tranquility along the shore of this quiet cove, head back up the hill and make your way toward the western tip of Yaquina Head to see the dramatic setting of the lighthouse and its surroundings.

◂ Birdsfoot trefoil (pictured here at Quarry Cove) may look pretty, but this invasive perennial legume is wreaking havoc on ecosystems across the Pacific Northwest by taking over the traditional domains of native plants.

YAQUINA BAY LIGHTHOUSE

The Yaquina Bay Lighthouse, Oregon's tallest at 93 feet, has been in constant operation since the original keeper walked up its 114 steps and first lit the oil-burning light under the French-made Fresnel lens in 1873. (The original Fresnel lens, visible from 19 miles out at sea, is still in use today, but the oil light has been replaced by a stack of 36 individual LED bulbs that flash in a unique pattern, telling mariners they are specifically near Yaquina Head.) Back when it was built, the Yaquina Bay and all lighthouses along the Oregon coast were constructed of wood from local forests. Today, Yaquina is the only one of 11 still in operation along the Oregon coast that has retained its historic all-wood structure. We can safely assume it was very well built from hardy timber to have stood up to thousands of winter storms off the Pacific over its century and a half. This is also the only remaining Oregon lighthouse with living quarters

▲ Climb up the 114 steps inside Yaquina Bay Lighthouse to get a terrific view of Yaquina Head and the central Oregon coast.

attached; the lighthouse keeper and family occupy the 2-story residence. In 1993 the lighthouse was placed on the National Register of Historic Places. You can go inside and climb up yourself for a spectacular view of the coastal ecosystems below. (Yaquina Bay Lighthouse is open noon–4 p.m. every day except holidays March–September; from October–February, it's open noon–4 p.m. Wednesday–Sunday.)

If the lighthouse is open, it's worth popping inside to check out the view from nearly 100 feet up. On a clear day from the top, you can see for hundreds of miles in every direction. Once you've checked the lighthouse off your to-do list, head down the long concrete stairway to nearby Cobble Beach, where millions of round basalt rocks make a clapping sound when waves roll over them.

If you are there around low tide (consult the tide chart for Newport, Oregon, for the date of your visit), you'll likely see plenty of ochre sea stars, giant green anemones, and purple sea urchins clinging to rocks as the seawater ebbs and flow around them. Look up and out and you might see Harbor seals popping out of the water to get a closer look at you before they head for any of a dozen off-shore islets just off Cobble Beach.

TSUNAMIS AND ECOLOGY

Up and down the Pacific Northwest coast, you'll see blue signs for tsunami evacuation routes. These point to roads where drivers can quickly get inland to higher ground above impending tidal surges. The National Oceanic and Atmospheric Administration (NOAA) and the National Weather Service work together to monitor for potential tsunamis hitting our coastlines. A network of open-ocean buoys and coastal tide gauges report information continuously to monitoring stations in each region. Meanwhile, this data is triangulated on the fly with tidal measurements along the coastline and seismograph sensors that detect tectonic activity. If a tsunami was heading your way, emergency warnings would be broadcast to all television and radio stations in the region as well as through wireless emergency alerts on cell phones. And if you hear loud sirens—they are placed up and down the coast as part of the tsunami warning system—head for higher ground immediately.

A huge earthquake off the coast of the Pacific Northwest in January 1700 sent tidal waves east into the coastline of modern day Oregon and Washington as well as west across the Pacific Ocean to Japan. We know this today not only from coincident American Indian stories passed down via oral tradition but also from studying the tree rings (dendrochronology) of coastal western red cedar stumps in isolated "ghost forests" of ancient, standing dead trees along the Pacific Northwest coast. The dendrochronological record shows the last year these trees lived was 1699. Biologists attribute their deaths to the sudden lowering of their coastal forest habitat into the new tidal zone created by the offshore earthquake's force and ensuing tidal surges.

As you can imagine, the tsunami of 1700 destroyed much more than just some isolated stands of western red cedar trees; it reshaped much of the natural structure of the 1000-mile coastline stretching from Northern California up into British Columbia. We know from the biological record that trees and plants were uprooted, destroying wildlife habitat that had been thousands of years in the making. Millions of birds lost their nest sites, while untold numbers of land animals were displaced or drowned.

While the Pacific Northwest hasn't suffered a tsunami of this magnitude since modern record keeping began, it could happen at any time given the instability of the Cascadia subduction plate. When this next "big one" does hit, shifting tectonic plates off the coast will likely send hundreds of miles worth of ocean water surging inland to finish off anything left standing, man made or otherwise, after the initial earthquake's jolting.

If you're a birder, Yaquina Head may just qualify as heaven for you. For starters, one of the largest nesting colonies of common murres (also known as common guillemots) makes their home here. As many as 65,000 of these handsome, crow-sized birds with black heads, backs, wings, and tails; white bellies; and yellow and black feet crowd together each spring on Yaquina's high cliffs to breed and incubate their eggs. These large members of the family Alcidae (like their puffin cousins) spend much of their time out at sea, where they feed by diving into schools of small "forage" fish such as polar cod, capelin, sand lances, sprats, and sandeels.

More graceful below the surface than above, common murres can dive 500 feet or more down into the water column in chase of prey. They can live into their twenties, returning with the same partner to the same cliffside nest site to breed every spring—they are monogamous and usually form lifelong pairs.

Common murres might be the poster bird of Yaquina Head, but many other avian species call the rocky headland home, or at least visit twice a year on their way up and down the Pacific Flyway. Barn

• Yaquina Head is home to one of the largest nesting colonies of common murres along the bird's entire range, from Northern California to the Aleutian Islands.

swallows and violet-green swallows nest along the many cliffsides around the peninsula. White-crown sparrows and song sparrows shuffle around in the brush alongside the park's woodland trails, as Caspian terns fly overhead, signaling the extent of their territory with their signature raspy calls. Northern harriers and American kestrels hunt for rodents in the grassy flats, while western meadowlarks hop around searching for beetles, grasshoppers, and crickets.

Peregrine falcons, red-tailed hawks, and bald eagles swoop down on unsuspecting shorebirds and other small prey near the lighthouse and on forested Salal Hill on the north side of the peninsula. Surfbirds and black turnstones feast on barnacles and snails out on the tidelands, while black scoters and western grebes dive for mussels, clams, crabs, marine snails, and sea squirts in the shallows just offshore. Pigeon guillemots, western gulls, black oystercatchers, and Brandt's and pelagic cormorants are just a few more of the 159 bird species seen around Yaquina Head. Certain sections of Yaquina Head are marked as off-limits to visitors at times, to give nesting wildlife some peace and quiet.

While you've got your binoculars out, train them far offshore in search of gray whales. These 50-foot-long, mottled black cetaceans pass by in the early winter and spring on their way back and forth between their winter calving lagoons along Mexico's Baja California peninsula and summer feeding grounds in the Alaskan arctic. While

Gray whales pass by Yaquina Head twice a year as they migrate 12,000 miles round trip between Mexico's Baja California and Alaska's Bering Sea. ▸

you won't likely get a close-up look at these behemoths from the land, look for their spouts—misty double-pumped jets of vapor shooting as much as 12 feet above the water surface—far offshore, where you might expect to see a tanker ship. (Several local outfitters in Newport take guests out on whale-watching expeditions if getting closer views is appealing.)

If you've still got energy left to burn, consider hiking the Salal Hill and Communications Hill trails, both of which are short but steep and cut through forest primeval on the north side of Yaquina Head. These classic Northwest temperate rain forest trails get you next to Douglas fir, western red cedar, and Sitka spruce trees, while western sword fern and salal spread out in the understory. Only in the Pacific Northwest can you be tide-pooling one minute and hiking through temperate rain forest the next.

With so much ecosystem diversity on such a small amount of land, Yaquina Head is indeed a microcosm of the Oregon coast. Whether you like to hike, birdwatch, explore tide pools, or just breathe in the freshest air in the country as it drifts in off the Pacific, Yaquina Head has you covered.

TAHKENITCH DUNES

Introduction to coastal dunes ecology
and invasive species dynamics

DIFFICULTY
Moderate

LOCATION
Gardiner, Oregon

LENGTH
2 to 4 miles

This trail is well maintained as it traverses second-growth forest before crossing onto the dunes. At the dunes it becomes tougher going, as your feet slip back in the sand a little bit with every step—so allot extra time if you plan to extend your adventure to cross the dunes and hit the beach. (Tacking on this latter section through the dunes and out to the beach and back adds 2 miles to the out-and-back mileage, making the hike 4 miles total.)

Most people visit in the summer when skies are reliably sunnier and temperatures warm enough for shorts and short sleeves. But the dunes are especially enchanting in winter if you can stand cooler temps and some clouds and rain. Leave dogs at home between March 15 and September 15 when snowy plovers, endangered shorebirds that live in the coastal temperate rain forest here, nest on the beach.

One of the nice things about Tahkenitch Dunes (versus other sections of the sprawling, 45-square-mile Oregon Dunes National Recreation Area encompassing it) is the absence of all-terrain vehicles (ATVs). These motorized 3- and 4-wheelers aren't allowed at Tahkenitch, so visitors here can enjoy the tranquility of nature without the noise pollution of

Pacific rhododendron leaves are often at eye level on the forested trail out to Tahkenitch Dunes.

Tahkenitch Dunes and the
Pacific Ocean at sunset.

revving engines or worries about getting run over that may accompany visits to other nearby dunes.

Pick up the trail at the well-marked trailhead near the parking area and entrance to Tahkenitch Campground, off U.S. Highway 101 just north of the little town of Gardiner. Judging from the size of the trees and the primeval quality of the forest, you wouldn't guess that the area was logged to stumps in the 1920s. It is classic Northwest temperate rain forest, with Douglas fir, western red cedar, and

▲ Evergreen huckleberry is ubiquitous both trailside in the woods as well as out on the dunes, where birds, bears, and other creatures enjoy its mid-fall berry offerings.

Sitka spruce trees reaching 150 feet and higher; Pacific rhododendrons draping their leathery green leaves, five to a cluster, across the midcanopy; and beadruby and sword fern lining the sides of the trail. A hike through this forest would be pleasure enough even without the rewards—the dunes and then the beach—at the end.

In a quick half mile, the trail descends suddenly via a couple of switchbacks and soon you'll see some light at the end of the forest tunnel with the trees opening up ahead. A few more steps bring you to the foot of the dunes. Close your eyes and listen for the sound of crashing waves which are another half mile ahead, across the dunes and through a small copse of shore pine trees. Venture forward out onto the dunes and look for footsteps of those who came before you to get a sense for where the "trail"—nonexistent because it crosses ever-shifting sand dunes—now leads. If you brought along a piece of cardboard (or even better, a snowboard), try your luck at sledding (or boarding) down the steepest slice of dunes uphill and to your left. Or if it's the golden hour, find a perch at the edge of the forest and watch the sun go down over the dunes, with the Pacific Ocean as a distant backdrop.

Given the repeated and dramatic shifting of their entire structure, the dunes are home to a dedicated and specially adapted group of native plants. Sitka spruces, shore pines, Port Orford cedars, and Jeffrey pines grow in small, erratically placed clusters, providing all-important cover for wildlife on the otherwise exposed dunes. Hairy manzanitas fill in some of the gaps, where they can grab a patch of

▲ Coming out of the forest, the Tahkenitch Dunes await.

soil amid all the shifting sands. Otherwise, the rest of the flora on the dunes—red fescue, sand verbena, seashore bluegrass, bog blueberry, tufted hairgrass, slough sedge, bearberry, skunk cabbage, and evergreen huckleberry, among others—sticks closer to the ground.

You may well see other footsteps in the sand besides those of humans. Of course, American black bear, Columbian black-tailed deer, coyote, cougar, bobcat, and raccoon roam freely through these wild and fecund coastal ecosystems. But some 393 other lesser-known wildlife species, some of them endemic (meaning they only exist here), scrape out an existence on the dunes.

The Siuslaw hairy necked tiger beetle, only 0.5 inches long with a tiger-striped, gray-and-white shell and white "hair" on its neck, is one example that you may see skittering across the sand at your feet. This rare denizen of the coast once ranged from Northern California up into northern Washington State, but now is only hanging on in a few coastal patches where the conditions are still just right—like this one. They can run as fast as 5 miles an hour in a sprint, which may not seem that quick, but it makes them one of the fastest species on the planet when you consider speed in relation to body size.

⌃ The Siuslaw hairy necked tiger beetle has benefitted from efforts to protect western snowy plover habitat.

⌃ Stay away from the dry sand areas of the beach along the Oregon coast during midsummer to give the endangered snowy plovers who nest there the best chance of survival.

Another seldom-seen native patrolling the dunes for squirrels, voles, eggs, and insects is the Humboldt marten (also called the coastal marten), currently under consideration for federal protection under the Endangered Species Act. The only subspecies of marten (which is in the weasel family) to live in a nonsnowy environment, these expert hunters are about as big as a small cat and live in the shrub thickets and woodlands at the edges of the dunes. They are busy, because they need to eat upward of 80 calories a day, roughly a quarter of their body weight, to survive in the wild.

Meanwhile, hundreds of bird species either live along this stretch of Oregon coast or pass through and stay for a visit twice a year on their way back and forth along the Pacific Flyway—the migratory bird airspace linking South America and the Arctic along the West Coast. Sanderlings, long-billed curlews, dunlins, and least sandpipers comb the beach and dunes in search of sustenance. Other small birds to watch for as they flitter across the dunes include pine siskins, belted kingfishers, chestnut-backed chickadees, wrentits, northern flickers, red crossbills, olive-sided flycatchers, and Anna's hummingbirds. Meanwhile, bald eagles, ospreys, northern harriers, and great horned owls patrol from on high, in search of easy pickings as rodents and other prey scoot between hiding places. Woodpeckers, herons, ducks, geese, and four different species of warbler also frequent the Tahkenitch area.

But of all the birds along this stretch of coast, none is more iconic than the otherwise unassuming little brown-and-white western snowy plover. Measuring only about 6 inches from beak to tail and weighing less than 2 ounces, these small, skittish shorebirds breed and nest in the dry sand of the upper beach during the summer—forcing thousands of human visitors to steer clear of certain sections of shoreline from mid-March to mid-September every year.

Some of the plovers spend the entire year here in the heart of their native habitat, where there's an abundance of their favorite foods, which include small crabs, clams, sand hoppers, marine worms, and aquatic insects. Others migrate north or south but return to the same patch of beach here in the late spring to breed and nest.

That process starts with a male scraping a nest out of the sand. He then bows next to the female he would like to impregnate while flashing the white part of his tail. Usually this is good enough for most females, who aren't too choosy, as they are trying to squeeze out 2–3 broods of 2–6 eggs each—typically with a different male each time—while the weather on the beach is accommodating over the summer.

Once the mom lays her eggs and is off to find another male, the dad takes over to rear the young. After hatching, the newborn chicks can't fly for 4 weeks, making them easy prey for other wildlife on the lookout for an easy meal. Dads distract predators and people away from their nest sites with various behavior displays in the opposite direction. These plover dads can also signal to their chicks to keep a low profile when predators are on the prowl. If the little fluff-ball chicks can make it through their first 6 days, their chances of survival increase dramatically. The birds reach maturity in about a year and can expect to live a full life if they make it to 10 or 12 years old.

Biologists have noticed a sharp decline in western snowy plover populations since the 1970s, and the bird was listed as endangered by the U.S. Fish and Wildlife Service beginning in 1993. The primary culprit in the plover's decline is habitat loss. Originally introduced a century ago to stabilize the dunes and facilitate road and train-track building, invasive species such as European beachgrass, American beachgrass, and Scotch broom have run wild and crowded out native

species, overtaking vast swaths where plovers used to nest. The encroachment of these invasive species have changed the structure of the dune landscape, opening it up to coyotes and other predators that used to avoid the sandy expanses as wastelands, where dinner didn't grow or run.

Luckily, efforts to remove these invasives and keep people and predators away from plover nesting sites have begun to pay off. A recent survey of the distribution and reproductive success of the plovers along the Oregon coast showed population numbers at their highest since monitoring began in 1990. But conservationists warn we have a long way to go before we can expect western snowy plover numbers anywhere near what they were before we started trying to "improve" on Mother Nature's work by tampering with her landscapes.

Once you're ready to move on from the dunes—some spend a few minutes; others spend a day luxuriating in the smooth, blonde sands—you can either turn around and head back to the parking lot (another 0.5 miles back) or keep trekking through the dunes, to the

▲ Introduced 100 years ago as a dune stabilizer, American beachgrass, a non-native invasive species, is wreaking havoc on coastal ecosystems along this stretch of the coast.

final leg of trail and the beach proper. If you choose the latter, do your best to follow others' footsteps in making your way across the dunes. (Even if you can't find others' footsteps, head due west and you'll get there). You'll cross through a small patch of shore pines before emerging onto the beach.

Experiencing the Pacific Ocean in person is awe-inspiring, whether it's your first time or your thousandth. Out on the beach it's almost always windier and more exposed than within the confines of the dunes back a few hundred feet. Watch for sneaker waves, avoid logs in the surf or on wet sand, and stay away from deep water and strong currents.

If it's between March 15 and September 15 (the endangered shorebirds' breeding cycle), the dry sand areas of the beach where western snowy plovers nest are off-limits. During this 6-month period, hiking and horseback riding is allowed on the wet sand areas only, but dogs, kites, and bicycles should stay home—or at least back at the car. And keep an eye on kids, so they don't run into plover nesting territory.

If it's near sunset, you may as well have a seat and wait for the golden orb to drop to the horizon before turning around and retracing your steps to the parking lot. (If you are staying late, make sure you have a headlamp or flashlight to light the way back.) Whatever time of day it is, you'll be glad you made the short trek and you'll surely feel invigorated by your immersion in one of nature's most elemental environments.

The sun makes its final descent over the Pacific Ocean horizon as shore pines separating the dunes from the beach stand by.

DEAN CREEK ELK VIEWING AREA

Elk and other wildlife in an idyllic 1000-acre landscape

LOCATION
Reedsport, Oregon

DIFFICULTY
Easy

LENGTH
0.25 miles

Dean Creek is backed by meadow and forest.

While it may seem like Roosevelt elk must have been in this spot since the beginning of time given how the landscape suits them, herds have only been making their home here since the 1930s. That's when construction of Highway 38 separated this parcel from the Umpqua River and farmers drained the native salt marshes and flooded the site with freshwater, in an effort to "improve" the land for cattle grazing. This landscape hack worked, and for decades cattle shared the wild and grassy acreage with elk, waterfowl, and other wildlife.

But between a decline in cattle ranching in the region, the elk's proclivity for the place, and the public's growing interest in wildlife viewing, the U.S. Bureau of Land Management took control of the site in 1991. Working with the Oregon Department of Fish and Wildlife and the local community to make it accessible to the public, they together created the site's outdoor, placard-based interpretive center, which explains the area's ecology and biology.

Unlike many of the sites covered in this guide, the Dean Creek Elk Viewing Area isn't so much about hiking as it is about observing. The visitor areas are paved (and wheelchair accessible); rough-hewn cattle fencing separates the elk pastures from the parking lot. You can get around just fine in any comfortable footwear; all you need to bring is a little curiosity. Given the mild climate of southern Oregon and the fact that the elk live here year round, any time of year is worth visiting. That said, time your visit for early

A herd of as many as 120 Roosevelt elk make their home along Dean Creek, an ideal habitat for the majestic ruminants because it combines a coniferous woodland with a riparian meadow chock-full of native grasses and other forage. ▾

morning or late afternoon if possible, as the wildlife are more active then—elk tend to seek the cover and shade of the forest during the middle of hot summer days, so don't expect many elk sightings then. If you're an action lover, stop by in mid- to late September, when the mating rut is on. Male elks (bulls) bugle loudly and clash horns to show off and win the loyalty of harems of females (cows) who are ready to ovulate.

▴ The O.H. Hinsdale Interpretive Center features stationary binoculars to help visitors get a better view of wildlife.

The well-marked turnout and parking lot for the Dean Creek Elk Viewing Area is 3 miles east of the town of Reedsport, along Oregon State Highway 38. Park in any of the dozens of marked spots and start your visit by touring the O.H. Hinsdale Interpretive Center, where a series of well-designed signs highlight various aspects of the elk's life cycle and the ecology of the landscape. Read up on the background of the elk on the interpretive placards, then train your eyes south out onto the meadows, drink in the view, and commence the search for wildlife.

Broadleaf cattails and Pacific reedgrass dominate the foreground, and chances are that at least a few Roosevelt elk—as many as 120 of the majestic beasts call this paradise home—will be roaming within sight. The largest of the North American elk subspecies, Roosevelts are wondrous creatures to behold. You can tell them from other elk subspecies (such as the Rocky Mountain elk they commingle with in the Cascades) by their heads, legs, and neck, which are a dark brown-black. The rest of their coloring is similar to other elk, with tan or light brown bodies and a beige or white rump. Roosevelt elk bulls average 875 pounds; cows typically tip the scales at a daintier 700 pounds. The second-biggest ungulate (hooved mammal) species (after moose), these elk bulls can be 10 feet long and 5 feet high at the shoulder, with their antlers adding up to 4 feet more in height—quite an imposing sight if you happen to get too close.

But don't worry, that's unlikely. Elk can smell you from some 600 yards away, and they want no part of human contact. Their sense of smell is around 1000 times more acute than ours. Those big,

▴ Roosevelt elk have darker necks and heads than other elk subspecies of North America.

broad, lateral nostrils can tell them a lot about a smell (for example, whether it's a potential threat or a food source, and from which direction it's coming); biologists call this survival tactic "stereo olfaction."

And if they do smell you (or hear you; their ears are great, too), they are likely to get away quickly, running as fast as 35 miles an hour. Of course, humans aren't the only predators they have to worry about; bears, cougars, coyotes, and even bobcats are also on the prowl here. On average, bulls can make it 12–16 years in the wild, while cows typically last up to 5 years longer (an injury or disease often leads to weakness and then predation).

Only the bulls grow antlers, which are made of solid bone and are covered in a fuzzy, skin-like, vascular layer called "velvet." In late summer or early fall, the protective velvet dries up and the elk scrapes it off by rubbing his antlers against trees and brush to get them ready for prime time. By the fall rut, after a summer of gorging on nutritious grasses and plants, bulls' antlers have come into their full glory. The antlers slough off in the late winter or early spring and new ones immediately start to grow.

It's no surprise that elk congregated in the area when farmers made the land more amenable for cattle grazing, because the two

Broadleaf cattails and
Pacific reedgrass are
plentiful at Dean Creek.

closely related species share similar digestive systems. Both are ruminant herbivores, browsing indiscriminately on whatever grasses, ferns, brush, shrubs, or brambles they can find. They constantly regurgitate this low-quality, hard-to-process forage by bringing it back up from their stomachs and chewing it over and over (chewing their "cud"). Their saliva contains a natural antacid that helps buffer the roughage and break it down more. Of course, the elk aren't just feeding themselves when they munch on various plants; they are providing a valuable environmental service in clearing understory vegetation from the forest floor, which in turn creates new openings for other plant and animal species.

Some 10 million elk inhabited North America prior to the arrival of Europeans in the 1500s; by 1907 there were only 100,000 left, mostly due to overhunting. But public awareness as well as forward-thinking hunting regulations have helped elk populations rebound. Today about a million of the animals roam wild across the continent; 60,000 of them are West Coast–based Roosevelts. The biggest threats to elk these days are habitat loss and fragmentation from logging and road building. Conservationists hope that enlightened forest management practices can help minimize disturbances that hurt habitat for elk and other wildlife. In the meantime, places such as the Dean Creek Elk Viewing Area are that much more valuable as havens for wildlife barely able to stay one step ahead of the bulldozer.

It may be called an "Elk Viewing Area," but you're likely to see other wildlife at this site as well. Waterfowl such a mallards, Canada geese, and American coots are common sights, while dozens of other ducks and geese fill the marshes.

Ospreys are big black-and-white raptors that, like their cousins bald eagles, love to nest in tall tree snags at the far edge of the meadows and fish Dean Creek for food. These master fishers dive-bomb their unsuspecting prey from heights of 30–100 feet above the water's surface. Spines on the pads of their toes and sharp, curved claws help them hold onto slippery fish. Osprey typically bring their fish meal back to the roost, draping it over a tree branch and dining in relative peace.

Cliff swallows, purple martins, killdeers, cedar waxwings, golden-crowned sparrows, black-throated gray warblers, and red-winged

Red-winged black-birds are some of the most abundant native birds in meadows and wetlands across the country, but there has been a 30 percent decline in populations since the 1960s—likely at least in part because of habitat loss. ▸

blackbirds flit about, filling the occasional quiet moment with sooth-ing whistles, songs, and chatter.

Majestic great blue herons in blue, gray, and white, along with their cousins great egrets (all white save for black legs and yellow beaks) stalk the shallows of little Dean Creek and the surrounding wetlands. Beaver, muskrat, and other rodents busy themselves feed-ing on cattails, water lilies, and whatever else they can source from this rich buffet.

It may be hard to believe there is so much industrious behavior going on when you look out over the Dean Creek meadows and all you can see are a few Roosevelt elk leisurely browsing on grass. But whether or not you care about all the hidden activity shouldn't affect your appreciation of this beautiful place. It's a delight for the senses that anyone can enjoy.

ROUGH AND READY BOTANICAL WAYSIDE

*Hundreds of rare plant species
and wildflower bonanza*

DIFFICULTY
Easy

LOCATION
near O'Brien, Oregon

LENGTH
1 to 3 miles

High in the Siskiyou Range of Southwest Oregon, near the California border, sits an anomalous creek-side flat teeming with life, despite soil conditions more akin to a desert. For lovers of plant and floral diversity, the Rough and Ready Botanical Wayside, a 19-acre preserve just outside of the small town of O'Brien, is a wonderland.

The Rough and Ready became part of the public trust in 1937. The was after lobbying by the Illinois Valley Garden Club convinced state officials to set it aside as a botanical preserve so that people would stop digging up exotic plants there to sell as oddities. The main trail follows the course of Rough and Ready Creek for 0.5 miles, to a bench and overlook of the flat, sandy expanse all around. On the outskirts of the flat, knob-like hills with soils more typical of this part of the mountainous West Coast (supporting dense Douglas fir–dominated forests) start stepping up to higher and higher peaks on the horizon. Most visitors go in the summer, but the spring wildflower bloom is second to none in the state of Oregon.

From the fenced-in parking lot off U.S. 199 (Redwood Highway), find the well-marked trailhead by a Bureau of Land Management sign. This marks the 19-acre section of the larger Rough and Ready Watershed in front of you as an "Area of Critical Environmental

Jeffrey pines have evolved to tolerate the thin, serpentine soils alongside Rough and Ready Creek better than most tree species, which helps give them the run of the place. ▸

◂ The blue-black berries of creeping barberry are a favorite treat for native wildlife such as sooty grouses, gray foxes, and coyotes, as well as lots of birds.

Concern." Walk west (straight) past a covered picnic table—you'll appreciate this slice of cover after your hike if it's a hot and sunny day, given how little shade there is in the preserve.

As you continue, if you are there in summer or fall, to your left you'll notice a small rise of sandy, rock-strewn soil separating the trail from the now-dry Rough and Ready Creek, full of huge boulders. You won't believe that this dusty creek bed ever hosts water. But winter and spring bring the substantial flows that support the spring wildflower explosion, although the water course is generally shallow and widely distributed across the mostly flat creek bed. Except for the profusion of plant life, you'd swear you were hiking along a permanently dry desert wash in the American Southwest rather than a riverbed in the typically green and wet Cascades. Indeed, this strange combination of dry and metal-laden soils, with plenty of precipitation and a diverse profusion of plants, explains why the Rough and Ready is often referred to as Oregon's "red rock rainforest."

How did this strange combination come to be? As you might guess, it's a long story. Some 40 million years ago, when the land now underfoot was actually underwater as part of the coastal sea floor, tectonic activity forced the subduction of the Juan de Fuca Plate off the West Coast under the larger continental North American Plate. The result of this collision was a massive coastal uplift and the creation of a line of ancient volcanoes up and down the West

The rock cobbles of the botanical wayside are a remnant of mantle rocks deposited eons ago into the Rough and Ready's alluvial fan. ▸

Coast that were precursors to today's much taller (and geologically younger) Cascades. To put this drastic change in context, the land underfoot here today along Rough and Ready Creek, formerly the bottom of the ocean, is some 30 miles east of where the Pacific coast sits now, near the present-day town of Brookings.

During this period of massive disturbance and uplift, rocks unearthed from the planetary mantle —the layer of rocks between Earth's super-hot core and the thin crust we live on—rolled and tumbled their way down the Illinois River Valley, spreading out here at the mouth of the Rough and Ready watershed. This type of geologic formation is known as an alluvial fan. Elsewhere, alluvial fans can yield rich soils that retain lots of water for plants, but that's not as much the case here. At the Rough and Ready, the deposits of mantle rock are what geologists term "ultramafic," which means they have relatively low concentrations of nutrient-rich silica but high concentrations of heavy metals, including chromium, cobalt, nickel, and iron. These low-silica, heavy-metal rocks weather down into what are called serpentine soils. (Traces of iron are what give many of the boulders and soil here their red appearance.)

Most plants are not able to grow in such a metallic substrate, and that's why the highly biodiverse Rough and Ready watershed is such an anomaly. The fact that this midlatitude temperate region is at the intersection of four mountain ranges (the Coast Range, the

• Sulfur buckwheat is one of five buckwheat subspecies that actually like the metal-laden serpentine soils of the Rough and Ready.

• Hall's violet is one of the many rare wildflowers in the Rough and Ready Botanical Wayside.

Klamath Mountains, the Siskiyous, and the Cascades) has something to do with it, as the occurrence of lots of habitat types in a relatively small geographic area fosters more gene flow and greater overall biodiversity.

Another factor in the rich biodiversity here is the self-selecting nature of the plants that survive. While the vast majority of vascular plants cannot eke out an existence in such poor soils, some species thrive in it—and the four winds have indeed blown many of them into the Rough and Ready watershed, making it home to possibly the highest concentration of rare plants in the Pacific Northwest.

While the rocky, fast-draining soils here may make it feel like a desert, a profusion of springs and seeps in the uplands and along the banks of the creek provide much more irrigation than meets the eye. Also, although it looks dry and sandy out there, a typical year brings 60–100 inches of rain to the wayside and surrounding lands. (Notoriously rainy Seattle, for comparison's sake, gets about 38 inches of rain annually.) These factors combine to make this section of the Rough and Ready watershed more of a lush oasis than a barren desert.

In spring, blooms pop across the red rock rainforest. A few of the many rare and endangered flowers you may encounter include Waldo rockcress, Koehler's rockcress, McDonald's rockcress, Hall's violet, two-eyed violet, Hooker's Indian pink, and Douglas monkey-flower. During April and May, plenty of other less-endangered yet nevertheless colorful blooms, many of which aren't typically found in this part of the Siskiyous, join the party. Wildflower chasers will delight in spotting deltoid balsamroot, harvest brodiaea, purple and white Chinese houses, coast larkspur, Henderson's shooting star, blue field gilia, large-fruited lomatium, naked broomrape, scythe-leaf onion, cat's ear, Tolmie's mariposa lily, moth mullein, showy phlox, Siskiyou mat, nodding arnica, and Siskiyou iris, among others.

The plant life here isn't restricted to wildflowers. Plenty of other shrubs and herbaceous plants live in the sandy soil, often squeezed between red rock cobbles. Six species of fescue (California, Idaho, Klamath, tall, small, and rat-tail) compete with five species of buck-wheat (goldencarpet, naked, wild, ternate, sulfur, and wicker) and lots and lots of Lemmon's needlegrass for real estate along the flats. Rising slightly above the fray of grasses are manzanita bushes. Three different subspecies (Siskiyou, hoary, and sticky whiteleaf) overlap and hybridize with each other here, much to the delight of visiting botanists.

Not surprisingly, the trees growing here on the serpentine wayside are more tolerant of poor soils than the assortment of conifers and deciduous trees you would find just a few miles away on nearby Siskiyou slopes. Here at the Rough and Ready, twisted and gnarled Jeffrey pines, some growing right in the flat shallow flow of the creek, are the most common trees dotting the landscape. You'll also encounter the occasional ponderosa pine, which looks similar to its Jeffrey pine cousin, albeit with more colorful reddish cream-colored bark and an even more gnarled presentation.

Oregon white oaks (also called Garry oaks) crop up alongside Rough and Ready Creek, sporting big acorns in the fall, beloved by the Siskiyou chipmunk. This endemic rodent makes itself at home along the Rough and Ready's generous shores as well as throughout the Siskiyous—but nowhere else. Other species that especially appreciate these scattered Oregon white oaks are butterflies. Several species use the tree as a larval host. Keep an eye out for the fluttering wings of gold-hunter's hairstreaks, California sisters, Propertius duskywings, and golden hairstreaks making their rounds pollinating the flowers and plants of the wayside.

While we're on the topic of the small stuff, let's not forget about the important role bees and other airborne insects—as well

• Oregon white oak is a big draw for several butterfly species, which use its leaves as larval hosts. Siskiyou chipmunks cache the tree's acorns for winter.

▲ Hoary manzanita is a constant companion along much of the short hike along Rough and Ready Creek.

as songbirds and hummingbirds, which depend on nectar for their nutritional needs—play in keeping the floral resources here pollinated. Meanwhile, mayflies, caddisflies, and midges on the surface of the creek attract hungry Chinook salmon, steelhead, and cutthroat trout, each of which spawn out in the crystalline waters of Rough and Ready Creek in late winter or early spring, when the water flow is at its annual maximum.

In terms of terrestrial wildlife, the usual cast of characters populating the nearby forests often wander down into the wayside in search of food. You may not see them, but rest assured that black bear, cougar, Roosevelt elk, coyote, mountain quail, gray fox, and Columbian black-tailed deer frequent the area. Pileated woodpeckers don't have as much woody raw material to work with here compared to some nearby upland forests, but they nonetheless spread out and do well on the tree-bound insects they can find. Also, beware of northern Pacific rattlesnakes, which fit in better along the desertlike Rough and Ready flats than in many parts of the Siskiyous, where they nevertheless persist regardless. While you can't live your life in fear, you can watch where you step. That said, if you stick to the wide and well-maintained crushed rock trail, you'll have little opportunity to disturb or surprise anything.

Keep moving, and at almost 0.5 miles in, you'll see a big Douglas fir partially shading a picnic bench on a little bluff overlooking the creek. Sit awhile and enjoy the panoramic view. The foreground looks positively Seussian with curled trees and, if it's spring, rainbow-hued blooms interrupted only by the spindly red branches of wide-spreading hoary manzanitas twigs. In the distance, the stately summits of Moores Ridge (such as Red Mountain and Vulcan Peak), 15 miles to the west in the Kalmiopsis Wilderness, rise some 3000 feet higher in elevation than where you now sit at approximately 1400 feet above sea level.

This picnic bench spot is the end of the universally accessible section of the trail, and is a good turnaround point for most people. Those who turn around here and head back to the parking area will hike (or wheel) a modest mile total on flat terrain and seen some of the best of the Rough and Ready watershed. If you're looking for more adventure, you can head another mile or so in, past several choice swimming holes, to Seats Dam, constructed decades ago to divert creek flow to power a now-defunct lumber mill just north of the wayside. The dam, at 1.5 miles in, is another good turnaround point, but you can hike still further and explore more of Rough and Ready's alluvial fan before heading into higher ground and more traditional terrain. Whether you make it a mile or lots more, you'll get a great feel for what makes this corner of the globe so special.

If you've been putting off visiting the Rough and Ready Botanical Wayside, now is the time, given the threat of future mining in the region and the havoc it could wreak on this unique and treasured ecosystem. Just because the site is part of the public domain as federal land owned by U.S. taxpayers—part of the watershed is on Bureau of Land Management territory, while the rest falls under the U.S. Forest Service's purview—doesn't mean it's protected from potentially

Jeffrey pine nee-
dles, with Moores
Ridge in the far
distance. ▸

harmful development. Mining companies have started making claims
on the mountainous, nickel-rich terrain upstream to assess their
prospects. Their plans include mining in a designated wilderness area
nearby, building miles of roads into and out of their operation right
through the wayside, and construction of a pollution-spewing smelter
to process the nickel ore on-site. If they are allowed to proceed with
their extraction plans, it would surely change the still-wild character
of the landscape forever.

   In 2010, Oregon's congressional delegation asked President
Obama to permanently protect the Rough and Ready ecosystem
from mining and other resource extraction activity, to no avail.
Today the area remains under dispute. Nature lovers (and botanists)
want to keep it the way it is in perpetuity, while profit-seeking mining concerns see the value of the land in question much differently,
continuing to push forward with plans to exploit what's below the
surface, no matter the ecological cost. Time will tell which side is
victorious in this small battle in the war to protect the integrity of
Mother Nature's domain.

LIMPY BOTANICAL TRAIL

Some 250 native plant species, including 43 species of shrubs and trees

DIFFICULTY
Moderate

LOCATION
near Grants Pass, Oregon

LENGTH
1 mile

Late May is a great time of year to see the blue camas blooming in its full glory on the Limpy Botanical Trail.

iven its unique climate and complex geologic history, the Siskiyou Mountains of southwest Oregon support the greatest diversity of plant species in the entire Pacific Northwest, and Limpy Botanical Trail in the Rogue River–Siskiyou National Forest is a great place to experience that diversity for yourself.

The trail itself is for hikers. Leave the flip-flops in the car and put on good socks and sturdy sneakers or boots. The loop gains about 200 feet in elevation over its first 0.5 miles, then gradually loses it on the way back around. Given the site's low elevation and the mild climate of southwest Oregon, you can visit the Limpy Botanical Trail any time of year, although early spring will give you a first look at the new season's wildflowers.

The parking area at the trailhead off Limpy Creek Road fits 8–10 cars; if the lot is full, park on the side of the road and walk in. A three-paneled kiosk featuring interpretive displays on the natural history of the area and a trail map lets you know you are starting out at the right place.

The first ecosystem you'll encounter is the mixed forest community, the most common forest type across southwest Oregon, with tall coniferous trees, expansive deciduous hardwoods, and widely dispersed thickets of shrubs. All these plants have evolved in the hot, dry summers that are characteristic of the region, which have included many forest fires. In fact, some of the plants here cannot reproduce without a fire, as extreme heat is required for seeds to germinate.

Time of year will determine which flora welcomes you. You'll see a lot of plant diversity no matter what the season, but the abundant wildflower blooms of spring yield the most colorful show. If it's February, look for spring queens, with their small clusters of light purple, bell-like flowers. A month later, graceful white and purple fawn lilies carpet the flats alongside the trail. In late May, blue camas, with its velvety purple-blue flowers punctuated by tiny, vibrant yellow anthers, quilts the forest floor. Blue camas was a staple food for local Indigenous people in the millennia before White settlement (Lewis and Clark wrote about camas fields as far as the eye could see and feasting on the plant's baked roots). Other shrub-layer plants that dominate the mixed forest here include evergreen huckleberry and Cascade barberry, both of which produce berries loved by birds, bears, and humans.

If you smell camphor, it may well be the crushed leaves of an Oregon myrtle (also known as a California laurel), a broad-leaved evergreen that grows 40–80 feet tall and spreads out its branches like a big shrub to catch as many rays as the large trees let through. The tree's signature scent is not actually camphor, but a mild toxin called umbellulone that irritates the mucous membranes and has been known to cause headaches in chemically sensitive hikers who get a big whiff walking by.

Native communities isolated this natural compound from the tree for use medicinally to treat headaches and menstrual cramps, and also to wash lice from the scalp. They also used the umbellulone-dense smoke from burning hardwood myrtle to get rid of fleas and to drive ground squirrels from their burrows. While these trees are native to this part of the state, you won't see them any farther north, as their range extends from southern Oregon down to the California–Mexico border.

Another iconic midcanopy tree of the mixed forest here is Oregon white oak (also known as Garry oak), which thrives in this diverse ecosystem despite being on the extreme southern end of its native range. Left unattended for a century, most forests on the wet west side of the Cascades end up being dominated by Douglas firs, but

↑ You don't necessarily have to ingest or even rub against some plants for them to affect you. Case in point is the Oregon myrtle, which has been known to give innocent passersby headaches as it off-gasses a mildly toxic natural compound called umbellulone.

↑ An acorn and leaves of an Oregon white oak (also called Garry oak).

Oregon white oaks, among other hardy native tree species, fight this by doing their best to propagate and claim more real estate on the forest floor, and within the canopy, for themselves. One of their key tactics for survival is being adaptable following disturbances such as forest fires, which happened much more frequently before our fire suppression efforts of the last century and a half. These periodic fires would prevent Douglas fir and most other conifer seedlings from getting established, allowing bunchgrass prairie interspersed with Oregon white oak and other fire-resistant trees and shrubs to persist.

PRESCRIBED BURNS

American Indians (the Takelma) populating this part of the Siskiyous learned from Mother Nature's lightning strikes that fire could be used as a tool to encourage the wild crops their community favored. Periodic prescribed burns by the Takelma helped perpetuate the grasslands that produced blue camas, chocolate lily, bracken fern, and Oregon white oak— all key food sources for those subsisting off the land—while also attracting grazing deer and elk for easy hunting.

In modern times, we have gotten so good at suppressing fire—at least until recently, when climate change has kicked wildfires into overdrive—that Douglas fir and other giants have been able to take root and eventually crowd out the other trees that would otherwise stretch their limbs into the middle and even upper canopy. But not necessarily here, where wildfires still roll through every few years. And locals are bracing for more frequent, more intense fires now that climate change is throwing weather systems out of whack. While such a scenario isn't good for people and may not be great for Douglas firs, it could be a boon to trees like Oregon white oak.

Also keep an eye out for Pacific madrone trees. These broad-leaved evergreens look a lot like their manzanita cousins, but have a brighter scarlet red outer bark that shreds away in strips, revealing a fresh medium green inner skin underneath. A widespread canopy of oval, glossy, light green leaves sends dappled light through to the forest floor below. Madrones are at the same time both highly adaptable (look for them growing out of cracks in the rock) and fickle, not taking root just anywhere. Many hikers consider it a rare treat to come across one in the forest, especially here, so far from the coast where they are more common.

The mixed forest has plenty of big trees, too. Douglas fir and ponderosa pine dominate the upper canopy, with some individual trees topping out at 200 feet tall. Their huge trunks sticking up throughout the forest look like Roman columns supporting some unseen heavenly structure. In a typical Northwest forest, these big trees would eventually crowd out the more diverse underlings, rendering the forest less diverse in its "climax" state. But not so here on the Limpy Botanical Trail, where the sheer volume of diversity means every nook and cranny is filled with life.

Just as you're getting used to the mixed forest, the scenery begins to change as you move into the rock outcrop ecosystem, where plants have adapted to living on bare rock with little to no soil in which to put down roots. The types of plants that

▲ Old man's beard lichen hangs off the trunk of a Pacific madrone tree. The madrone's unmistakable red bark peels away to reveal a fresh green inner bark.

▲ It wouldn't be the Pacific Northwest without at least a few huge Douglas fir trees, this one labeled in case there is any question.

can thrive in such a challenging setting are different from those just a few hundred feet back in the mixed forest, where soils retain and share more water and nutrients. Epiphytes—organisms that source their nutrients from the air—are right at home here, glomming to any old rock or wood as a substrate. As you traverse through the rock

▴ Stick your nose into the patterned bark of a ponderosa pine tree and you will likely get a pleasant whiff of its vanilla-scented sap.

outcrops look for little white cup lichens crowding together like hungry open mouths. Common dragon moss, haircap moss, fork moss, and eurhynchium moss jockey for territory.

More complex plants are forced to put roots down in small pockets of soil trapped in cracks in the rock. One example is broadleaf stonecrop, a rare Northwest succulent that stores water in its leaves for use during the dry season, rather than depending on soil moisture. Some other plants that thrive in such a setting include lungwort, licorice fern, chickweed monkeyflower, California mistmaiden, and canyon desert-parsley.

The rock outcrop ecosystem isn't devoid of soils completely, though, and there is plenty of flora that thrives in it regardless of its predominantly rocky bottom. Two such trees are canyon live oaks and manzanitas, both of which can take root in shallow, sandy soils and have thick, leathery leaves that help them retain water.

Soon the trail becomes a boardwalk, and you'll know you've entered the serpentine community, the most unique and ecologically diverse section of the hike. (The U.S. Forest Service has constructed the boardwalks to protect this ecological treasure from the footfalls of hikers.) It may seem like the flora all around you has morphed into new shapes, but what's really going on is the composition of the soil beneath your feet has invited in a whole new set of plants and trees.

The difference here comes down to geology. The rock underlying this particular area is ultramafic, which means it's composed primarily of heavy metals with relatively low concentrations of nutrient-rich silica. Over the eons, this rock has broken down into nutrient-deprived but mineral-rich soil, which many plants cannot tolerate. But just as no opportunity goes unnoticed in the animal kingdom, plants that thrive in such an alternative scenario rush in to

◂ When you get to the board-walk—and incense cedars and Jeffrey pines become the dominant trees around you—you'll know you've entered the serpentine ecosystem.

Drought-tolerant Jeffrey pines can survive in the harsh and shallow soils of the serpentine ecosystem. ▸

fill the niches. And therein lies the reason why serpentine soils tend to support more diverse plant communities than so-called healthier granitic soils.

As you progress into the serpentine, you'll notice fewer big trees, and those that are present are not quite as tall as the ponderosa pines a few hundred feet back. Here on the serpentine, the smaller but related Jeffrey pine reigns supreme. The bark patterns of the two species are similar, but the Jeffrey pine's bark is more muted and monochromatic. While you'll find ponderosa pines as far north as British Columbia, the Jeffrey pine, like many plants along the Limpy Botanical Trail, is at the extreme north limit of its range.

Another tree that does well in the shallow, iron-laden soils of the serpentine is the incense cedar. Slightly shorter than the Jeffrey pine and with splayed (instead of conical) needles, incense cedar is well adapted to fire-prone zones such as this part of Oregon and plays an important role in forest succession. Look for the tree's furrowed reddish bark, more akin to a redwood than a Douglas fir.

Some of the other novel native species you might see along this stretch of trail include Brewer's oak, a shrublike subspecies of Oregon white oak, and California coffeeberry, a shrub which produces edible berries with seeds that look like coffee beans. Also keep your eyes peeled for the tiny violet blooms of Waldo rockcress and its cousin Klamath rockcress.

▲ Incense cedar's bark, up close.

◄ Limpy Creek cascades over boulders on its way to the Rogue River.

One plant you can't miss thanks to its perky, leathery green leaves is western azalea, which offers up sweet-smelling white, pink, orange, yellow, or mixed-color blooms in early May. Other beautiful spring bloomers on the serpentine are yellow iris, common selfheal, buttercup, common woodrush, shooting star, Hall's violet, mariposa lily, wedgeleaf violet, and short-lobe Indian paintbrush with its signature cluster of a dozen or so tiny scarlet flowers. You'll also likely encounter wild onion, Bolander's onion, Siskiyou mat, and common yarrow.

Take your time enjoying the diversity of the serpentine, then continue on as the trail loops back through the final ecosystem of the journey, the forest edge community. This area contains species from both the serpentine and mixed forest. Ponderosa pines re-enter the mix alongside Jeffrey pines, while California black oaks spread their big black boughs wide and checkerblooms send up violet blooms midspring. Take the opportunity to splash your face—or cool your feet—in Limpy Creek, which the trail crosses on a series of wooden footbridges. Revel in tiny waterfalls as the creek cascades over boulders. (As tempting as it may be, don't drink the creek water, which seems pure but could contain giardia, a microscopic parasite from human or animal waste that causes intestinal distress).

More familiar Northwest trees—red alder, bigleaf maple, vine maple—start to fill in the gaps in the forest and soon enough, you're back at the parking lot. Although the hike is only a mile long, it feels as though you've traveled through several different worlds—and indeed, you have experienced four distinct ecosystems.

OREGON CAVES, CLIFF NATURE TRAIL

Splendid spelunking and a diverse, marble-laden forest hike

DIFFICULTY
Easy

LOCATION
Oregon Caves National Monument and Preserve, near Cave Junction, Oregon

LENGTH
1 mile

O regon Caves National Monument and Preserve is open year round, although sometimes the access road is closed in winter during and after big snow storms. If you're interested in touring the cave interiors, plan to visit between March and October (when the U.S. National Park Service runs 90-minute, ranger-led tours throughout the day); explorers looking to go deeper can arrange for a customized off-trail cave tour with rangers. If you do make the trip in winter, consider hauling in some snow-shoes to facilitate getting around the trails and forest surrounding the closed-off cave.

Even if you're more a hiker than a caver, this is still a great place to explore. The 1-mile Cliff Nature Trail leads through some of the most diverse forest in the Pacific Northwest on its way over the top of the monument's namesake marble-bound caverns.

Park at the day use area and walk past the rustic entry station and down the paved road for 800 feet, to the middle of

▲ Pacific madrone's peely green and red bark is unmistakable—and unforgettable.

A member of the heath family, Pacific madrone has leathery, evergreen oval leaves that adorn the forest's midstory year round. ▸

the elaborate visitor and maintenance complex. Peely barked Pacific madrone boughs wind their way through the straight and tall conifer trunks that dominate the forest all around. The buildings here, constructed between 1924 and 1936 in the rustic style of architecture often associated with America's national parks, all share rough-cut Port Orford cedar bark sheathing, wood-shingled roofs, and granite-block masonry. Take a peek inside the 6-story Chateau, a National Historic Landmark that features guest rooms as well as a restaurant, coffee shop, and gift shop. The lobby features a large double-sided rock fireplace, dark wood paneling, picture windows looking out into the treetops, and tree-size log posts supporting an open-beam ceiling. An offshoot of Cave Creek, the creek that also runs through the cave itself, has been rerouted through the adjacent dining room in an impressive display of bringing the outside in. After marveling at the Chateau, make your way across the driveway to the smaller yet still impressive Chalet, where a covered indoor-outdoor breezeway welcomes visitors bound for either a cave tour or a hike on one of the monument's three main (aboveground) trails.

If you timed your visit to do a cave tour, get ready to go subterranean. Rangers lead small groups on 90-minute excursions covering about 0.5 miles of the 3-mile cave network underlying this small Siskiyou slope on the outer flanks of Mount Elijah. Even if you're not taking a tour, it's worthwhile to walk a few feet into the cave entrance (until you reach a locked access gate) to get a feel for what it's like inside. The first thing you'll notice, even just inside the cave entrance, is the ambient air temperature differential between inside and out. Whether the outside temperature is below freezing in February or sweltering in July, inside the cave it stays around 44 degrees F year round.

Going deep into the cave system, you'll get to see another world that is dominated by mineral-laden dripping water. This dripping creates a wide variety of speleothems (stalagmites and stalactites) on the various surfaces of the cave's dark recesses. You can hear the moving water of Cave Creek, the first underground river to be designated as "wild and scenic" by the federal government in 2014, as it flows through and under the cave floor, carving new holes into the underlying limestone ("karst") along its dark and mysterious course. In fact, the creek is sometimes referred to as the River Styx, in reference to the river in Greek mythology that served as the border between earth and the underworld.

The cave network here came to be as a result of vertical cracks and cross-fractures in and between rock layers. These breaks grew wider over time, some forming spaces tall enough for humans to stand in and walk through. While the cave has existed for millions of years, it wasn't "discovered" until 1874, when local hunter Elijah Davidson chased his dog into a dark hole in the rocks. To his amazement, the hole led to a mysterious netherworld. After wandering inside without a light, he was only able to find his way out by following the sound of water he heard from Cave Creek below.

It would take another 35 years for the site to become open to the public. In 1909, President William Howard Taft invoked the Antiquities Act in setting aside the cave and its surroundings as a national monument. This move precluded future commercial development in the area and ensured the preservation of the natural and cultural treasures found here.

▲ Deep in the cave, water full of minerals creates stalactites (shown here) and stalagmites, together known as speleothems. A ranger-led cave tour is the only way to see this deep inside the cave network—well worth the 90-minute commitment.

The formation of the 3-mile cave network is a long story. Going back some 180 million years, this part of Oregon was not part of the North American continent yet, but was instead a shallow arm of the Triassic-era Panthallassic Ocean. Dinosaurs roamed the earth and volcanoes occasionally spewed ash and lava over the landscape. In the ocean, coral, clams, and fish extracted a mineral called calcium carbonate from the water column and used it to build their own skeletons, shells, and bones. When these marine animals died, their hard parts settled on the ocean floor, gradually building up in layers. Meanwhile, ocean plants were extracting carbon dioxide from the water, generating even more calcium carbonate in the process and further adding to the significant load at the bottom of the sea. Over time, these layers of calcium carbonate and other sediments on the ocean floor compressed under their own weight and the constant pressure from the water column above.

It would be millions of years before tectonic shifting raised this part of modern-day Oregon out of the sea. The intense heat and pressure of these upheavals metamorphosed the different layers of rock here into new forms: shale became slate, sandstone became quartzite,

▴ Pockets of erosion that didn't become full-fledged caves are called "blind leads" by geologists.

The Cliff Nature Trail traverses over the top of the cliffs that others tour below.

and limestone turned into marble. You are standing today on the resulting jumble of these interbedded rock layers known to geologists as the Applegate Group, a 4-mile-long tilted slab on the slopes of Mount Elijah (and home of this extraordinary site). Subsequent sporadic tectonic uplift followed by glaciation helped steepen the hillsides, which facilitated more erosion from running streams and turned the landscape into something more like we see today.

While caves aren't usually known for their biodiversity, due to the lack of sunlight and the organic nutrients that light helps create, the Oregon Caves are an exception, harboring upward of 160 different species. The most iconic cave residents are bats, and eight different species are found within the cave complex. The most common here are Townsend big-eared bats, but Yuma, long-eared, fringed, and long-legged bats can also be found inside, where they rest between trips outside to forage for insects and seek out mates. They also congregate inside more in the winter, when the insulation of the old-growth tree bark under which they typically roost doesn't keep them warm enough. Some hibernate inside the cave all winter long. The National Park Service's barred "bat gate" at the entrance keeps people and other big predators out of the cave during winter to protect the flying mammals.

In spring, the bats wake up and head out to gorge themselves on newly hatched beetles, moths, flies, wasps, and mosquitoes, among other insects. They typically hunt at night, using echolocation to navigate and locate prey. A single bat on a feeding mission can eat as many as 500 insects per hour, and will typically consume its body weight in insects overnight.

Like just about all of Mother Nature's creations, bats provide vital ecosystem services wherever they live, including keeping local insect populations in check, pollinating plants, and dispersing seeds. While predation by hawks, owls, and snakes have been bats' biggest worries through the ages, habitat loss due to human encroachment and development is perhaps today's most pressing challenge, as bat population numbers decline worldwide.

Of course, climate change is also affecting the bats' range and the availability of prey insects. The increased variation in climatic extremes wrought by climate change could potentially—or perhaps has already begun to—alter the timing of when bats wake up from

Eight different bat species utilize the cave, but the Townsend big-eared bat, shown here, is by far the most common. ▸

their winter hibernation. If they come out too early, there might not be enough insects hatched yet for them to eat, which would not only affect the success of their foraging efforts but would also limit nutrients for their newborn pups. The results could be devastating for generational survival rates.

National Park Service biologists here are also worried about human visitors unknowingly transferring a fungus that has afflicted large numbers of bats in the northeastern U.S. and elsewhere east of the Rockies (as well as throughout Europe) with a terminal disease called white-nose syndrome. Infected bats develop a chalky white fungus on their noses while they hibernate, then behave erratically—like flying outside in winter—until the disease eventually kills them.

While white-nose syndrome hasn't reached the bats of the Oregon Caves yet—or bats anywhere on the West Coast—rangers warn that it's up to cave visitors to keep it that way. If you've visited any mines or caves east of the Rockies or in Europe prior to visiting Oregon Caves, leave any backpacks, clothes, or shoes you wore behind on your visit here. The fungal spores that cause white-nose syndrome are easily transferred via such items, even if they've been washed.

Beside bats, the cave complex hosts other wildlife as well. No other cave in the country has as many endemic species of troglobites—small animals that have adapted to cave life and now couldn't survive on the surface. Two of them are cave crickets and springtails, both insects that find their way around in total darkness with long, slender antennae and utilize their body fluids as natural antifreeze to keep them functioning in the cold. Another of the cave's endemics is the pseudoscorpion, an arachnid that looks like a tiny scorpion missing its tail. Some other cave dwellers include bushy tailed woodrats, harvestmen, tissue moths, and an assortment of beetles, slugs, and snails. And more than 30 different antibiotic-rich microbes coat the walls of the cave with various shades of gray, light green, beige, and off-white.

Douglas fir is king throughout the forest here, as it is across much of the Pacific Northwest's west side. ▸

While the cave system may be the main attraction at Oregon Caves National Monument and Preserve, what's outside may be just as fascinating to those interested in ecology. The Siskiyou Mountain region, at the intersection of the Cascade, Klamath, and Coast ranges, is one of the most ecologically diverse areas of the Northwest and North America, because of the various habitat types bumping up against one another here.

Find the trailhead through the Chalet's breezeway and make your way southeast, climbing on a trail that briefly parallels the park road then climbs higher into the classic-looking Northwest forest. Trail makers used boulders lodged deep into the earth as giant steps. Towering Douglas fir trees, with their red and brown ruffled bark,

◂ Start the hike on Cliff Nature Trail by hiking up the stairs and through the Chalet's breezeway to the trailhead.

look like colonnades and dominate the forest here. But unlike other parts of the Northwest, many other tree species coexist with the usual suspects. Port Orford cedars, ponderosa pines, noble firs, sugar pines, white firs, western white pines, and knobcone pines all find good homes on this remote Siskiyou ridge.

Pacific dogwood branches stream in and out of the conifer trunks. In late spring or early summer, look for their pretty, 4-inch white flowers that are actually bracts (modified leaves) and reflect light around the otherwise dark understory. Meanwhile, the swooping, leathery, green-leaved branches of Pacific madrone, a tree that loves the thin, rocky soils of the cliff sides here, dresses up the midstory nicely.

Oregon grape, with its pointy green leaves and late-season red berries, can be mistaken for holly, an invasive scourge throughout the Northwest, but rest assured that Oregon grape is native and a key source of nutrients for a number of forest birds here, including Steller's jays, cedar waxwings, and dark-eyed juncos.

Lower down, 11 different species of fern thrive. Like elsewhere in the west-side forests of the Northwest, you'll see plenty of sword fern

▲ The view out across the Illinois River Valley includes neighboring Siskiyou peaks.

and maidenhair fern, but keep an eye out for more obscure species given our lower latitude, such as parsley fern, lady fern, brittle bladder fern, and serpentine fern. Western trillium's white spring flowers add a splash of color to the forest floor when they turn violet as they fade during the mid- to late summer.

While the grade starts out gradual, eventually switchbacks prevail. Follow the well-maintained trail, which now has you pointed southwest. Just when you are starting to tire of the uphill grade, the trail flattens out at a beautiful overlook spot perfect for a rest. Drink in this sublime view across the densely forested Illinois River Valley and across to a panorama of neighboring Siskiyou peaks, including Fiddler Mountain, Pearsoll Peak, Eight Dollar Mountain, and Squaw Peak.

On the sun-drenched cliff face behind you, an impressive panoply of life clings to the surface of the marble. Broadleaf stonecrop—a mat-forming succulent with spindly red stems and overlapping, red-tinged petals surrounding a light green or pale yellow center— retains water in its fleshy, engorged flowers. This accommodates its preference for growing in very little soil along cracks in rock faces. Marbled outcroppings are covered with thick beards of green moss, as Cascade barberry fills occasional patches of soil between the prevailing hardscape. In other spots, pale green lichen blobs stretch themselves across 2-inch diameters.

If you hear some rustling in the forest near the trail, it's most likely one of the many Columbian black-tailed deer that live here. If you're visiting between mid-May and July, you may even stumble

▲ Broadleaf stonecrop is rooted in small cracks in the marble atop the Applegate Group rock formation along the Cliff Nature Trail.

upon a fawn trying to blend in with its surroundings. Mothers tuck their fawns into secluded spots for hours on end while they are out foraging for food. The fawns have little if any scent and their light brown coloration with white spots helps them blend in; they instinctively lie still to avoid attracting potential predators such as coyotes, cougars, and black bears. If you see a fawn lying motionless in the woods, it's merely exhibiting normal behavior. Take a good long look, then keep moving.

‹ Columbian black-tailed deer may not seem scared of humans but give them plenty of space anyway.

‹ A dead Douglas fir snag mingles with vanillaleaf and moss-covered erratic rocks (stones and boulders left behind by glaciers).

Northern spotted owls can live here thanks to the profusion of old-growth trees still standing. They make a nice life, hunting Douglas squirrels, Townsend's chipmunks, and northern flying squirrels, themselves hunting for seeds, berries, and nuts in this diverse forest. Red-white-and-black-headed pileated woodpeckers create a racket in search of ants and other tasty insects inside the bark of living or dead trees. Their pecking action not only keeps them fed and puts a check on populations of ants and other insects but also helps break down wood into nutrients that other plants can use.

Be careful where you step as you hike the beautiful forest trails at Oregon Caves. The hardy but not invincible Roth forest snail might be gliding along beneath your feet. This unique subspecies of land snail is, so far, only known to be found in this location. As it slimes itself across rock faces and along the forest floor, it uses its four tentacles to detect light and odor to help it navigate and find food. Like other forest snails of this region, it feeds on moss, decaying plants, algae, and fungus, using a rasp-like tongue with thousands of tiny scraping hooks to pull nutrients into its mouth. On warm days the snail retreats into its hard shell, which it keeps for life and maintains through the constant extraction of trace amounts of calcium from the area's marble rock.

The Roth forest snail is hardly the only creature struggling to hang on here. Several other species found within the preserve's borders are considered at risk by conservationists. Five of the eight bat species inhabiting the cave network are suffering from unprecedented population losses in recent decades. Outside, northern goshawks, olive-sided flycatchers, little willow flycatchers, California mountain kingsnakes, Del Norte salamanders, and tailed frogs are also on the ropes but holding on within the protected confines of this 7-square-mile preserve. While you would have to be incredibly lucky to see any of these threatened and generally elusive species, it's comforting to know they are still out there.

Keep hiking and soon enough the Cliff Nature Trail swings by the exit of the cave network, where a man-made door delivers cave tour participants at the end of their 90-minute subterranean sessions. The remaining 0.25 miles of the Cliff Nature Trail's loop is paved to accommodate tour participants.

ROGUE RIVER NATURAL BRIDGE

River disappears into prehistoric lava tube, re-emerges in primeval forest

DIFFICULTY
Easy

LENGTH
1.5 miles

LOCATION
near Prospect, Oregon

This short hike offers a remarkable intersection of geology, volcanism, and ecology. The trail leads to a series of overlooks of the Rogue River and the gorge it has carved through volcanic basalt, including a short underground detour through an ancient lava tube. If you just want to see the lava tube, a 0.5-mile out-and-back stroll delivers. For more of a leg stretch and a better sample of the forest ecosystem around the river, make it a clockwise loop by crossing over the river after the Natural Bridge overlook, and return via the trail through Natural Bridge Campground on the other side of the river. This makes for a 1.5-mile loop. The trail network is open June–October.

Start at the well-marked trailhead at the west side of the large parking lot and follow it for 500 feet to a wooden footbridge across the raging Rogue River. In the early 19th century, French fur trappers dubbed the rough river *La Riviere aux Coquins* after local natives whom they considered *coquins* (French for rogues). But looking upstream from here, you'd swear it was named after the tumultuous path and roguish rapids of the river.

⬩ Lodgepole pine has a distinctive bark pattern; here it resembles a face.

• The Upper Rogue River corkscrews its way down through basalt canyons from its headwaters near Crater Lake.

Descending for 215 miles from its headwaters near Crater Lake (around 15 miles east of here) to its mouth at Gold Beach, Oregon, the Rogue was one of eight original rivers protected by the Wild and Scenic Rivers Act of 1968. Botanists have recorded some 3500 different plant species along its course, making the Rogue basin one of the most diverse temperate coniferous forest ecosystems in the world.

WILD & SCENIC RIVERS

In 1968, the U.S. Congress passed the Wild and Scenic Rivers Act to preserve the American rivers (and their immediate environments) that had outstanding natural, cultural, and recreational values. The Act ensured that these rivers would be protected and kept in a free-flowing condition for the enjoyment of current and future generations. The legislation was carefully worded to safeguard what's special about each designated river, while also allowing for potential "appropriate use and development."

Since the Rogue, Clearwater, Eleven Point, Feather, Rio Grande, Saint Croix, Salmon, and Wolf Rivers were originally designated, 201 more U.S. rivers have joined the list, translating into protection for upward of 12,000 miles of rivers across 40 states and Puerto Rico. While this represents great progress, environmentalists point out that 75,000 large dams across the country have modified some 600,000 miles—around 17 percent of the total flow—of all American rivers coast to coast.

Turn right after the footbridge crossing and head north on the paved path as the forest closes in on the trail. Douglas fir, white fir, lodgepole pine, ponderosa pine, incense cedar, Shasta red fir, and bigleaf maple dominate the forest here, but also look for Pacific dogwoods, tanoaks, Pacific madrones, vine maples, and western hemlocks. Epiphytes hang off any available branches while a wide variety of lichens colonize just about all the bark substrate available.

Beaked hazelnut, Pacific rhododendron, Oregon boxleaf, and Greene's mountain ash occupy occasional real estate in the midcanopy. Meanwhile, down low between the trees and along the edges of the trail, Oregon oxalis, western sword fern, salal, western maidenhair fern, and evergreen huckleberry fill in available gaps.

If you are visiting in late spring or early summer, keep your eyes peeled for woodland wildflowers. Western columbine, ocean spray, western starflower, American trailplant, common vetch, snow queen, and Suksdorf's woodsorrel are just a few of the dozens of colorful blooms thriving in this diverse, high-Cascade riparian ecosystem.

If you're lucky, you might see the white flower rein orchid. This unassuming but endangered green flowering plant grows to about 2 feet tall and sports around six stem bracts, each with small white blooms in late spring. While this orchid ranges from Northern California all the way to Alaska, it's still rare enough throughout its range to warrant the concern of conservationists.

Red tree voles, northern flying squirrels, Douglas squirrels, and Townsend's chipmunks scurry about collecting nuts, seeds, and forbs to store for the long winter. These rodents have evolved to be

◂ Wooden foot-bridges along this paved stretch of the Rogue River Trail make checking out the natural bridge that much easier.

A rare sighting of a white flower rein orchid.

Large sections of the Rogue River's watershed are off-limits to logging because of the "near threatened" status of the resident northern spotted owls.

vigilant, though, as Pacific fishers and northern spotted owls, among other predators, could be lying in wait.

You may remember the northern spotted owl from headlines in the 1990s about the death of the logging industry at the talons of this bird, whose habitat and existence were threatened by the wholesale elimination of the old-growth temperate rain forest. The result of the hubbub was the closure of upward of 20 million acres of national forest to logging operations beginning in 1993. A move to reopen 3.4 million acres by the outgoing administration in early 2021 is currently being challenged in court to retain full habitat protection. The original closures helped slow the bird's decline, but other factors, such as colonization by more aggressive barred owls, have prevented a wholesale recovery.

Keep hiking for another 0.1 miles, following the rushing river as it tumbles over basalt boulders, creating mini-waterfalls at every step down. If you think you saw a fish jump out of the corner of your eye, you're probably not imagining it: the river is alive with native salmonids. Rainbow, brook, brown, and cutthroat trout as well as Chinook and coho salmon, the two salmon listed as endangered, make the Upper Rogue and its tributaries a big draw for black bears, bobcats, river otters, bald eagles, ospreys, and human anglers. Depending on the subspecies and life cycle stage, these fish indulge in the buffet of the Upper Rogue, feeding on a variety of aquatic insects (caddisflies, mayflies, stoneflies), crayfish, and minnows.

Not surprisingly, the fish runs aren't what they used to be. According to the folklore of local communities whose ancestors have inhabited the Rogue basin for at least the last 8500 years, you could cross the river on the "backs of kings" (Chinook salmon). Researchers estimate that before 1850, coho runs in the Rogue could reach 2.5 million fish each year, while Chinook numbers topped 500,000.

▲ Look for rainbow trout, with their signature silver, pink, and red striping, in the cold, clear waters of the Upper Rogue River.

Today the runs should be diminished by as much as 70 percent for coho and 45 percent for Chinook in the Upper Rogue, factoring in the obvious habitat loss due to a century and a half of development following White settlement. The fact that these runs are in fact diminished much further means other factors are contributing to the drastic salmonid decline in the Rogue. The primary offenders are a dozen dams constructed along the river's 215-mile run over the last two centuries. Even with most of these troublesome concrete blockages now gone thanks to the hard work of environmental activists and a healthy dose of biological common sense, other threats remain, including logging, agriculture, urban development, and increasing water temperatures as a result of climate change.

Keep moving and look out across the river for a cave on the other side, where the river flows in and then back out. This is the end of a collapsed lava tube and a preview of things to come farther ahead on the trail. The raging river water roils in and out of this cave mouth before swirling around again and moving along downstream.

Another 100 feet ahead along the trail, you'll notice the river has disappeared from view. Welcome to the natural bridge, where the Rogue hides from sight as it travels through a 200-foot-long underground tunnel carved by basaltic lava flowing from fissures in Earth's surface some 8000 years ago. This was part of the eruptive phase that blew up Mount Mazama and created Crater Lake, 15 miles east and 3000 feet higher in elevation.

Lava tubes like the one hiding the Rogue below you formed when the upper surface of a basalt flow cooled, causing the outer

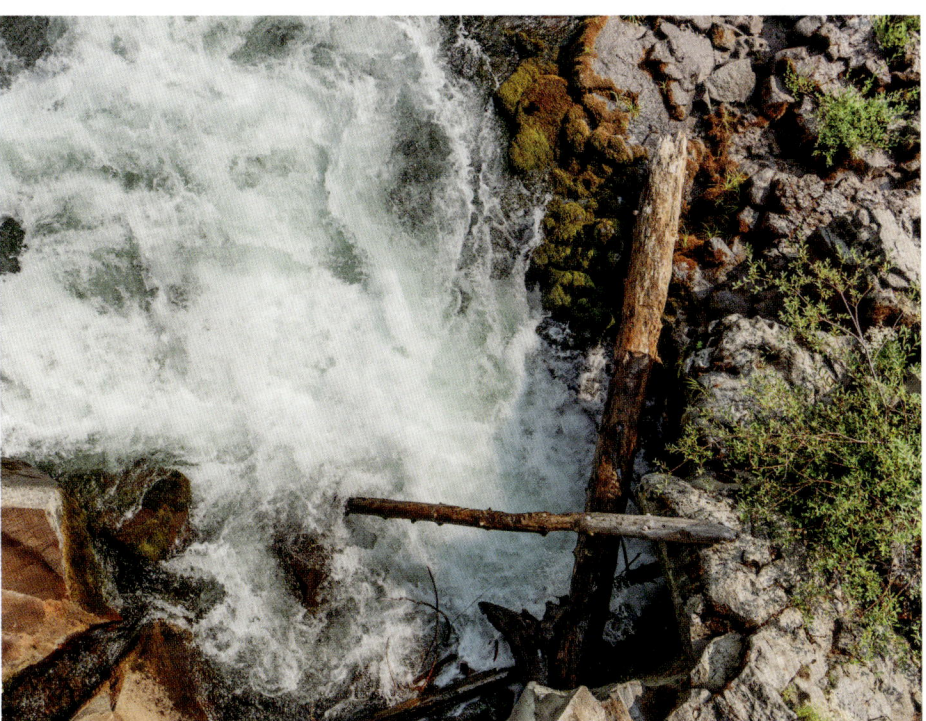

▲ The Rogue River disappears into an old lava tube on the right side of this photo taken from the Natural Bridge viewing deck.

edges to solidify, while hot lava continued to flow underneath. When the flows subsided and the hot lava finally drained out for good, it left behind this long, hollow tube. Eventually the river eroded its way through its basalt channel to meet up with this lava tube and go for a 200-foot subterranean ride. American Indians used the resulting natural bridge to cross over from one side of the river to the other long before the U.S. Forest Service erected the fancy steel and wooden footbridges now connecting the trails along both sides of the raging Rogue.

You'll notice strange, rounded pockets in the basalt, some of them filled with river water and others higher and drier. These "potholes" form when pebbles and small rocks are spun around and around in minor depressions in the underlying basalt by fast rushing river water, eroding the basalt below in a circular fashion like a vortex. The deeper the pothole gets, the harder it is for the rocks at the bottom to get out—and the deeper the rocks carve the pothole. Be careful walking on the basalt over the natural bridge and along the edges of the river; it's easy to sprain an ankle or worse stepping

‹ Douglas fir down! This ancient fallen tree will serve as a nurse log for new seedlings. Look for a neat row of younger trees growing along its course in 100 years.

errantly into one of these depressions. (The Forest Service recommends staying on the trail, not only for your own safety but to not trample fragile plants and lichens.)

Revel in the fact that you are staring into the roiling tumble of one of America's original wild and scenic rivers near its wild and scenic source. At this elevation and above, humans haven't modified or altered the river flows at all, as they have below with dams and other ecologically questionable projects undertaken in the name of progress.

From the natural bridge, the river must travel another 184 miles before it finally meets the Pacific Ocean. The rest of the journey will be fraught with challenges brought on by development, encroachment, and pollution, but up here in the high Cascades the water is still pure, coming out of Crater Lake at 32 degrees F, filtered by alpine forest soils and scraped by basalt on its fast run down, down, down. Drink in this pure scene (but not literally—there is always a slight risk of giardia or other parasites in freshwater rivers, lakes, and streams whenever wildlife is present). Then retrace your steps back to the parking lot, or opt for a longer walk and continue north, then east to cross the river and return via the other side.

Seeing the Rogue River Natural Bridge so close in such a pristine forest setting yields a newfound appreciation for the workings of the natural world.

ERRATIC ROCK STATE NATURAL SITE

90-ton rock once embedded in an iceberg, transported by Missoula Floods

DIFFICULTY
Easy

LENGTH
0.5 miles

LOCATION
near McMinnville, Oregon

This well-traveled glacial erratic rock now watches over the Willamette Valley.

If you've ever felt a little out of place, you'll sympathize with Erratic Rock, a boulder left behind by a traveling iceberg on a hillside near the South Yamhill River in the Willamette Valley. Measuring 15 feet by 5 feet and standing 6 feet tall, this stone is made of argillite. During the Missoula Floods of the last ice age, it was transported within an iceberg on the back of a slow-moving glacier down the Columbia River Gorge. When the ice receded some 10,000 years ago, this rock ended up stranded on a hillside more than 800 miles from its home. Since then, it has become the center of a small ecosystem of lichens, fungi, and plants that are able to capitalize on a geographically unique substrate and setting.

Driving along Oldsville Road on the way to Erratic Rock Natural Area, you'll pass bucolic farms and vineyards. The residents of this fertile valley have been growing corn, hazelnuts (or filberts), walnuts, berries, and other staple crops for generations; more recently wine grapes have come on strong.

Anyone who can do a short walk uphill can make the 0.5-mile out-and-back trek to see this lonely glacial erratic. Also, given the mild climate of the Willamette Valley and the fact that the site isn't so much about seasonal blooms and features means it's worth a visit any time of year. That said, late August is always a nice time to be out and about in the Pacific Northwest, with the invasive, non-native Himalayan blackberry bushes yielding their sweet black treats then.

Enter the trail via a well-marked trailhead and information sign across the street from a pullout with four parking spaces. The trail, paved all the way, heads uphill to start, fenced in on both sides by fruit trees (cherry, pear, and apple), blackberry bushes, and other plants overflowing from the edge of the vineyard it bisects. Rows and rows of grapevines run up the hill to the left of the trail, while a bucolic farm,

▲ Keep an eye out for the sign marking the trailhead to Erratic Rock Natural Area.

▲ Pink flowers on an everlasting pea plant greet visitors along the trail to Erratic Rock.

complete with a classic farmhouse, geese and chickens, and scattered fruit trees, is on the right as you ascend.

A huge, gnarled cedar elm marks a left turn in the trail on the way to the big rock. More blackberry bushes line both sides of the trail, along with profusions of pink flowers on viney everlasting pea plants. Views of a neighboring farm open up to the right; oak groves separate crop fields while chokecherry trees form a border on the left.

As you proceed over the final 500 feet of trail to the big rock, the sides of the trail open up into a manicured, parklike setting, with seldom-mowed grass and a picnic bench. Stands of knee-high Queen Anne's lace, each stem with its own radial crown of small white flowers, fill in the unkept areas along the edge of the state land (the site is a State Natural Area, meaning it is publicly owned and maintained, like a state park). This non-native invasive is common on disturbed or recently cleared lands across the Pacific Northwest, where it can take root quickly and outcompete many native species that are slower to mature. Don't worry too much about the Queen Anne's lace—we've got much bigger environmental problems to address—and keep moving on, as the glacial hitchhiker is coming into view.

The trail ends in a lollipop shape around Erratic Rock, big and bold and multi-colored, with metallic highlights thanks to its high aluminum and silica content. Circle around it on foot, and if you so dare, climb aboard and check out the wondrous 100-mile view, looking south over the Willamette Valley and east to snowcapped Mount Hood. You'll feel like you're standing on top of the world.

While this glacial erratic didn't choose to be here, it sure ended up in a nice spot to spend eternity (or until the next cataclysm moves it along). Of course, glacial erratics are all over this region, but what makes this one different is not only its huge size but also the fact that it's the only example of an argillite erratic ever documented outside of Canada.

Argillite is a fine-grained sedimentary rock consisting of a mix of clay and silt particles hardened over time through the cementation of soil into its pores and cracks in a process known as lithification. This ancient "mudstone" is typically high in silica, which can sparkles in the rock's veins. Argillite degrades into shale when exposed to erosional forces, which has made it easy for amateur rockhounds and irresponsible souvenir hunters to chip away and steal chunks of it. Indeed, the rock today is only about 60 percent of the size it was when settlers first took note of it in the 1840s.

And just how did this big hunk of argillite end up right here exactly? It's a bit of a long story, but not in geologic time. The rock started as mud and silt 600 million years ago, on a seafloor under what is now the Canadian Rockies. This ocean covered the northwestern section of the continent. Various tectonic events uplifted, compacted, and exposed what started as essentially an earthen ball; over eons that ball lithified into rock and settled south of its primordial home in what is now western Montana, where it likely remained for millions of years.

But things started to change for the rock about 13,000 years ago. A giant ice dam that had blocked the Clark Fork River in what is now

▲ The shale-like surface of Erratic Rock is interspersed with lichens.

northern Idaho burst, due to warming temperatures at the beginning of the end of the last ice age. The ice dam kept reforming and rebreaching over the next 2000 years, each time releasing tremendous torrents of water across modern-day eastern Washington and down the Columbia River toward the Pacific Ocean. These massive walls of floodwater—the Missoula Floods—traveled at speeds topping 60 miles an hour, and flowed with 10 times the combined annual volume of all Earth's rivers combined. Besides scouring away the cliff sides and river bottom of what we now call the Columbia River Gorge, these floodwaters carried with them tons of boulder-laden icebergs. As temperatures started to rise, the ice melted, leaving the boulders stranded on hillsides and in fields all along the route of the floods, which extended from the gorge south into the Willamette Valley. The Erratic Rock here is the largest of hundreds of glacial erratics left behind in the region.

Even though Erratic Rock doesn't provide much of a soil substrate, some organisms still manage to eke out an existence on it. In this case, it's the lichens. Look for the lichenized fungi family Rhizocarpaceae, with its signature light green blobs and black outlines. Another big player on Erratic Rock is the crustose lichen genus *Lecidella,* which has little fuzzy black dots, typically on a white background. Yet another, *Xanthoria elegans,* is nicknamed the elegant sunburst lichen, because of its orange-yellow coloration. Several

A close-up view of Erratic Rock's multi-hued face. Iron lends a reddish hue and silica provides some silvery sparkle. ▸

other lichens compete for relatively limited space on this rare substrate (officially Canadian argillite).

Lichens are able to live where no other organisms would dare because they are not just one organism but a form of mutual symbiosis between two or three different species—a fungus and an algae and/or cyanobacteria. The body of a lichen can be considered a small ecosystem unto itself, as it's composed of fungal filaments around cells of green algae and/or blue-

▲ Lichen from the family *Trapeliaceae* on Erratic Rock.

green cyanobacteria. The fungus provides its partner(s) with protection and gets nutrients in return, much in the same way that fungi and tree roots work symbiotically below the forest floor for mutual benefit. Biologists classify lichens as members of the kingdom Fungi, even though they are technically a multi- or dual-species organism, because the fungal partner is the dominant player while the algae and/or cyanobacteria are secondary.

After examining these fascinatingly intricate and colorful lichens and taken in one last panoramic view (or snapped one last photo), turn around and head back down the way you came to the trailhead and parking area.

Looking out as you start to descend, it's hard not to contemplate the striking contrast between the manicured agricultural land all around and the prehistoric, timeless boulder at the top of the hill. If the cultivation of crops represents the point when we humans became civilized, the line between Erratic Rock State Natural Site and the vineyards surrounding it may as well be a before and after of geological time.

Interestingly, the timeline between past and present eons is more connected than it may seem. The Missoula Floods transported boulder-laden icebergs hundreds of miles back then, but also flushed along huge amounts of gravel, sand, silt, and clay. It's these very soil elements that make the Willamette Valley one of the most fertile agricultural regions in the United States today. The ancient floodwaters left behind much more than this albeit noteworthy rock.

The 0.25-mile walk back down goes much quicker heading downhill. Stop to admire any lingering oxeye daisies or lupine that might be sticking out under the fruit trees and blackberry bushes.

WINES & ANCIENT FLOODS

The Willamette Valley has become one of the leading viticultural (grapevine cultivation) areas in the nation over the last two decades, in large part as a result of the rich grape-growing soils created in the wake of the Missoula Floods 13,000–15,000 years ago. Some of the most prized pinot noir, pinot blanc, and pinot gris in the world comes out of this little valley. Here, just an hour outside of Portland, vintners specialize in the Burgundian style of winemaking. If you're so inclined, stop in at one of the local wineries for a tasting or to pick up a bottle of wine made from the soils of the Missoula Floods.

▲ Vineyards surround Erratic Rock State Natural Site.

CAMASSIA NATURAL AREA

A 22.5-acre nature preserve perched on bluffs overlooking the Willamette River

LOCATION
West Linn, Oregon

DIFFICULTY
Easy

LENGTH
1.4 miles

Named after the common camas plant, which blooms across the preserve's meadows in spring, Camassia Natural Area is a 1.4-mile loop trail leading hikers through the preserve's labyrinth of woodlands, wetlands, meadows, and outcrops.

Some 300 different plant species have been recorded at Camassia, a testament to how well the shallow soils of the basalt bluff here retain water and make a nice substrate for photosynthesis. The land, a rare remnant of native Oregon prairie, was protected from development in 1962 when local activists convinced The Nature Conservancy (TNC), a leading international nonprofit conservation group, to buy it and turn it into a preserve to protect dwindling populations of camas and other native plants, as well as for the public to enjoy. Given the prodigious camas blooms, April and early May are the best times to visit the preserve, but it's open year round and the mild climate of Northwest Oregon means any time of year is fine for strolling through.

Look for the marked trailhead at an opening between two fence posts at the edge of the small parking area off Walnut Street in West Linn. At the fork, go left to follow the loop trail in a clockwise direction (although hiking it the other way is fine, too). The first section of the preserve you'll encounter is where trail crews from AmeriCorps cleared overlapping mats of English ivy, thus freeing up hundreds of trees from the vines' chokehold and clearing acres of forest floor for native plants to recolonize. Since then, Oregon ash trees, black cottonwoods, and vine maples—all natives with a right to be here—have reclaimed this stretch of forest.

As you hike, be on the lookout for poison oak around ankle and knee height; it is prevalent here. If your bare skin brushes up against this climbing shrub with tan stems and three shiny leaves, you'll likely suffer an itchy rash that can take a few days to dissipate. Staying on the trail is one way to avoid coming in contact with it, but wearing long pants or knee socks can also help prevent direct skin exposure to the plant's irritating oils.

Keep moving and soon you'll find yourself amid the grassy plateau in the middle of the preserve, where the camas blooms are most heavily concentrated. If you time your visit right, you'll feel like you're floating on a sea of flower petals as you cross through the

‹ Back in 1962, The Nature Conservancy purchased the land that became Camassia Natural Area to preserve dwindling populations of native common camas plants (the violet-purple flowers here) that used to blanket the landscape across the Willamette Valley. The pink wildflower is rosy plectritis.

▲ Beware of poison oak along the sides of the trail.

▲ Common camas was the inspiration for the Natural Area's name.

preserve's highlands. The violet-purple, six-petaled blooms surround a light green-yellow stigma, while bright yellow anthers seem to orbit around the center.

Prior to White settlement in the 1800s, camas was very common throughout the Willamette River Valley as well as elsewhere in the Pacific Northwest. Humans have been here for at least 8000 years, and local communities like the Kalapuya made extensive use of camas plants as a staple food. The plant's nutrient- and antioxidant-packed root can be eaten raw, roasted, boiled, fried, or dried, and it keeps well in storage for long periods of time, which was important to help Indigenous peoples make it through the long, rainy winters when nothing was available to harvest fresh.

Camas is far from the only bloom during spring at Camassia. The pink flowers often seen alongside the camas blooms are rosy plectritis. Other beautiful bloomers include fool's onion, blue-eyed Mary, false Solomon's seal, fawn lily, Indian hellebore, western trillium, and harvest brodiaea. While the violet-blue of the common camas blooms dominate the view, these other blooms contribute a lot of complementary color bling to the scene.

Keep walking across the wildflower-filled plateau and at the other side you'll enter a small grove of quaking aspens, rare this far west but thriving here in the thin volcanic soils. All the aspens in this grove spring from a single rhizomatic root system, so are technically one organism, not many trees.

• Plenty of other blooms join common camas in springtime on Camassia's grassland plateau, including (from left) fawn lily, blue-eyed Mary, and false Solomon's seal.

This is a great place to stop and look for wildlife. Anna's hummingbirds frequent the preserve grounds and the transition here between forest and grassy plateau gives them plenty of nectar options to sample. Other avian species to watch for include spotted towhees, cedar waxwings, Bewick's wrens, and golden- and ruby-crowned kinglets.

Other wildlife at Camassia include lots of ants, beetles, spiders, and other creepy-crawlies, but also the 2-inch-long green or brown Pacific chorus frog, a master of camouflage that can change its skin tone to match its chosen surface.

Camassia is also a haven for the western gray squirrel, which has been extirpated from much of its former range in California and Washington State. Conservationists are looking at ways to expand the range of the western gray squirrel in its native range, but stiff competition from hardier invasive squirrels coupled with human development of any remaining habitat make preserves like this one essential for wildlife (and plants) on the brink.

At the junction in the trail, go right to continue on the loop trail. In another 200 feet or so you'll pass through a savanna ecosystem dominated by old, lichen-encrusted Oregon white oaks. Peely barked Pacific madrone boughs snake out horizontally to catch more sunlight on their leathery evergreen leaves. This type of sparsely wooded meadow, with an even mix of sun and shade, is increasingly rare—even though it was once common throughout this part of Oregon.

It's unusual to see quaking aspen trees this far west, but they seem to love the thin, rocky soils above the Willamette River.

‹ Most people don't realize that the western gray squirrel is a threatened species up and down the West Coast. Much of its habitat has been either paved over or taken over by more aggressive eastern gray squirrels and other wildlife.

A small side trail to the left here leads to an overlook of a cell tower just east of the preserve's boundary, where a pair of ospreys has been returning to nest every winter since 1997. While these fish hawks will occasionally dine on a rodent or other small, terrestrial mammal, they are pescatarians by choice, preferring fish. This perch gives them access to a healthy supply of both surf (from the nearby Willamette River) and turf (from the meadows and forests of the preserve).

Return to the main trail and keep heading east. In another 100 feet or so you'll start walking on exposed basalt bedrock that hardened into place from lava flows here some 15 million years ago, following major volcanic eruptions to the east. This outcrop was then further scoured by waves of rock-laden flood water traveling at 60 miles per hour, following the collapse of Lake Missoula's ice dam. Humans couldn't have designed a better way to showcase the geologic past of this land. The exposed bedrock here tells the tale of those two major geological events—and their local effects right here—more succinctly than any interpretive sign ever could.

Continue hiking as the trail hooks to the right and you'll come to a clearing with a direct view to the east, showcasing 11,249-foot Mount Hood, Oregon's tallest peak and an impressive poster child for the Cascade Range. If you brought a picnic lunch or a snack, this would be a great place to enjoy it while enjoying a sublime view.

‣ Talons ready, an osprey descends to nab a fish.

Back on the main trail, the next attraction is a series of study plots, where Nature Conservancy researchers are testing different methods of controlling invasive English ivy. This aggressive vine topples trees and displaces native vegetation. Formerly covered in ivy, this stretch of forest is now being restored to its former glory, much like the area you passed through at the beginning of the loop.

Continue on another 400 feet or so through the forest and return to the start of the loop at the trailhead. Congratulations: you've seen it all. And hopefully you've learned a thing or two along the way, or at least enjoyed a relaxing stroll through a beautiful natural area.

SALT CREEK FALLS

Dramatic 286-foot waterfall and mossy canyon carved from basalt

DIFFICULTY
Easy to diffi-
cult options

LOCATION
near Oakridge, Oregon

LENGTH
0.5 to 2 miles

With the bustling university town of Eugene only an hour's drive west, it's hard to believe how remote and wild the forest and canyon surrounding Salt Creek Falls remains today. Even though there is evidence of human occupation in the region as far back as 7000 years, Salt Creek Falls, nestled in a desolate pocket of the Cascades at more than 4000 feet elevation, wasn't officially discovered until 1887—some four decades after nearby Eugene was settled by French fur trappers and their families. These days it's an easy stop off Highway 58 over Willamette Pass, one of Oregon's major Cascade-crossing routes. While it may not be untouched wilderness anymore, it sure feels like it as you hike around the site. The short path to the main falls overlook is paved, but if you want to venture deeper down into Salt Creek Canyon for even better views, bring sturdy shoes suitable for hiking. You can stop to visit the falls any time of year, but the parking lot won't be plowed out in winter (in which case you can park by the locked gate, or at the nearby Salt Creek Sno-Park, and walk—or snowshoe—the 0.5 miles into the falls overlook).

Starting out on foot from the far reaches of the circular driveway and parking area, you can't miss the elaborate trailhead kiosk that explains the ecology, history, and recreational activities of the region. The visitor facilities, including an elaborate wheelchair-accessible paved trail to the main viewing area, railings along the canyon edge, picnic spots carved out of the forest, and stairs to facilitate different viewing angles of the falls, were built by the Civilian Conservation Corps, the Depression-era work program that put 3 million

Columnar basalt fills in the upper canyon behind majestic Salt Creek Falls. ▸

unemployed Americans to work on parks infrastructure and other related projects.

Continue down the wide paved path, passing through a lush forest of Douglas firs, Greene's mountain ashes, western hemlocks, Pacific dogwoods, rhododendrons, silver firs, vine maples, subalpine firs, and thimbleberry bushes. Beargrass and pinemat manzanita colonize open stretches where the trees subside. Map lichens spread out over the faces of glacial erratic rocks. The pine-scented setting is classic, midelevation Oregon Cascades forest.

In 150 feet you'll arrive at the first fenced overlook of magnificent Salt Creek Falls. You'll have to crane your neck a bit to get a good look at the falls as they drop precipitously down the side of a steeply graded cliff into the canyon below. Salt Creek Falls has long been known as Oregon's second-tallest waterfall (after 620-foot Multnomah Falls in the Columbia River Gorge, near Mount Hood), but more accurate contemporary counts list it as fifteenth tallest in the state.

This beautiful scene was millions of years in the making. The first step in the geological process was the Cascades uplift, which started some 4 million years back and concluded only a few hundred

▸ The Civilian Conservation Corps constructed the visitor facilities and trails at Salt Creek Falls as one of many projects around the Pacific Northwest during the 1930s.

▴ On the way to Salt Creek Falls, you'll pass through quintessential mixed-age Cascades forest.

▴ Map lichens colonize lots of territory on glacial erratic rocks.

▴ The bottom of the upper canyon, now filled in with columnar basalt, is visible above the top of the mossy, green lower canyon stratum behind Salt Creek Falls' thunderous veil.

thousand years ago. This uplift occurred as successive eruptions throughout the West Coast volcanic arc (from Northern California up through British Columbia) built up the mountain range we now know as the Cascades. As these massive mountains formed, winds off the Pacific Ocean delivered lots of precipitation to the region (much like today); all of this running water sculpted the still-fresh landforms of the Cascades into the serrated ridges and V-shaped canyons so familiar to us now.

Following this volcanic uplift, an ice age enveloped the planet, turning Salt Creek into a 150-foot-thick river of glacial ice. This slow-moving ice flow widened and further eroded out the creek bed, turning it from a V shape into a deeper U shape. Another subsequent period of volcanism around 600,000 years ago filled Upper Salt Creek Canyon with a layer of basalt some 300 feet thick. As this lava-derived, volcanic rock cooled, chunks of it contracted and shrank. Meanwhile, the advance and retreat of glaciers multiple times in the intervening eons further scrubbed the underlying, weaker pyroclastic rock. The combined results of all these stresses are the columnar basalt cliffs we see filling in the upper canyon today behind Salt Creek Falls. The rocks' telltale starburst patterns reveal their geological fingerprint.

⏵ Black swifts prefer to dwell on ledges, especially those behind waterfalls.

Revel in the majesty of the falls, which first tumble over a series of smaller cascades before finally falling 286 feet in one final horsetail swoop. While Salt Creek Falls may be the fifteenth tallest waterfall in Oregon, it's third when it comes to largest single drops. And what a drop it is, with some 50,000 gallons of water making the dramatic jump every minute of every day. Mists fill up the canyon below year round, feeding the plants, lichens, and mosses competing for limited vertical space on the canyon walls.

Keep an eye out for black swifts flying back and forth through the voluminous veil of Salt Creek Falls to their nests in dark caverns on the rocky ledges behind the waterfall. These unique ledge-dwelling birds—about 7 inches long and blackish from beak to tail feathers, with sickle-shaped wings—feed in midair, preferring winged ants but settling for any flying insects. On clear days the birds forage in airspace so high that they look like little black specks in the sky, but when the clouds roll in you can spot them cruising at a much more viewable altitude. They spend most of their time on the wing, traveling as far as 50 miles daily in order to find enough food to sustain themselves. The best time to look for them here at Salt Creek Falls is just prior to sunset, when they return home to roost.

DIAMOND PEAK WILDERNESS

As you are approaching Salt Creek Falls on Highway 58, look south and you'll no doubt be delighted by the view of jagged Diamond Peak, which punctuates the horizon at an elevation of 8744 feet on the crest of the Cascades. The peak, an extinct shield volcano, formed slowly over time during an eruptive phase thousands of years ago, as layers of fluid lava successively built up and cooled over and over again. Once the peak was formed and the volcano dormant, glaciers started wearing it down into multiple cirques, dividing the summit into several peaks connected by pinnacled lava ridges.

▴ Diamond Peak is visible from Oregon Highway 58.

If you love getting away from it all, make time to visit the wilderness area around and including Diamond Peak. There are only two ways in: 20 miles of rough U.S. Forest Service roads from Highway 58, or 10 miles of hiking (or snowshoeing, or skiing) from Willamette Pass. Once you're immersed in this magical backcountry, far from any cell tower or convenience store, you'll spend your time exploring game trails and dipping your toes in any of the dozens of alpine lakes dotting the topographic map. Backcountry skiing down the snowfields of Diamond Peak's cirques is a favorite winter pastime for locals and Eugene residents as well. The Diamond Peak Wilderness is also one of the scenic highlights of the Oregon section of the Pacific Crest Trail—you just may run into some through-hikers if you are there in summer or early fall.

While the hardscrabble birds have been around a lot longer than humans, conservationists are worried about their future. Black swift population numbers have dropped precipitously from about 3.5 million birds in 1970 to only 200,000 today—a decline of 94 percent in a half century. At their current rate of decline, the birds will lose half of their existing population within another decade. Beyond that, it's impossible to know if our great-grandchildren will ever be able to see one, except in the pages of a history book. No one knows for sure what's causing the mysterious decline. The usual suspects include the success of pesticides in killing off large numbers of insects (the birds' primary food source), habitat loss as a result of human encroachment on habitat, and, of course, climate change.

Whether or not you see black swifts coming and going, you won't be disappointed by the landscape view in front of you as you stare out into the green and gray canyon below. Some 300 feet below you, Salt Creek Falls hits the canyon floor and meanders in a serpentine fashion on its way toward its mouth at the Middle Fork Willamette River, 22 miles to the west—and 3000 feet lower in elevation—near the small city of Oakridge, an outdoor recreation hot spot in the Willamette National Forest. Salt Creek itself is named for a series of springs downstream from the falls that are rich in salt and loved by local fauna such as Roosevelt elk and Columbian black-tailed deer in search of a sodium fix.

If you want to check out the canyon floor and the base of the falls for yourself, walk up the stairs to the right and find the start of a hiking trail that zigzags precipitously down the opposite side of the canyon over the course of a vertiginous 0.5 miles. But the best view of Salt Creek Falls—looking directly across to the middle of the great

▴ The canyon floor is accessible via a short but challenging 0.5-mile trail to the bottom.

cascade—comes after only about 800 feet down the trail (in case you want to turn around at that point).

Another short side trail heads off in the other direction from the main overlook and traverses the canyon rim, culminating at a picnic spot on a ledge near the top of Salt Creek Falls. There just isn't a bad view within this small corner of the Willamette Pass area, and the constant crashing sound of falling water is strangely soothing, despite the ruckus. Even if your visit to Salt Creek Falls is brief, the view of the majestic waterfall, its lush green canyon, and the surrounding forest will remain burnished in your memory.

TRAIL OF THE MOLTEN LAND

Otherworldly ancient lava flow used by
NASA to train moon-bound astronauts

DIFFICULTY
Easy

LOCATION
Newberry National Volcanic Monument, near Bend, Oregon

LENGTH
1 mile

People say that the Pacific Northwest—with its high desert plateaus, glacier-clad peaks, and rugged coastlines—is a land of extremes. But the fact that the region plays host to jagged, red-brown and black, volcanic-bouldered moonscapes really cements that reputation.

While this harsh landscape would be difficult to navigate on foot given the size and sharpness of the lava rocks all around, the U.S. Forest Service has made it easy with a paved, wheelchair-accessible trail. Anyone who can walk a mile (the entire trail, with its central loop, is 1.1 miles long, with only 135 feet of overall elevation gain) should have no problem making this short, rewarding journey through the once-flowing lava.

Keep in mind that you'll be at 4500 feet elevation, so make sure you have acclimated to the altitude before doing anything too strenuous. Late spring through early fall is the best time to visit, with midsummer bringing the best wildflower blooms (and color shows).

Park at the Lava Lands Visitor Center 13 miles south of Bend off Highway 97, and look for signs pointing to the trailhead, which is to the right of and behind the complex of visitor facilities. Follow the paved feeder trail and go right at the junction to the Trail of the Molten Land.

• The Trail of the Molten Land leaves from behind the Lava Lands Visitor Center, off U.S. Highway 97 south of Bend, Oregon.

▴ Pacific rhodo-
dendron adorns
the forest on the
access trail leading
out toward the
basalt lava flows.

(The left fork follows the 0.25-mile Trail of the Whispering Pines that loops through a ponderosa pine forest adjacent to the lava flows; it's well worth an extra few steps if you have the time later.)

After another 100 feet of hiking, the trail leaves the forest and enters the rock-encrusted terrain of the lava flows. This landscape as we now know it was created about 7000 years ago, when Newberry Volcano erupted, sending hot lava out of some 400 different vents and cinder cones—more than any other volcano in the world—across the 17 square miles encompassing the heart of the huge, mostly underground volcano. (The entire volcano stretches underground across some 1200 square miles, roughly the size of the state of Rhode Island.) One of those cinder cones was Lava Butte—1.75 miles north of here and worth a drive to the top for the view—which sent wave after wave of hot lava some 5 miles to the north and west, decimating verdant virgin pine forests. The lava cooled as it spread, settling into jagged basalt chunks that now form a perennially choppy sea of black rock all around you.

Basalt is a hard, black, extrusive igneous rock. (Igneous means it's of volcanic origin; extrusive means it's derived specifically from

an eruptive event.) Igneous rocks come in many forms, determined by their mineral content and where they cool and harden, but basalt is the most common. Compared to other igneous rocks, it is low in silica (sand and glass)—a function of its origins as flowing lava that can't get bogged down with lots of sand. This low silica content makes it appear less brilliant than, say, obsidian, another igneous rock, which is more valuable to rock hounds.

On the Trail of the Molten Land, at Newberry National Volcanic Monument.

    The reason NASA came here back in the mid-1960s is that basalt chunks similar to those found here are also found on the surface of the moon, as a result of lunar lava flows. (Likewise, Mars has similar basalt on its surface.) The astronauts training here had issues with falling on the basalt, which led to not only sprained ankles but also ripped space suits. As a result, important improvements in the design and ruggedness of the suits were made—but the moral of the story for us today is that it's tough going out on those sharp rocks, and to stay on the trail as much as possible.

NEWBERRY VOLCANO: STILL A RISK

Although you can't see any fresh, glowing lava today, Newberry Volcano is still seismically and geothermally active. The caldera you are walking on sits over a shallow magma body only 1–3 miles below the surface. The last major eruption was 1300 years ago—a blink of an eye in geologic time, and not reassuring to those living within a 30-mile radius who would potentially be in the volcano's path of destruction. If tectonic forces were to stir up the volcano's lava reserves and pressure built inside, a larger eruption could ensue. The result could be as simple as a few area roads being consumed by lava—or as devastating as nearby towns being wiped off the map and ash being blown into Earth's orbit. The latter could impact skies around the world for days, weeks, or even months. Given the risks, volcanologists from the U.S. Geological Survey's Cascades Volcano Observatory and the University of Washington's Pacific Northwest Seismic Network are keeping a close eye on Newberry, monitoring it for hints of potential eruptive behavior. Rest assured that if an eruption were to become imminent, the public would be warned and access to the Newberry National Volcanic Monument as well as surrounding public lands would be restricted.

Just because the landscape is harsh and dry doesn't mean nothing grows here. In fact, several species well adapted to such conditions prevail, albeit in small numbers. These xeric plants have evolved with different techniques for retaining water during long seasons of drought. Examples include limiting the size of leaves to reduce energy needs, growing special tiny hairs to catch morning dew, and developing waxy coats to reflect sunlight and prevent unnecessary drying.

The sun sets over Lava Butte, the cinder cone that blew out all this lava some 7000 years ago.

itself up out of the jagged, black rock "waves." This tree is likely more than 2000 years old and still going strong. The environment here in the high desert is so dry year round that the basalt rocks, even at 7000 years old, don't erode much. Because of this, trees here must adapt to living on small pockets of soil. Ponderosa pines adapt to this environment by sending out a single moisture-seeking taproot, then growing in a spiral fashion so that fluids and nutrients are distributed evenly around the entire trunk and to all branches. Any secondary roots act only as "feet" to help anchor the tree; they don't actually access and spread nutrients like the main taproot does.

In a more typical setting, such as the ponderosa pine forest just a mile to the west (and barely out of the path of the lava flow 7000 years ago), trees send down multiple roots, all of which access water and soil and feed branches directly above them. Those trees grow straight and tall.

Also due to the harsh conditions here—lack of water and other nutrients, no protection from heavy winds—these twisty pines grow very slowly and end up looking more like the bristlecone pines of California's eastern Sierra than like the stately ponderosas they are.

‹ A fallen, twisted, "dwarf" ponderosa pine trunk is surrounded by rubber rabbitbrush and wax currant.

It's hard to believe these "dwarf" trees are hundreds of years old, given how much smaller they are then their neighbors along the Trail of the Whispering Pines.

There are far more remains of dwarf ponderosas than living examples out on the lava these days. As a tree matures, its single taproot has trouble supporting all that woody mass and eventually can't bear the weight of the trunk and branches anymore. The resulting downed wood isn't going anywhere anytime soon, though, given the lack of erosional forces. Yet these twisted tree carcasses still contribute nutrients to the ecosystem and serve as roosting and cover sites for animals brave enough to live on the basalt.

There's not a lot of wildlife out on the lava flows, due to the lack of nutrients. The animals that do make a go of it mostly stay out of sight, so you probably won't see a long-tailed weasel as it slithers between rocks under the cover of darkness in pursuit of its next rodent meal. Likewise, pallid-winged grasshoppers blend in with their surroundings and are seldom seen by hikers—but if you're here in late summer, listen for their signature mating call: short spurts of repetitive clicks that sound like an intermittent water sprinkler at work.

If you hang around long enough, preferably toward the edge of the day (early morning or late afternoon), you stand a better chance of seeing wildlife. While larger mammals tend to stick to surrounding forests, it's not unheard of to see black-tailed deer or Rocky Mountain elk prancing around. Cascade golden-mantled ground

Yellow-pine chipmunks are very cute, but for their own good, don't feed them. ‣

squirrels—with reddish brown heads and bodies and broad black-and-white stripes running the length of their backs and tails—are likely to follow along on your tour of the Trail of the Molten Land.

You can expect similar behavior from the yellow-pine chipmunk, smaller than its ground squirrel cousin and with narrower black-and-white racing stripes that extend all the way from the tip of the nose to the end of the tail.

If you see a larger rodent with grizzled brownish fur, small round ears, a whitish spot between the eyes and a yellow belly, say hello to a yellow-bellied marmot. These large, burrowing rodents feed on leaves and blossoms as well as whatever grains, legumes, and fruit they can scavenge. They'll even tolerate the occasional insect when times are tough.

DON'T FEED THE WILDLIFE

It's never a good idea to feed wildlife, as they do just fine on their own and giving them human food can only serve to make them less able to forage on their own, which hampers their long-term survival odds. Another reason to keep your food for you is that your bread or crackers or candy could actually cause the squirrels, chipmunks, pikas, and marmots here to starve if they include some of it in their food caches. There, it could contaminate naturally foraged foods with unusual bacteria, yeasts, or chemicals.

Meanwhile, American pikas—the so-called rabbits of the rocks—often signal their presence with a whistle. These lagomorphs, like their rabbit and hare cousins, are strict vegetarians and are known to always cache a portion of the herbs and shoots they harvest in a hay pile to save for the long, cold winter, when fresh food is nonexistent. Pikas move these hay piles around to keep them safe from the elements and from other wildlife raiders.

Rock wrens actually nest among the basalt boulders of the lava flows. ▸

Many bird species can be found around the moonscape—mountain chickadees, evening grosbeaks, red-breasted nuthatches, pygmy nuthatches, and red crossbills, to name a few—pass over and some—red-tailed hawks, golden eagles—can be seen diving for an occasional squirrel or pika. If a turkey vulture is circling, there could be an animal carcass nearby, so steer clear.

While most birds avoid nesting on the lava flows because of the lack of resources and protection there, the rock wren is an exception. This small, unassuming brown-and-white songbird with a long, slightly curved beak nests within cavities in the basalt and, for some unknown reason, creates stone walkways to its nest entrance.

As you round the final curve of the central loop, hang a right on the access trail back to the parking lot. The visitor center is worth a visit if it's open, and you can ride the shuttle bus or drive yourself up to the top of Lava Butte for a 360-degree view of the extent of the Newberry Volcano's terrestrial impact. It is amazing how much an ancient volcanic eruption can still dominate landscapes and ecosystems to this day. While the forest that once stood here must have been wild and beautiful, now a whole new set of plants and animals have been able to colonize these lands, further enhancing the biological diversity of the Pacific Northwest.

RIMROCK TRAIL

Volcanic spires rising 600 feet
above the Crooked River

DIFFICULTY
Easy

LOCATION
Smith Rock State Park, near Redmond, Oregon

LENGTH
0.5 miles

Central Oregon's high desert plateau is blessed with a pleasant climate year round, including more than 300 days of sunshine and only 9 inches of rain annually, which makes Smith Rock worth visiting any time of year. Summer, when temperatures routinely soar above 80 degrees F, is the most popular time, but spring is the locals' favorite, thanks to wildflower blooms across the canyon floor and upland trail sides. You're more likely to have the trails to yourself in fall and winter, but temperatures can dip below freezing, so bundle up.

The Rimrock Trail, a level 0.5 miles, follows the ridge overlooking all of this splendor, with a few park benches strategically placed along the way. They are good places to contemplate the Zen beauty of the monolithic rock and its surrounding scenery.

Starting behind the green yurt that serves as a visitor center, pick up the crushed gravel Rimrock Trail as it skirts the edge of the canyon. Of course, the main attraction here is the view of Smith Rock itself. More an aggregation of connected spires and cliffs than a single rock, this Central Oregon natural landmark started to take shape as a result of a series of volcanic supereruptions over a 2-million-year period beginning about 29 million years ago. When the dust (and magma and ash) settled, the cliffs of Smith Rock rose over the surrounding landscape at the western edge of the newly formed Crooked River Caldera, a

▲ The Rimrock Trail hugs the side of the canyon overlooking Smith Rock.

400-square-mile depression in the land representing the collapsed mouth of a now long-extinct volcano. Looking at a map, you can find the edge of the huge, ancient, bean-shaped caldera by tracing your finger clockwise from Smith Rock in the far west to Gray Butte, Grizzly Mountain, Barnes Butte, Prineville Reservoir, and Powell Butte. Each of these outcrops shares the same beginning—as what is called "welded tuff," which forms when still-hot particles of volcanic ash fuse together after settling on the surface, eventually cooling and turning to rock.

While this welded tuff relief at the edge of the caldera was no doubt here to stay, it wasn't until around 400,000 years ago that a new round of volcanism again reshaped the landscape of present-day Central Oregon. That is when the general form of the Smith Rock we know and love today took shape. At that point, the eruption of the Newberry Volcano some 40 miles to the south sent wave after wave of hot lava across the landscape, covering Smith Rock as well as just about every other surface within a 1200-square-mile radius. This lava eventually cooled to rock-hard basalt.

The force of these flows also pushed the Crooked River right up against the cliffs along Smith Rock. In the intervening millennia, the river's flow, plus wind, precipitation, and gravity, have helped chisel the flanks of Smith Rock. When heavy rocks come loose, they fall

The still-eroding welded tuff of Smith Rock is a great substrate for rock climbing. White markings are from the chalk climbers use for a better grip. ▸

One of the natural wonders of the Pacific Northwest, Smith Rock looks like the ancient ruins of a castle, with the meandering Crooked River encircling it like a moat.

down, eventually breaking into smaller and smaller pieces and eventually, soil fragments.

The jagged skyline of Smith Rock today is the result of all of these volcanic insults and subsequent erosional forces combined. Of course, geologic time includes right now, and the cliffs and hoodoos of Smith Rock aren't done crumbling. Hopefully the increasing visitation numbers in recent years—as the population of nearby Bend grows and more people head out to see the wonders of nature—won't expedite the erosion process. This is a spot where "leave no trace" guidelines are essential for keeping nature natural.

Move west on the trail, and soon you'll be looking directly across to Morning Glory Wall, a rock formation famous for its wide range of climbing routes. See if you can spot any climbers on the sheer rock face. Smith Rock is known as the birthplace of the sport climbing movement in American rock climbing, and today remains a prime destination for practitioners of the sport from all over the globe.

After watching these human spiders defy gravity, train your gaze down into the canyon below. The ribbonlike course of the

▴ The pinnacles at the top of Smith Rock are worn down by wind, weather, and gravity.

The welded tuff walls of Smith Rock are reddish thanks to lots of iron ore within.

Crooked River glistens in the seemingly ever-present sunlight. The relative abundance of floral diversity here is surprising given how parched the landscape seems; Central Oregon lies in the rain shadow of the Cascades. With only 9 inches of rain a year here, it's a wonder there is so much greenery everywhere you look.

Like much of the Intermountain West (between the Rockies and the Cascades), this is sagebrush steppe country, dominated by big sagebrush and to a lesser extent three-tip sagebrush. The profusion of these plants casts an almost-fluorescent light green shadow as far as the eye can see.

Of course, between the sagebrush, lots of other plants have found their own niches. Great Basin wild rye, sulfur buckwheat, and narrowleaf mock goldenweed are among the more Plain Jane–looking plants at your feet. Black cottonwood trees crop up on the creek flat below, while occasional western junipers and ponderosa pines interrupt the otherworldly views from along the ridgeline you're traversing. The tiny scarlet flowers of drought-tolerant curl-leaf mountain mahogany are easy to miss but well worth examination if you happen to spot them.

Tall Oregon grape's leathery barbed leaves prevent mule deer and Rocky Mountain elk from grazing and help the plant store water during summer droughts. Its berries are favorites of greater sage-grouses, cedar waxwings, dark-eyed juncos, spotted towhees, gray foxes, and raccoons, among other wildlife—and humans have been making Oregon grape berries into jam for generations. Native communities in this part of the world (including the Tenino and Northern Paiute) used tinctures from tall Oregon grape's bark and berries medicinally to treat liver, eye, and gallbladder issues.

The real show around Smith Rock starts to happen as spring dawns and dozens of wildflower species start to flash their colorful blooms. Hood's phlox, mock orange, bicolor lupine, arrowleaf balsamroot, morning glory, desert Indian paintbrush, sagebrush mariposa lily, Nootka rose, and white-stemmed frasera are among the many blooms dressing up the otherwise reddish, sand-colored landscape.

All that nectar is far from overlooked by local insects. Orchard mason bees come for the widespread availability of pollen. Painted ladies, monarchs, and several other butterfly species alight on blooms and stems briefly, always flying away just before you can snap a picture. Anna's hummingbirds and rufous hummingbirds make a habit of stopping by on their travels, getting sips of nature's energy drink where they can while spreading pollen far and wide.

▲ The sagebrush mariposa lily is one of the showier blooms of Smith Rock in springtime.

Other birds abound in this oasislike setting that offers habitat niches for everyone. Look for canyon wrens in the cliffs pulling ants, beetles, and spiders out of rock crevices with their long, pointy bills. White-throated swifts also nest in the cliffs and subsist on insects and spiders, but these hunters snap up their flying prey in midair. Small flocks of American bushtits patrol the rock hoodoos, also hunting for insects and spiders. Northern flickers dart between snags and curling western juniper boughs, hammering for insects crawling around under the bark.

Soon you'll be facing another iconic rock formation called the Dihedrals—tall, sharp-angled columns—where you'll also likely see climbers. Directly below, examine the top of a big ponderosa pine growing near the banks of the Crooked River for a bald eagle's nest. You may even glimpse one of our national symbols as it commutes

▲ Seen from above, it's no wonder the Crooked River is so named.

back and forth on feeding missions. These iconic brown-and-white, yellow-billed raptors live well here, dining on a healthy assortment of small mammals (mountain cottontails, yellow-bellied marmots, Merriam's ground squirrels) that they pluck from the surrounding

◂ Smith Rock seems to jut into the air from the Crooked River Canyon. Bald eagles sometimes nest in the ponderosa pine on the left.

boulder fields and canyon walls. Fish from the river are also often on the menu.

When the eagles do prey on fish, they are helping transfer some of the nutrients of the river into the sand and soils of the surrounding land, reinforcing the oasislike feeling along the banks of the Crooked River, an aquatic ecosystem unto itself. In fact, those very trout beloved by bald eagles and human fishermen are indicator species for the health of the river. While the fish runs aren't anything like they were before White settlement and the widespread damming of the American West, the Crooked River still supports impressive numbers, with some 8000 fish per mile during the height of the fall runs. Mayflies and caddisflies float on top, ready for plucking by fish and birds. Down in the water column, shallow as it may be in parts, olive scud, which are essentially freshwater shrimp, create a perpetual buffet for these hungry anadromous fish on their way downstream and out to sea.

Where the Rimrock Trail starts to curve south back toward the parking lot, take another look out at Smith Rock and see if you can make out Snoopy on top of his dog house at the top of Asterisk Pass.

• Can you see Snoopy in the rocks of Asterisk Pass?

• Yellow rabbit-brush colonizes open or disturbed patches of desert, such as under this fence alongside the Rimrock Trail.

Down below, horses and their riders could be fording the river en route to greener pastures on the north side of Smith Rock.

After 0.5 miles of hiking, you'll come to a junction with the Rope-de-Dope Trail that snakes its way down into the canyon. Following the trail down to the river and back up will add about 0.6 miles to the hike (and coming back up is a switchback-laden slog), but dipping your toes or more in the friendly shallows of the Crooked River may be worth it.

Otherwise, proceed along the Rimrock Trail as it winds back to where you parked. Yellow rabbitbrush spreads out in the openings between the sagebrush, coloring in the landscape in the fall with its tiny yellow flower clusters. Western fence lizards speed away if you surprise them on the trail—or they might stay still on a rock as you pass, hoping not to be noticed. Be wary of rattlesnakes concealed under rocks or behind bushes as you hurry to finish this last section of the trail.

In an easy 0.5 miles, you'll have seen some of the best views in Central Oregon, while learning a thing or two about the interconnectedness of nature. No doubt, as you drive away and see Smith Rock in your rear-view mirror, you'll start daydreaming about your next visit.

CLARNO PALISADES

Age-old mudflows, fossilized plants, and a natural stone arch

DIFFICULTY
Easy to moderate

LOCATION
John Day Fossil Beds National Monument, Clarno Unit, near Clarno, Oregon

LENGTH
1.3 miles

The Geologic Time Trail, flanked at every turn by big sagebrush plants, yields epic views of the Palisades rock formation.

At the Clarno Palisades in the John Day Fossil Beds National Monument, visitors can journey through tens of millions of years in geologic time over the course of just a few short hiking trails. Winding along and into the iconic crumbling rock faces that dominate the landscape for miles around, these trails offer wondrous views, fossilized plants, and a dry waterfall.

While the Pacific Northwest is a land of extremes, a hot and sandy desert isn't what usually springs to mind. But that's just what visitors to Eastern Oregon in general, and the John Day Fossil Beds National Monument in particular, will find. Take a step or two off-trail and you may just brush up against a spiky plant of one sort or another, or even a rattlesnake, so do your best to stay on the path. The Geologic Time Trail, first of the three trails traversing the Palisades, is relatively flat. On the Trail of Fossils and the Clarno Arch extensions (mileage includes all three), however, be prepared for a bit more scrambling up sandy switchbacks to get close to the Palisades.

The Geologic Time Trail starts at the Palisades picnic area (and main parking lot) and traverses 0.25 miles carved between sagebrush and other brushy desert understory. Interpretive signs along the way spell out the geologic history by describing how the environment here changed over millions of years. For instance, 50 million years ago, the site where the Palisades now stand looked more like a semitropical rain forest than a dry and dusty desert. Magnolia and palm trees dotted the landscape. Tiny 4-toed horses browsed on understory vegetation, while carnivorous possum-like creodonts ate anything they could catch and stuff into their powerful jaws. Annual rainfall totaled around 120 inches per year then; today some 13 inches a year is normal. The rock formation that eroded down to become what we know as the Palisades formed in this period initially as volcanic mudflows (lahars) were expelled from a massive volcano on the site.

Things cooled over the next 10 million years, and forest cover became more deciduous and eventually died back. As the landscape turned to grassland, North America's original primates went extinct. Soon thereafter, at least in geologic time, tectonic forces cracked the ground open, with molten basalt lava pouring out of the resulting fissure and incinerating everything in its path. Successive fracturing and basalt floods covered the land, until over 10,000 square miles of what is now parts of Washington, Idaho, and Oregon were buried up to 3 miles deep. After another few million years, early elephants—arrived from Asia over the Bering Land Bridge?—first appeared in a landscape now transformed into wooded savannas. Soon prehistoric single-toed horses appeared, migrating

▲ A fallen Rocky Mountain juniper branch adorns the desolate landscape.

from the Great Plains, where most of their species was concentrated. Substantial species intermingling happened around 3.5 million years ago, when the Panamanian land bridge formed, connecting previously detached North America and South America. Tortoises and other traditionally southern wildlife colonized new lands. The earliest evidence of human habitation in this region was some 15,000 years ago, but our presence really began to be felt once the glaciers of the last ice age finally started melting, around 13,000 years ago. That's when the ecosystem we see today started to take shape.

The way the rocks have eroded over the years have made them a treasure trove for fossil hunters. Fossils form in different ways, but the most common is when a dead plant or animal is frozen, dried, or somehow else encased, typically by sediment. The ensuing heat and pressure from being buried can cause the tissue of organisms to release hydrogen and oxygen, leaving behind a carbon residue. This process, known as carbonization or distillation, results in a detailed carbon impression of the dead plant or animal that paleontologists, amateur and otherwise, are able to examine tens of millions of years later. Paleontologists working this site have discovered fossilized remains of dozens of long-extinct wildlife species as well as more than 300 plant species, including 175 species of fruits and nuts.

Cut to the present, and it's the sage-steppe ecosystem all around that dominates the ecology of this locale and the region in general. The perky gray-green leaves of big sagebrush, which grows up to 9 feet tall, and three-tip sagebrush, which grows to 7 feet tall, are omnipresent. Besides painting the desert a shimmery gray-green, they also lend a uniquely sharp but sweet-smelling aroma to the

▲ The Clarno Arch hike gets visitors up close to the Palisades.

air—crush a few leaves in your hand and smell for yourself—instantly conjuring olfactory memories of previous visits to the high desert or creating new ones if you've never been before.

Rocky Mountain junipers, with their swirling branches, lacy-leathery foliage, and little pale blue berries, dot the trail and pop up in the distance. The tree and its produce are an important source of forage and cover for many species of desert wildlife. Numerous birds and mammals eat the berries and mule deer practically subsist on it over the winter, when other browse isn't available.

Antelope bitterbrush, named for its attractiveness as browse for antelope and other mammals, is another shrub common in Eastern Oregon (and elsewhere across the West). Bitterbrush can be a dead ringer for big sagebrush, except when it blooms in the spring and reveals itself as more akin to wild rose, with its pretty five-petaled yellow flowers. Another native lending additional yellow to the sandy scene is broom snakeweed.

Even the rocks serve as a substrate for life. Eggyolk lichen thrives on the sharp volcanic chunks, coloring them from ochre to pea-green to, you guessed it, egg yolk–yellow. This composite fungus-alga organism ekes out a living, like other fungi, from the nutrients in dust and moisture floating by in the air, along with whatever minerals it can scrape up from its substrate. But lichens' secret sauce is their ability to also derive energy from photosynthesis, thanks to their algal partner that can take in sunlight and convert it like other plants. Incidental bird and insect dung also contribute to the nutrient intake of lichens.

Lichens are one of the few organisms adapted to life on every continent, growing in those leftover spots that are either too harsh or too limited for other organisms to colonize. They just need a substrate—rocks are ideal but dead wood, animal bones, rusty metal, or even undisturbed plastic will do—plus air and sunlight. Some lichen species can survive astounding temperature extremes: Antarctic lichens can survive stretches at -300 degrees F, while desert varieties—such as the eggyolk lichens on display around the Palisades—can survive heat blasts as high as 200 degrees F. Living in such extremes isn't for every organism, but some lichens are happy to call these spots home.

⏴ Rocky Mountain juniper bark has a rough, sectional appearance.

⏴ Ochre-tinged eggyolk lichen congregates on a volcanic rock.

Lichens grow very slowly—less than a millimeter a year is typical—by extending their thalli (the main vegetative "bodies" of their tiny structures) outward from tips or edges. Some ecologists consider them "immortal" given that a detached thallus can colonize new substrates and continue to reproduce vegetatively. Also, when two members of the same lichen species meet, they can commingle into one larger individual, which makes it difficult to distinguish or age any given patch of lichen. Regardless, the average eggyolk lichen probably lives for hundreds of years on its boulder edge.

LICHENS: NATURAL ANTIBIOTICS?

Lichens produce upward of 500 metabolic byproducts that scientists are still struggling to understand but which we think are linked to controlling light exposure, dictating color shades, repelling herbivores, killing attacking microbes, and discouraging competition from nearby plants. Researchers have confirmed what traditional healers have known for millennia: many lichens contain natural antibiotics. Aboriginal societies have used extracts from lichens not only for dyes but also to treat fungi found on the body (such as athlete's foot) and bacterial infections including boils, scarlet fever, and pneumonia. Exploring these still mysterious biochemical compounds further—and their potential applications for human health—seems like a promising line of research for biotechnology.

While not many humans can stand living in the harsh environment of the high desert—this part of Oregon is one of the least populous and most desolate areas of the Lower 48—some 350 species of wildlife are dependent on thriving sage-steppe ecosystems for their very survival. The icon of this environment of course, is the chicken-like, ground-nesting greater sage-grouse. This largest of North America's grouse species is plump and round and mottled brown and white with gray speckles. The larger males weigh as much as 7 pounds, and stand about 2 feet tall. At dawn in spring, they put on a unique mating display, puffing up the yellow air sacs on their chests by thrusting their bodies forward, resulting in an otherworldly popping sound. You may hear it as a show of territorial defense if you inadvertently stumble upon a grouse's nesting ground. It's especially surreal if several birds are at it simultaneously.

Many biologists and environmentalists believe that based on the science alone, this unique bird should be recognized and protected as an endangered species. Sharp declines have been found in its population and "area of occupancy" across its range—which connects 11 states across 175 million acres of public and private lands throughout the American West. According to U.S. Fish and Wildlife Service data, the species population declined some 3.5 percent per year on average between 1965 and 1985. From that point forward the decline has been slowed but not stopped or reversed. Biologists fear that if major threats continue unabated—such as disturbances from recent upticks in oil and gas development in the desert, which can cause degradation, fragmentation, and loss of habitat—the greater sage-grouse could become a casualty of the indomitable march of "progress."

But to date, federal officials at the U.S. Fish and Wildlife Service do not agree that the bird's conservation status warrants endangered species protection. Furthermore, many human denizens of the rural West—especially those who derive their incomes from farms, ranches, logging, mines, and other land-based endeavors—oppose endangered species status on the grounds that it unfairly impinges on the ability of human residents to make a living. The debate is far from settled, and the conservation status of the greater sage-grouse is sure to continue as a hot-button issue across the West for years to come.

▲ During mating season, the male greater sage-grouse puffs out two sacs on its chest in an attempt to attract females.

Plenty of other birdlife resides in or at least passes through the region. If you see a flitting small bird with pale yellow eyes, a gray back, streaked breast and wing bars, and white tail corners, you've spotted a sage thrasher. These small songbirds breed exclusively in sage-steppe environments, using the extensive sagebrush for concealment while they forage for ants, grasshoppers, beetles, and, when they can get them, berries. While conservationists aren't worried about the fate of the sage thrashers thanks to the birds' safe numbers and large range, their population has declined by some 52 percent since the late 1960s, according to the North American Breeding Bird Survey.

Other iconic wildlife of the sage-steppe include pronghorn antelope, Rocky Mountain elk, mule deer, sagebrush lizards, pygmy rabbits, Great Basin spadefoot toads, and golden eagles. All of these species, and hundreds more, are vulnerable to the habitat loss and fragmentation going on across Eastern Oregon. Livestock overgrazing, residential development, agricultural conversion, herbicide and pesticide treatments, and changes to fire management regimes are combining to put the entire ecosystem on the ropes. While today there is plenty of pristine sage-steppe landscape remaining, it won't last forever given current human use and abuse trends. Native sagebrush thickets are being replaced by invasive species such as cheatgrass and crested wheatgrass. Native wildlife cannot survive on these invasive plants, so trying to control how we use the land—or even better, how we can best leave it alone—is the optimal option for preserving this unique environment for future generations.

If you started at the main parking area (by the picnic tables and bathrooms) and have hiked the 0.25 miles to where the Geologic Time Trail ends, move on to the two looped side trails that lead up into the rocky terrain at the foot of the Palisades. (You can also turn around at this point and retrace your steps back to the car, making it a 0.5-mile, out-and-back hike).

The Trail of Fossils is a 0.25-mile loop off of the Geologic Time Trail that leads up into the rocky terrain at the foot of the Palisades. The astute observer on this trail will catch glimpses of fossilized plants along the cliff walls and edges of boulders that have tumbled down from the Palisades over the millennia. The other trail is the 0.5-mile, out-and-back Clarno Arch Trail, which climbs even higher into the base of the Palisades—also past many fossilized plant remains— to an unusual stone chute capped by a natural arch. Tens of millions

of years ago, rushing water carved this chasm in a weak vein of the Palisades. You can still see the structure of the (long-dry) waterfall today. Also visible are petrified fallen logs in the rock face.

On this short cluster of trails, you'll get a full dose of epic high desert plateau scenery, not to mention an education about the formation of landforms and the plants and animals that inhabit them, both historically and in the present. It can be hard to believe you're in the wet and wild Pacific Northwest when the views in every direction look more like parched portions of the Four Corners region 1000 miles to the southeast. But it's this very diversity of ecosystems that makes the Pacific Northwest one of the best places to visit if you love to see nature work its magic in a wide variety of ways.

▲ The Clarno Arch is a delicate natural stone arch created by erosion over time.

ISLANDS IN TIME TRAIL

Crumbling hoodoos and fossils
of long-extinct animals

DIFFICULTY
Easy

LENGTH
1.3 miles

LOCATION
John Day Fossil Beds National Monument, Sheep Rock Unit, near Dayville, Oregon

The fact that this psychedelic moonscape in the Blue Basin section of the John Day Fossil Bed's Sheep Rock Unit is only a few hours' drive from two major metro areas (Portland and Boise) makes its wild qualities that much more enticing. Be prepared for exposure on this dry and sun-bleached hike; even though it's short, bring plenty of water and don't rush it. Take advantage of the occasional bench under the shade of a western juniper tree when you can—they are relatively few and far between. You'll gain 220 feet in elevation all told, but most of it is gradual. It's worth noting that there are 13 metal bridges along the Island in Time Trail to facilitate the crossing of dry gullies; your dog won't like them, so be prepared to carry your furry friend over these otherwise convenient connectors. Also keep an eye out for rattlesnakes and watch where you step.

Spring is the best time to visit—for the moderate temperatures and wildflower blooms—but fall is also nice. With winter lows below 0 degrees F and summer highs topping 110 degrees F, you should think twice about making this trip, and plan accordingly, during one of these extreme seasons.

At the well-marked trailhead on the east side of the parking lot, follow the Island in Time Trail sign pointing to the right. (The left fork leads to the Blue Basin Trail, a 3.25-mile loop around the same section of the monument that climbs higher and affords a bird's eye view down into the blue-green canyons for miles down the John

The Islands In Time Trail gets you deep into the Blue Basin, named after the blue-green cliff walls. These colors are the result of weathering celadonite in ancient lava and ash flows.

Day River valley—save it for later if you have extra time and energy.) Heading south, the Island in Time Trail climbs gradually out of the parking area and into a little valley, up and up, past twisted western juniper trees, the occasional wispy netleaf hackberry, and a coterie of low-lying shrubbery, including big sagebrush, three-tip sagebrush, rubber rabbitbrush, and broom snakeweed.

Broom snakeweed is easy to distinguish in the late summer and early fall as it lights up the desertscape with its small, yellow tubular flowers arranged in dense clusters to attract insect pollinators. It sends down relatively deep roots, so excels at stabilizing loose soils. Lots of leaf litter delivers nutrients from the deep roots to the desert surface. The business end of the plant's scientific name (*Ericameria nauseosa*) refers to the slightly nauseating smell given off when the leaves or flowers of the plant are crushed or trampled. Some describe the smell as like pineapple; others complain it's more of a rotten, rubbery odor. It's not a major browse for fauna because of the odor

▲ There is little shade along the Islands in Time Trail save for the occasional western juniper tree.

Blue-green hoo-doos (columns of weathered rock) are a frequent companion on this hike through the Blue Basin. ▸

(unless the mule deer can't find anything else), but it does provide lots of valuable cover for small mammals. Americans Indians made use of the plant's flowers to make yellow dye and ground its leaves for medicinal tea. These days, researchers are looking into ways to harvest its oil as a form of natural insect repellent, among other potential applications.

Soon you'll see fencing on the right that protects the hillside from erosion and views of the blue-green cliffs open up straight ahead. What makes the rock such a unique shade of blue-green? It was formed from layers of ash that built up as a result of volcanic eruptions throughout the region beginning around 16 million years ago. The unique seafoam-green color of the cliffs is a result of the weathering of the mineral celadonite that predominates in much of the Blue Basin's clay stone, as water moved through the alkaline ash beds that formed following volcanic eruptions.

The blue-green cliffs represent just one strata of the geological layer cake in this section of the John Day Fossil Beds, however. While the Painted Hills Unit of the monument (50 miles to the west) is more famous for its multi-hued landscape views, there is plenty of color variation here as well. While blue-green may be the signature tone of the Blue Basin, layers of red, yellow, and blue-gray also proliferate, each representing the differing mineral content of lava deposits, ash flows, and soils during different geological

epochs—and each yielding fossilized remains of distinct types of long-extinct plants and animals.

Maybe the only thing more colorful than the cliff walls around you are the wildflowers, at least if you are there in spring. One of the earliest to bloom—they say it's a harbinger of the snow melt up in the mountains—is the pretty yellow fritillary, a small lily also known by the common name yellowbell because of its bell-shaped flower. Tailcup lupines send up stately purple stems, often clustering in big patches and fixing lots of nitrogen into the desert soils for other plants to use as fertilizer. Munro's globemallow is almost poppy-like in appearance, with orange petals enveloping bright yellow anthers.

Applegate's Indian paintbrush colors the landscape red with its late spring blooms. This showy, flowering plant is actually a root parasite, which means it has modified roots called haustoria that penetrate another plant's roots, from which it derives extra nutrients. An Indian paintbrush plant doesn't need to glom onto another host plant to survive, but the individuals who manage to do so grow bigger and live longer.

▲ Not everything is blue-green here. Different colors of the strata tell us what minerals were prevalent in the ancient ash and lava flows.

A hoary aster bloom lends a splash of color to the desert floor.

Sandhill cranes migrate through the John Day Fossil Beds National Monument twice a year.

A wide variety of lichens find the volcanic rocks around the John Day Fossil Beds to be excellent habitat.

Some of the less common blooms you could see here include purple sage, common yarrow, prairie clover, blazing star, western goldenrod, and hoary aster. A pleasant surprise this far north is the hedgehog cactus—stubby, green, and spiny for most of the year, until spring, when it sends up glorious violet or scarlet blooms, beckoning bees and other flying insects to its pollen-covered, yellow-green anthers.

While the wildflowers steal the show come spring, herbaceous perennial grasses are taking care of business year round. Basin wildrye, bluebunch wheatgrass, Idaho fescue, and Thurber's needlegrass are the most common in this stretch of desert, but Sandberg bluegrass, big bluegrass, needle-and-thread grass, Indian ricegrass, sand dropseed, and bottlebrush squirreltail also pop up frequently.

Non-native invasive grasses are increasingly a problem throughout the monument. Cheatgrass is the main offender—it sets seeds much earlier than native desert grasses, outcompeting them and then drying up later in the summer, just in time to fuel wave after wave of brushfire in the desert. Cheatgrass also loves to colonize newly disturbed stretches of the desert, such as recently burned areas. Medusahead rye, toadflax, Russian knapweed, and spotted knapweed also pose problems for land managers around the monument and across the high desert of the wider Columbia Plateau.

As for wildlife, the animals here have to be comfortable with extremes, given temperature swings of more than 100 degrees F between winter and summer and very little precipitation (between 9 and 16 inches a year). Those that can come and go easily, like migratory birds, can take what they need from the land and then move on. For example, sandhill cranes, trumpeter swans, and mute swans pass through twice a year on their annual migration paths. Many other birds hunker down and stay put in their preferred habitat here year round. Red-tailed hawks, American kestrels, great horned owls, common nighthawks, rufous hummingbirds, black-billed magpies, and great blue herons are just a few of these regulars.

In summer, when it's time to search for mates, listen for croaking northern leopard frogs and western toads that are hanging out by nearby springs and seeps. If you think you might have seen a lizard skitter away in your peripheral vision, you're not seeing things. Sagebrush lizards and leopard lizards here dine on beetles, flies, ants, caterpillars, spiders, ticks, and mites.

A diverse array of mammals inhabit these parts as well. Columbian white-tailed deer, mule deer, pronghorn antelope, and Rocky Mountain elk coexist, peacefully sharing the same habitat. You probably won't see them, but coyotes, cougars, and American badgers are stealthily on the hunt, and the healthy rodent population here keeps them well fed. Northern pocket gophers, Belding's ground squirrels, and yellow-bellied marmots are among the juicier prey for skilled carnivores.

This kind of life-and-death interplay between wildlife species isn't anything new in this part of the world. Indeed, the extensive fossil evidence throughout the area proves that similar types of predator-prey and ecosystem dynamics have been going on here for tens of millions of years. The earliest fossils paleontologists have found date back 30–40 million years and tell the tale of a much different landscape—one that was wet and subtropical, with close to 175 types of nut and fruit trees supporting dozens of species of ancient mammals, birds, amphibians, and insects.

But instead of cougars chasing deer, it was their distant ancestral precursors—saber-toothed nimravids pouncing on oreodonts—engaging in the timeless predator-prey dynamic. Meanwhile, rhinoceros and mouse-deer browsed their way through lush forests of prehistoric redwoods, maples, and alders, as lemur-like primates dangled from the ancestors of today's oaks and elms.

We know all of this thanks to fossils first uncovered here in the 1860s by soldiers stationed nearby to protect government mining camps from raids by local Paiutes. Since then, paleontologists have discovered fossils of more than 100 different prehistoric mammals—including not only oreodonts and nimravids but also the ancestors of dogs, cats, horses, camels, and rodents. Likewise, nearly 60 plant species—hydrangea, pea, hawthorn, and mulberry, just to name a few—are fossilized in the strata of the Blue Basin.

Paleontologists working at the monument are constantly on the watch for fossils that come to light as a result of erosion. Once exposed to oxygen, these ancient samples will break down just like regular organic matter, so researchers are careful to properly preserve them.

Replica casts of fossils at three different spots along the Islands in Time Trail show what these remnants looked like when paleontologists originally found them here. One example is a replica oreodont fossil. Oreodonts were a diverse family of herbivores similar in size to modern-day sheep and, given the sheer number of unearthed specimens, as prevalent as today's deer. An interpretive sign points out that the way paleontologists find fossilized remains yields clues as to how the given animal may have died, which in turn often reveals something about its lifestyle or what kinds of threats it may have faced. The fossilized oreodont skeleton on display is missing a forelimb and a hindlimb, while its shoulder blade is dislocated and its spine and neck are twisted. We'll never know if these abnormalities tell the story of a horrific death at the claws and jaws of a carnivore or are merely the result of post-mortem scavenging by other animals. Paleontologists can sometimes make assumptions based on multiple finds of the same or related prehistoric species.

The fossil record can also help us track how the environment here has changed over geologic time, given the different types of plant and animal remains that show up at different sediment layers. You would never believe that the patch of desert where you now stand once lay on the bottom of a prehistoric ocean, and later was part of a subtropical coastal rain forest, unless it was written in stone

‹ This replica cast shows a fossilized tortoise shell found nearby. It is from an animal that lived tens of millions of years ago.

in the form of fossilized plants and animals that could only live in such ecosystems.

After 0.6 miles of hiking, the Islands in Time Trail dead-ends smack in the middle of Blue Basin—you'll know you're there by a conspicuous End of Trail sign just past the last fossil replica cast and interpretive display ("The Search Continues" details how paleontologists continue to look for and find fossils here). You are standing in the middle of a blue-green, walled, natural amphitheater at an elevation of just over 2400 feet, some 200 feet higher than you started back at the trailhead. Breathe in another lungful of the dry air and relish the notion that the return hike is predominantly downhill, albeit at a slight grade. Turn around and retrace your steps back to the parking lot—and watch out for any stray nimravids along the way.

ZUMWALT PRAIRIE PRESERVE

Rare 51-square-mile ecosystem of pristine, temperate grassland

LOCATION
near Joseph, Oregon

DIFFICULTY
Easy

LENGTH
1.9 mile

The spring wildflower displays across Zumwalt Prairie in northeastern Oregon's Wallowa Mountains are some of the best across the Pacific Northwest.

Zumwalt Prairie Preserve offers an easy 1.9-mile loop trail through some of the most beautiful prairies and meadows in the Pacific Northwest, if not North America. Anyone in moderate shape should be able to walk the loop, though some of it requires trudging through soggy meadows and stout stands of bunchgrass, so bring sturdy footwear. Wood cairns made from old fence posts bear blue trail markers to guide hikers through the sometimes confusing fields of bunchgrass. With winter temperatures consistently below freezing in this high, dry desert, most visitors take to the trails at Zumwalt during summer. Spring yields the best wildflower displays, while fall offers solitude and an autumnal color palette.

Part of what makes the Zumwalt so special is that temperate grasslands like this are among the most threatened biomes on the planet—and the most altered ecosystems in North America. Also extremely special, of course, is Zumwalt's spectacularly beautiful and vital landscape, with its galloping elk herds and million-wildflower vistas against a backdrop of the 9000-foot peaks of the Wallowas. Humans seem to feel right at home ambling through these bunchgrass prairies, maybe because they are reminiscent of the African savannas where humanity first started.

Park at the small pullout across from the well-marked trailhead along Zumwalt-Buckhorn Road (about 1.5 miles south of the town of Zumwalt), and cross through a small wooden stile to enter the preserve and begin hiking the Horned Lark Trail. Enjoy the open sight lines and extended views out to the Wallowa Mountains, beyond the Findley Buttes to the southwest. Bunchgrass prairie spreads out as far as the eye can see, giving you a newfound appreciation for what the settlers experienced on the Oregon Trail when they came upon these lands. Not much has changed here since then, although everything has changed around it—which is exactly why The Nature Conservancy (TNC) stepped in to preserve it back in 2000. At that point, the nonprofit conservation group purchased 27,000 acres in the heart of the 330,000-acre Zumwalt grasslands, adding another 6000 acres in 2006. Besides being TNC's largest land acquisition to date in Oregon, the 51-square-mile preserve is also the biggest private nature sanctuary in the state.

The Nature Conservancy's ownership of the heart of the Zumwalt prairie means continuing conservation and stewardship of this unique ecosystem and its native biodiversity. Just as important, it means research is being conducted here that will help biologists and land managers elsewhere prepare for changes wrought by non-native species, human development, and climate change, among other threats.

Keep moving as the Horned Lark Trail gradually descends into the Pine Creek drainage. At 0.75 miles in, you'll reach a wildlife exclosure protecting a thriving young clonal colony of quaking aspen saplings from the grazing mouths of ungulates (cattle, mule deer, Roosevelt elk). TNC erected this and other similar exclosures around the Zumwalt Preserve to give young native plants a chance to get established before their fresh young shoots get gobbled up. The fencing consists of crisscrossed logs built up all around the protected plants in a pyramid shape (so animals stepping across one rung would then have to deal with another, making it too frustrating to navigate). An exposure-bleached cattle skull sits firmly atop one of the fence posts, either as decoration or to warn still-living ungulates intent on grazing to steer clear of this exclosure.

▲ The Wallowa Mountains provide a striking backdrop to the Zumwalt Prairie.

A shed elk antler is evidence of the wildlife found on the Zumwalt Prairie. The Nature Conservancy has installed wildlife exclosures around the Preserve to protect young stands of native plants from grazers. ▸

Luckily, there are plenty of other grasses and young shoots for these grazers to chew their cud on. While the bunchgrasses of the prairie may be ungulates' primary source of nutrition out here, come spring, one of nature's biggest salad bars opens across the Zumwalt Prairie. If you are lucky enough to be visiting during this most optimistic of seasons, brace yourself for one of the best wildflower displays this side of the Cascades' alpine meadows. Early bloomers (starting in late February or early March) include sagebrush buttercup, yellowbells, bigseed biscuitroot, cous biscuitroot, lanceleaf springbeauty, and small bluebells. Many other blooms start to pop open in late April and early May, including bulbous woodland-star, dwarf hesperochiron, inflated grasswidow, Bonneville shootingstar, creeping barberry, darkthroat shootingstar, hairy clematis, arrowleaf balsamroot, cushion phlox, Virginia strawberry, old man's whiskers, largehead clover, Wallowa onion, nineleaf biscuitroot, hoary balsamroot, and Douglas buckwheat.

Even more wildflower species bloom later in the spring here on the Zumwalt. During May and June, keep your eyes peeled for dwarf yellow fleabane, lambstongue ragwort, shaggy fleabane, parsnipflower buckwheat, hookedspur violet, yellow evening-primrose, spiny phlox, Canadian milkvetch, woodland strawberry, wholeleaf saxifrage, sunflower mule-ears, ballhead waterleaf, low pussytoes,

A few of the wildflowers you can expect to see at Zumwalt Prairie in spring include (from left) lance-leaf springbeauty, Bonneville shooting star, pearly pussytoes, and scarlet gilia. ▾

Cusick's Indian paintbrush, pearly pussytoes, elkweed, sticky cinquefoil, Cuddy Mountain onion, common woolly sunflower, tobacco root, Tolm's onion, rush pussytoes, western stoneseed, roundleaf alumroot, largeflower triteleia, scarlet gilia, globe penstemon, and meadow deathcamas.

Such great floral diversity also means non-natives creep in and can crowd native plants out of their own habitats. Sulfur cinquefoil, meadow hawkweed, and common bugloss have been particularly problematic across the Zumwalt Prairie. TNC has initiated vigorous eradication efforts throughout the area it controls, but there is only so much it can do outside its domain.

Past the exclosure the trail turns sharply to the right, following the course of Pine Creek downstream. Look across what seems like acres of bunchgrass for the next blue trail marker, which is just a speck in the distance.

Besides being beautiful and ecologically significant, the Zumwalt Prairie is also a mecca for birds, with its oasis-like setting amid the otherwise arid Columbia Plateau. The trail you are walking is named after the horned lark, one of the iconic bird species here. Flocks of the small, reddish gray and white songbird—which sports a black beak, matching throat, and tufted feather "horns" on both sides of its head—walk and run across the prairie, looking down at the soil and

• The golden eagle is much less famous than its bald eagle cousin, but is just as fierce a hunter.

rocks in search of errant seeds they can pilfer. If you get too close, the larks will make haste to the sky in twisting flight patterns, while sounding warning calls to other birds nearby. The only lark native to North America, horned larks nest early in spring right in the bunch-grass fields spread out before you; males performing singing flight displays to attract mates.

Perhaps the most famous avian residents of the Zumwalt Prairie are its raptors. Ospreys, bald eagles, golden eagles, northern gos-hawks, turkey vultures, northern harriers, sharp-shinned hawks, Cooper's hawks, Swainson's hawks, red-tailed hawks, ferruginous hawks, and rough-legged hawks all nest within this prairie, patrolling its typically blue desert skies in search of their next meals.

If you do see a raptor circling above, chances are it's stalking a nearby rodent. Look out into the grass to see if you can spot any nervous-looking Belding's ground squirrels.

Waterfowl also flock to this natural haven. Wood ducks, American wigeons, blue-winged teals, northern shovelers, northern pintails, canvasbacks, redheads, ring-necked ducks, lesser scaups, buffleheads, ruddy ducks, gadwalls, snow and Canada geese, and tun-dra and trumpeter swans are among the webbed-foot set frequenting Pine Creek and its associated riparian areas and ponds alongside the Horned Lark Trail.

The horned lark is the trail's namesake.

Seeing a wood duck close enough to distinguish its rich coloration is enough to make any nature lover's day.

Other birds known to frequent these parts according to TNC's most recent avian census include Columbian sharp-tailed grouses, chukars, wild turkeys, gray partridges, ring-necked pheasants, sora rails, Wilson's snipes, Bullock's orioles, red-winged blackbirds, American white pelicans, and great blue herons. Ruffed and dusky grouses, three types of grebe (pied-billed, horned, and eared), and two types of quail (mountain and California).

The next landmark to look for is a cattle pond where local bovines can hydrate some distance from sensitive rare plants. Pass the pond, turn up the hill, and continue to the top, which places you back where you started at the trailhead.

Once you've hiked through the Zumwalt Prairie and experienced this captivating environment, you can't help but think what a shame it is that we've lost so much of the temperate grassland that once blanketed some 40 percent of the contiguous U.S. landmass. While The Nature Conservancy seems to have this little slice of heaven covered, it's up to you and me to follow their example. By working to make our outdoor spaces more friendly to wildlife and the environment, we can help preserve vital ecosystems everywhere.

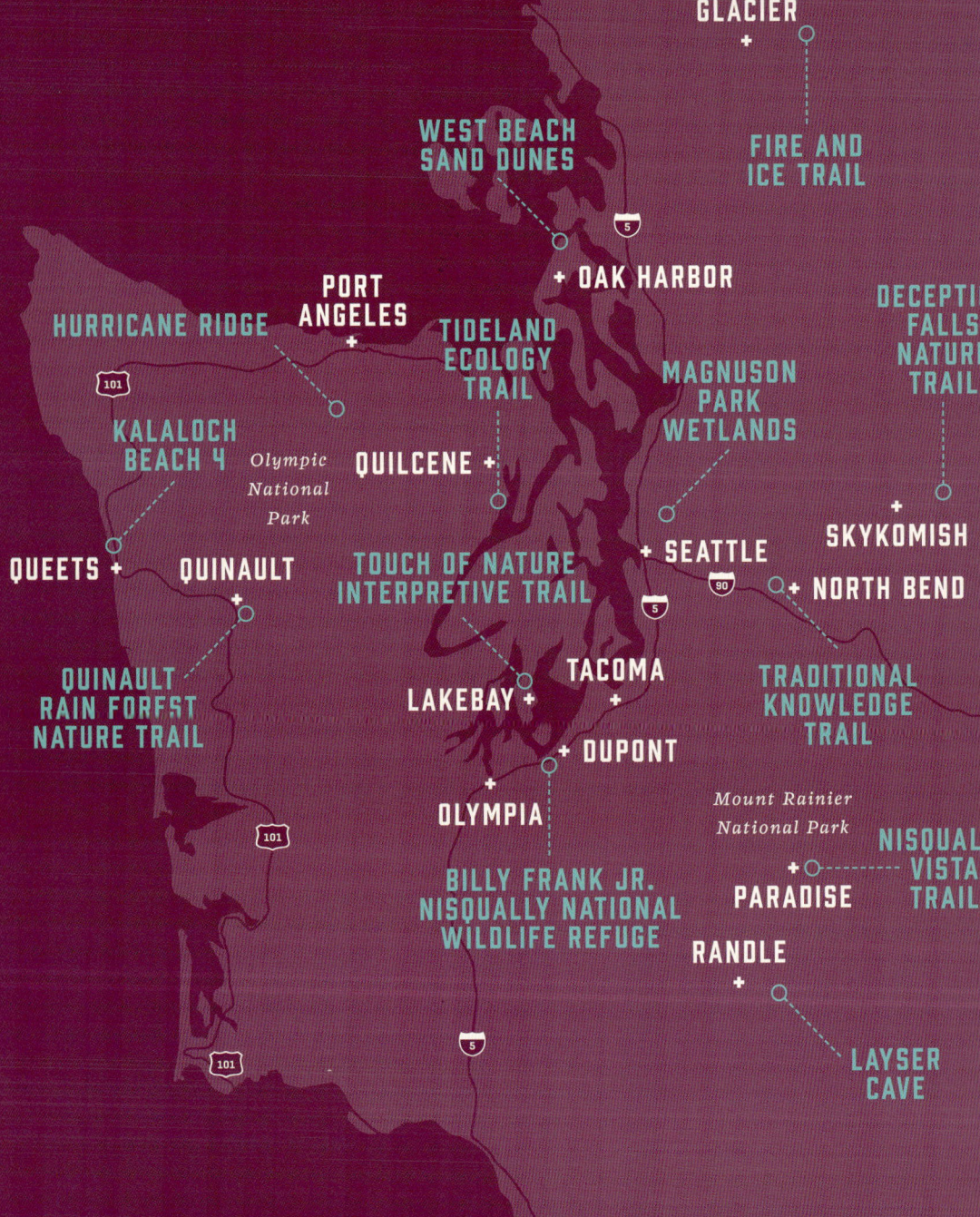

GLACIER

FIRE AND
ICE TRAIL

WEST BEACH
SAND DUNES

OAK HARBOR

DECEPTIO
FALLS
NATURE
TRAIL

PORT
ANGELES

HURRICANE RIDGE

TIDELAND
ECOLOGY
TRAIL

MAGNUSON
PARK
WETLANDS

101

KALALOCH
BEACH 4

Olympic
National
Park

QUILCENE

SKYKOMISH

QUEETS

QUINAULT

TOUCH OF NATURE
INTERPRETIVE TRAIL

SEATTLE

NORTH BEND

90

5

QUINAULT
RAIN FOREST
NATURE TRAIL

LAKEBAY

TACOMA

TRADITIONAL
KNOWLEDGE
TRAIL

DUPONT

101

OLYMPIA

Mount Rainier
National Park

NISQUALL
VISTA
TRAIL

BILLY FRANK JR.
NISQUALLY NATIONAL
WILDLIFE REFUGE

PARADISE

RANDLE

5

LAYSER
CAVE

VANCOUVER

WASHINGTON

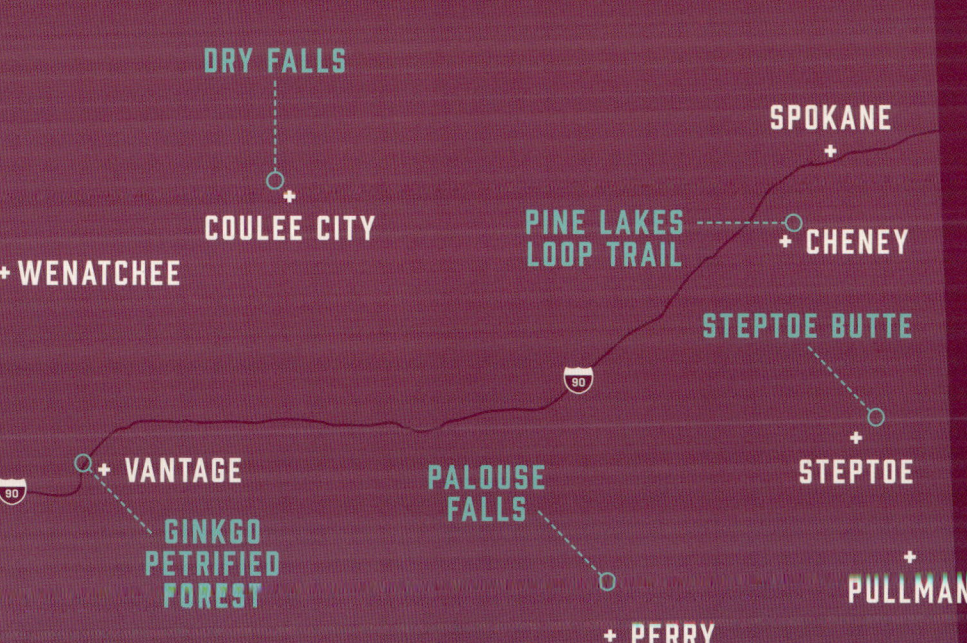

DRY FALLS

SPOKANE
+

COULEE CITY
+

PINE LAKES
LOOP TRAIL

CHENEY
+

+ WENATCHEE

STEPTOE BUTTE

90

STEPTOE
+

+ VANTAGE

PALOUSE
FALLS

90

GINKGO
PETRIFIED
FOREST

PULLMAN
+

KIMA
+

+ PERRY

KALALOCH BEACH 4

Sandstone sea stacks, teeming tide pools, and panoramic views

LOCATION
Queets, Washington

DIFFICULTY
Moderate

LENGTH
0.8 miles

Looking west over the Pacific Ocean from Kalaloch Beach 4.

Kalaloch Beach 4 is one of the wildest and most remote spots south of Alaska, and the fact that it's just a short hike from the parking lot makes it that much more appealing as a lunch-time or sunset destination for those traveling in and around the Olympic Peninsula.

While the hike from the parking lot down to the beach isn't long—your toes can touch the sand after just a 0.3-mile jaunt through the woods—it does involve traversing some two dozen stairsteps carved into a small creek-side gorge. The trail is well maintained and if the weather is nice, you won't be alone. Sneakers or hiking shoes are recommended but you'll make it in whatever comfortable shoes you're wearing. Summer is the most popular time to visit the Olympic coast, and for good reason, as winter brings rain and lashing winds that can make for treacherous wayfaring.

From the trailhead kiosk in the southwest corner of the parking lot, proceed a few feet and you'll face a fork in the trail. Take the short spur to the right for a quick look over the beach from a bluff above it—and get a sense of what your ultimate destination looks like. Retrace your steps (about 150 feet) back to the fork, and take the other path, past three interpretive signs, and down to the beach via a 0.25-mile stairstep hike. The hard-packed dirt trail is framed in most sections by 4 × 4 timbers to prevent erosion along the edge of the gorge that the trail traverses. Soon the framed-in trail turns to neatly framed timber stairsteps for the quick descent to the beach.

It's worth a quick off-trail detour on the way down to Kalaloch Beach 4 to check out the peaceful little freshwater creek buffered on each side by tall, vibrant stands of Pacific reedgrass. ▾

Vine maple branches drape over the trail while epiphytes (plants that derive all their nutrients from sunlight and dust particles floating by on the air) swing in the breeze off the nearby ocean. Western hemlock and Sitka spruce trees, along with the occasional western red cedar and Douglas fir, take up the mid- and upper-story layers of the canopy. The sound of an unnamed tributary of nearby Kalaloch Creek creates a nice tinkling backdrop to the sounds of birds chirping and your own footfalls.

After about 0.1 miles of descending stairs, the trail starts to bottom out. Understory plants—including salal, skunk cabbage, beadruby, western sword fern, arctic sweet coltsfoot, bracken fern and red elderberry—start to close in on either side of the trail as you approach the opening to the beach.

The sound of waves crashing and the tide surging back and forth starts to take your ears' attention away from the gentle, flowing sounds of the creek. Watch out for the occasional banana slug crossing the trail underfoot; you wouldn't want to squish this little yellow ambassador of the wet and wild Northwest with those thick-soled hiking shoes. Just past a sign warning about the dangers of surf and riptides, the trail empties out onto a footbridge made of regular 2 × 4 planks on the bottom but with curved and twisted driftwood branches for railings. Crossing this little footbridge primeval is like going through a portal to another world.

▴ Red elderberry thrives in the wet conditions of the coastal forest and provides many environmental services, including stabilizing soils, keeping erosion in check, supplying food for dozens of bird species, and offering cover for other wildlife.

At the end of the footbridge, pick your way through a labyrinthine grotto where lots of smooth, rounded river rocks meet layered waves of sandstone and shale worn down by eons of erosional forces. These strange, layered rocks tilting up at odd angles—geologists call this unusual type of rock formation an "angular unconformity" composed of "overturned turbidites"—first formed under the water column offshore

▴ Beadruby and arctic sweet coltsfoot are among dozens of native ground cover plants competing for precious space on the forest floor in the woods leading down to Kalaloch Beach 4.

when countless sediment-rich currents got compressed and cemented together by pressure. In a process called lithification, the result was solid rock. These rocks were "born" underwater some 80 miles to the west as part of the Juan de Fuca tectonic plate, and were eventually pushed eastward and subducted under the North American tectonic plate before being uplifted to sea level and then planed off by wave erosion. The current geological state of Kalaloch Beach 4 has been

▴ Overturned turbidites mark the transition between coastal forest and beach.

▴ Smooth river rocks that spent years upstream being polished by the constant trickle of creek water are now deposited haphazardly on the beach below.

▴ Piddock clams bore their way into the sandstone rocks along Kalaloch Beach 4.

a process some 22 million years in the making, with each high tide playing a small role in continuing the sculpting process to this day.

Much of the sandstone is pock-marked with little holes 1–2 inches in diameter, the result of Pacific rough piddock clams, also known as boring clams, taking up residence by glomming onto rocks, growing serrated-edged shells, and rocking back and forth to make a depression big enough to move into. These filter feeders can live as long as 20 years in their little holes, but more often get flushed out to sea in big storms, at which point other species like snails, peanut worms, brittle stars, and gumboot chitons may move into the abandoned cavities.

Like elsewhere on the Olympic Peninsula coast, bleached driftwood is everywhere, and some of it can be loose, so be careful where you step. You wouldn't want a 100-foot-tall western hemlock

log to roll over on your ankle—
or worse. It's hard to believe
that many of these huge drift
logs, now so firmly settled on
the beach, lived out their days
far upstream in the temperate
rain forest. Winter storms,
with wind blasts topping 40
miles per hour, topple many
of them. Meanwhile, spring
rains can swell creek beds and
rivers, undermining the banks
and sending riparian trees into
the ensuing floodwaters on
their way to the river mouth
and beach below. Other shore-
bound downed trees emanated
from eroding headlands near
the beach.

Once you've made your
way over the twisted wall of
sandstone and driftwood and
onto the beach sand proper,
head north toward the tide-line
sea stacks you can see about
0.25 miles to the right. You can

▴ A battered sword fern catches some early
morning rays through the forest.

make the walk from the end of the footbridge to the sea stacks in 10
minutes, but most people take double or triple that amount of time to
enjoy the sights and sounds along the way.

The beach here is bejeweled with tiny pebbles that have come
from the creek and keep getting washed back and forth on the
beach with the shifting tides. Seagulls flap their wings overhead and
huge fallen trees with their root balls intact line the shore. Bull kelp
strands, identified by their shiny bulbous brown tips and graceful
curling tails, mingle with other ocean detritus along the dark brown-
gray sand boulevard. Rockweed, which looks like little primate hands
with double yellow "fingertips" and is a favorite seaweed snack for

limpets, entangles with bull kelp tails, but also straggles on its own above the midtide line, eagerly awaiting the next nutrient-filled wave.

You'll certainly see the abandoned gleaming white and pearlescent purple shells of Pacific razor clams adorning the beach, but don't touch—you could cut yourself on their surprisingly sharp edges. The crafty bivalve mollusks survive by siphoning microscopic plants and animals from the surf, submerging quickly beneath soft sand as needed to evade predators like crabs and humans.

CLAM DIGGING

Shellfish harvesting has been going on along Washington and Oregon coastlines since long before there were states, and today the practice continues much like in the past. Digging for and eating razor clams is practically a rite of passage for Pacific Northwest kids and their parents.

But in order to ensure against overharvesting and to protect people from getting sick, both Washington and Oregon Departments of Fish and Wildlife regulate shellfish harvesting. Clam digging is only allowed on specified days of the year and requires a state permit. Check the agencies' websites for information on allowed digging dates and obtaining permits.

One reason you want to follow state guidelines is to avoid ingesting a neurotoxin that could permanently damage your nervous system and paralyze parts of your body. Paralytic shellfish poisoning is a foodborne illness that can develop after eating clams or mussels contaminated with saxitoxin, a toxic by-product of dinoflagellates in algae blooms. State officials monitor shellfish for contaminant levels and issue closures accordingly.

Driftwood relics in varying states of decay, most bleached white from their time bouncing around at sea before landing on the beach, host countless barnacles and provide tired walkers with lots of natural bench space.

Before you know it, you're at the sea stacks. The scaly rock structures have beautiful abstract patterns that come from outer layers flaking off because of salt, water, and wind erosion, not to mention temperature extremes, piddock clam burrowing, and myriad other exposure-related factors. (No one said being a sea stack was going to be easy.)

These impressive sandstone structures are accessible even at high tide, but you'll see more intertidal life in the shallow crevices during a low tide. Consult a tide chart and try to time your visit with an especially low minus tide (a math minus sign will appear in front of the listed tide height). While this natural jungle gym is fun to climb around on no matter your age, watch your step and don't venture onto spots being washed over by incoming waves or you could become a casualty of the coast.

Acorn barnacles and gooseneck barnacles attach themselves to surfaces by secreting a form of natural cement with a bond not even slamming ocean waves can break, covering every substrate that isn't sand. Most barnacles stay put for 5–10 years or more once they have found a suitable host site, suspension feeding on nutrients (phyto-plankton, zooplankton, bacteria, and detritus) out of the constantly flushing water column. It's no fun to break a fall by landing hand-, elbow-, or head-first on a bed of barnacles, so proceed with caution if you are climbing around the sea stacks.

Trekking over barnacle-encrusted rocks is all worth it once you see your first group of giant green sea anemones clustered just below the waterline. Even though these little psychedelic green blobs look unassuming, they are voracious carnivores, feeding on the steady diet of crabs, mussels, urchins, and small fish that the shifting volley of frothing seawater delivers to their doorstep with every wave. While often solitary, sea anemones will also huddle up in groups, with as many as 14 per 3 square feet. This can reduce evaporation, crowd out competing organisms, and optimize their collective take of prey. Marine biologists estimate anemones can live to around the ripe old age of 150 years.

Another star of the intertidal stage is the ochre sea star, a starfish colored either purple or its namesake ochre shade of orange (also sometimes yellow or even reddish brown). These brainless crawlers grow to about 14 inches across and use a spiny network of

An ochre sea star and giant green sea anemones wait for the next wave to bring them more to eat. ▸

nerves to direct their activities. Their tubelike feet have suckers on the ends that allow them to affix themselves to rocky substrates and live and feed in the to-and-fro of heavily wave-swept intertidal zones.

While it may seem like a sea star wouldn't have much to eat down there, the opposite is in fact true; the intertidal zone is a veritable all-you-can-eat buffet for these underwater predators. A sea star's favorite meal may be mussels, but chitons, limpets, tube worms, snails, barnacles, urchins, and even crabs will do in a pinch. Most sea stars live to at least 4 years old, with some hearty survivors making it into their 20s. And, if one or more of their arms gets chopped off, they can just grow it back, although the process does take several months.

Marine biologists consider ochre sea stars to be a keystone species, in that they serve as an indicator for the wider health of their coastal ecosystems. As such, when large numbers of West Coast sea stars began to mysteriously die off in 2013, environmentalists and wildlife lovers were rightly worried. But after countless hours and millions of dollars spent on research, we still aren't sure what's causing Sea Star Wasting Syndrome, although conditions improved in 2015. Researchers are keeping an eye on the problem, as it still affects smaller percentages of sea star populations, and fingers are crossed that new efforts to clean up the oceans will help make the problem just a bad memory.

These types of estuarine areas—where saltwater and terrestrial ecosystems merge—are by nature more biologically diverse, given the sheer variety of food sources and habitats present. Adroit naturalists will find many other subjects worthy of observation in the intertidal zone, including hairy hermit crabs, red rock crabs, wolf eels, pricklebacks, brittle stars and sea snails, among others. Black bears and raccoons prowl the beach and nearby woods, so don't leave any food or sweet-smelling items unattended.

Up in the sky and perched on every outer sea stack are gulls galore. While some gulls fly south for the winter, many stick around the Washington coast, where the fishing is good year round. Look for Bonaparte's, glaucous-winged, Heermann's, herring, mew, Thayer's, and western gulls finding plenty to eat at the shifting tideline on the western edge of the continent.

While gulls may be the most common birds of the coast, other forms of avian life abound. Bald eagles occasionally swoop down from the heights of coastal evergreens for a quick snack. Keep your eyes peeled for brown pelicans, black oystercatchers, wandering tattlers, and black turnstones. Lucky birders might even get to see the elusive marbled murrelet, a 9-inch-long endangered seabird (closely related to the auk) that lives in the tall trees of the temperate rain forest, but forages for small fish and marine invertebrates offshore. Meanwhile, dozens of other migratory bird species trekking between southern winter homes in Latin America and northern summer digs in Alaska stop over along this stretch of coast, so don't be surprised if you see something more exotic.

Depending on the tide and seasonal conditions, you can spy sea otters frolicking in kelp beds and doing the backstroke in the tide pools. If you brought binoculars, take a look offshore for whale spouts. This stretch of beach is one of the best terrestrial whale-watching spots in Washington. Orcas and humpbacks make occasional appearances both inshore and farther out along the coastline. Gray whales migrating from Mexico's Baja California to Alaska in April and May occupy lanes far offshore, but occasional big spouts betray their locations as they pass.

Fishing in the morning mist for redtail surfperch at Kalaloch Beach 4 is a favorite pastime of many Olympic Coast locals. ▾

At the north end of the sea stacks, look for anglers in hip boots and chest waders casting long lines from light and bendy 9-foot-long rods questing for redtail surfperch. These silver-scaled fish with pinkish red fins grow to about 10 inches long and weigh about a pound. They love the action of the crashing waves of the coast, and fishing enthusiasts come from far and wide to indulge in the sport—and catch dinner. (A Washington State saltwater fishing license is required.)

Once you've wandered around the sea stacks to your heart's content, head back along the beach, through the driftwood and sandstone, over the footbridge, up the stairstep trail and to the parking lot. Total hiking distance out and back is just under a mile; you can do it all in less than an hour, but if the weather is tolerable give yourself at least double that so you can take your time and fully explore this precious stretch of coast. Or stay to watch the sunset; there is hardly a better vantage point in the entire Pacific Northwest.

QUINAULT RAIN FOREST NATURE TRAIL

Primeval temperate rain forest with 300-foot-tall trees

DIFFICULTY
Moderate

LENGTH
1 mile

LOCATION
Quinault, Washington

Besides gargantuan trees, this trail also showcases hanging air plants—epiphytes—that derive nutrients from passing breezes, plus a coterie of wildlife specially adapted to life in the wet and wild Olympic rain forest.

Even though it's a short interpretive trail, be prepared for muddy and slippery conditions along the way. There is hardly any elevation gain in aggregate, but every step seems to be up or down in order to avoid roots, rocks, and other impediments. Decent footwear—hiking boots or sneakers—are de rigueur. Part of the trail is on Douglas fir boardwalk with a rough-hewn wood fence, the only thing saving you from falling down into the verdant green gorge below. Per Olympic National Forest rules, stay on designated trails only, as bushwhacking or blazing your own trails could damage fragile native flora and wildlife habitat. The rain forest is alive—and worth visiting—any time of year, but especially in winter when most of the massive rain amounts the Quinault region gets per year falls (bring a raincoat!).

Washington State is a land of varied terrain, but one of its most iconic natural features is the temperate rain forest of the Olympic Peninsula. Nowhere else in the contiguous U.S. is as lush, as green, or as wet. Indeed, the west-flowing rivers of the Olympics—the Bogachiel, Hoh, Queets, Quinault—and their valleys get upward of

‹ This western hemlock tree makes itself right at home growing adjacent to a larger Douglas fir tree.

140 inches of rain annually. With so much moisture at their disposal, the trees grow big and tall. You won't find Sitka spruce, western hemlock, Douglas fir or western red cedar as big anywhere else in the world. In fact, some of these goliaths live to 1000 years and beyond, reaching heights over 300 feet and diameters as wide as 18 feet across. No wonder this region dominated the American timber industry for so many decades during the latter half of the 20th century.

This short but wild hike follows the rough and tumble course of Willaby Creek, a gorgeous tributary of the larger Quinault River watershed system that commences high in the glaciers surrounding Mount Olympus before flowing southwest, through the lush green temperate rain forest lowlands, and finally emptying into the Pacific Ocean at the Quinault tribal village of Taholah.

Representing just one small slice of this mighty alpine-to-ocean watershed, Quinault Rain Forest Nature Trail zigs and zags for 0.5 miles through magnificent old-growth forest. Just steps from the trailhead, Willaby Creek feeds into scenic Lake Quinault, a 6-square-mile symbol of the ultimate advance of the Quinault Valley glacier, which disappeared toward the end of the last ice age. Lake Quinault formed from ice melting at the "snout" (the colloquial word for a terminal moraine on a glacier's tip) as the climate warmed up.

The alpine glaciers that formed millennia ago in the Olympics' high country ground their way down the path of least resistance—preexisting river valleys—morphing themselves into valley glaciers and supercharging the grinding forces of erosion already at work. Glacial erratics (boulders left behind by retreating glaciers) and other natural debris give scientists a clear view of the pathways taken by various ice sheets. These mammoth features once dominated landscapes dozens of square miles across, but these days look like lush river valleys—such as the gorge surrounding Willaby Creek.

Around every corner is another example of textbook temperate rain forest flora, and if you're lucky you'll get to see some fauna (wildlife) as well. Whether or not you know they're nearby, red-backed voles, black bears, marbled murrelets, minks, banana slugs, American dippers, cougars, coyotes, winter wren, northern flying squirrels, varied thrushes, Roosevelt elk, bald eagles, river otters, pileated woodpeckers, bobcats, osprey, raccoons, ruffed grouse, and martins, among other wildlife species, are going about their business all around you and providing essential services to the rain forest ecosystem along the way. Of course, many of these species are nocturnal, while others only venture out at the edges of the day, which explains why we rarely see them as we trudge around under the midday sun.

The hike starts out with a fork and a polite suggestion to go left in order to follow the loop trail clockwise (although either way will do). Front and center at this initial crossroads is a classic example of one tree growing its roots around another, in the plant world's version of a wrestling survival quest. One western hemlock tree has enveloped another as the two trunks pretzel for access to sunlight, even if it means growing sideways. In 2020, the most sideways bough was becoming a hazard over the trail and had to be removed,

▴ Two western hemlocks jockey for position at the beginning of the Quinault Rain Forest Nature Trail's loop.

but what remains of these intertwined Escher-esque hemlocks sets the stage for a hike full of surprises, especially for those new to temperate rain forest ecology.

A few zigzags later, you'll wind your way up to a massive old-growth Douglas fir around which the Forest Service has built a wooden viewing platform, so visitors can get up close and personal. Rangers estimate this gargantuan specimen, which measures 302 feet tall and 13 feet in diameter, is over 800 years old—and it's still going strong. Douglas fir seedlings thrive in open space, and this tree probably got its start accordingly in a clearing created by a large forest fire. You don't see many young Douglas firs in a mature old-growth forest because they're unable to get enough sunlight and water to make it through their baby years if a thick understory of competing plants is already in place.

While this particular king-size Douglas fir dominates its surroundings, there are lots more where it came from. According to tree-ring analysis, this part of the forest really began to take root around the year 1600, when a tremendous fire swept through the Quinault

▴ Want to hug a tree? A viewing platform around this hulking 800-year-old Douglas fir makes it easy.

River Valley, leaving a jumbled legacy of snags, stumps, and downed logs filled in with low-lying shrubs and broad-leaved trees. Douglas fir seedlings capitalized on the opportunity and took root, eventually rising above the understory and becoming the dominant canopy layer tree in lowland forests of the Olympics some 200–300 years ago.

Around the same time, other conifer seedlings began to fill in. The result is a much more diverse forest nowadays than it was two centuries ago. While Douglas firs, which average 200 feet in height, are no doubt still the tallest trees in the temperate rain forest, three other tree species—Sitka spruce, western hemlock, and western red cedar—crowd the upper canopy with their conifer needles competing for sunlight.

Named for the town in Southeast Alaska where it's prevalent, the scaly barked Sitka spruce averages 175 feet tall and can live to 800 years of age, thriving in the coastal fog belt stretching from Northern California to British Columbia. The single largest example of any kind of spruce tree in the world, a mammoth Sitka spruce standing 191 feet tall, measuring 17.7 feet across in diameter, and more than 1000 years old, is nearby on another short interpretive trail not far from the shores of Lake Quinault.

Another big player in the temperate rain forest ecosystem is the western hemlock, which like its compatriot the Sitka spruce favors wet soils and tolerates the shade of the midcanopy as it grabs whatever sunlight the taller Douglas firs let slip through. The official state tree of Washington, western hemlock is considered the most humble of the temperate rain forest's "Big Four," as its top (and even its dark green needles) tends to droop downward in the shadows of slightly taller trees. Humility aside, these big boys also average 175 feet in height and can live beyond 500 years of age. They thrive in soggy lowlands—like this area of the Olympic coast—but can survive up to about 4000 feet in elevation, where their relatives, mountain hemlocks, start to take over.

Last but not least among iconic temperate rain forest trees, western red cedars get to be only about 160 feet tall on average, but what they lack in height they more than make up for in girth. It's not uncommon for millennia-old specimens to be 20 or more feet across and at least 60 feet in circumference. Unlike some tree species that clump together in groves, the western red cedar is more of a solitary figure. As the saying goes, there are no cedar forests but many cedar trees. They do best in dappled shade in forlorn soggy bottomlands, where they can absorb lots of water through their roots.

Long venerated by Pacific Northwest Native communities for its usefulness in making practical things, the relatively soft and pliant wood of the western red cedar is particularly resistant to rot. Because it evolved to grow in boggy environs, the tree contains a natural aromatic fungicide that resists rot and insects.

The items Indigenous peoples made from the bark and wood of the western red cedar included diapers, capes, hats, skirts, baskets, sails, masks, bowls, spoons, rope, and cord, as well as planks and beams for totem poles, longhouses, and, of course, canoes. Given the relatively light weight of its wood, not to mention its rot resistance, cedar was by far the best choice for canoes—the primary form of transportation for many Natives.

While there may be debate as to which specific tree is the biggest western red cedar, there is no question that it's on the wet and wild west side of the Olympic Peninsula. Why do trees get this big in this

▲ Western sword fern hangs down while Oregon oxalis creeps up along the sides of the gorge along Willaby Creek.

corner of the universe? In essence, these pillars of time are just doing what nature programmed for them. The fact that the environment in this protected bioregion is fed by prodigious amounts of fresh air and moisture off the Pacific Ocean—largely without the impact of humankind and its pollution—helps the trees live long, full lives.

Every schoolkid knows you can determine the age of a tree by counting its growth rings, but it might be news to you that a lot can be learned about the natural history of a region by looking even closer at the clues hidden in tree rings. For instance, blackened scars from forest fires show up encased between annual ring layers; researchers can use this data to pinpoint the years when specific fires occurred in the forest. We can also now tell when earthquakes and tsunamis struck by taking a look at tree rings. Douglas firs pump out pitch (also known as sap or resin) as a natural form of antibiotic when they get infected areas, and researchers can see that pitch residue in the tree rings; this has been useful in drawing conclusions about the historical prevalence and impact of diseases or blights affecting trees throughout the ecosystem.

Back on the trail, about 100 feet or so past the 800-year-old Douglas fir, take a gander at a western red cedar with its exposed roots sprawled out all over an equally impressive, gone-to-rot, old-growth stump. This excellent example highlights how important dead trees are to temperate rain forest ecology. With their wood broken down by fungi, lichens, mosses, and insects, these dead stumps, snags, and fallen logs are rich in nutrients that new plants need to get started. Believe it or not, the wet and soggy soils of the temperate rain forest are relatively shallow and don't provide nearly the nutrients big trees need to thrive. Because it harbors nutrients the flora of the rain forest needs to grow, dead wood is an essential part of the ecosystem.

It's not uncommon to see a straight line of trees in this forest that were all "nursed" by the same fallen log. Teeming with fungi, bacteria, and insects, these nurse logs provide an elevated nurturing environment in which plants, shrubs, and tree seedlings can take root relatively undisturbed. As the nurse log decomposes over decades, a few hearty trees hold on with their roots. Once wrapped around the log, these roots eventually support their trees like stilts planted into the soil below. According to the National Park Service, 96 percent of all spruce and hemlock seeds across the Olympic Peninsula's rain forest break open and germinate on nurse logs.

Meanwhile, standing dead trees (also known as snags) play a similarly important role in the rain forest ecosystem, providing shelter, food sources, and perching locations for some mammals as well as dozens of bird species and thousands of insect species. Broken down and softened by microbes, insects, and the elements, these snags are ripe for colonization by opportunistic life-forms. The tree itself might be dead, but it surely harbors uncountable numbers of living organisms. Deep inside such snags you'll find not just rodent burrows, bee hives, and ant colonies, but miles of fungal strands that are part of an unseen network moving nutrients through the ecosystem. An eagle or osprey might use the broken top of a snag (or one of its higher branches) as a nest site, or even just as a spot to scout for prey.

A Douglas fir tree in these parts might live 500 years (give or take) and grow 200 feet tall. But once it dies, it could take another 200 years to break down into a snag just a few feet high. Along the way, the dead wood that caves in or sloughs off won't go to waste as it's mined for nutrients and then slowly disintegrates into surrounding soils. Listen closely and you may hear the sounds of a pileated woodpecker helping this disintegration process along, as it knock-knock-knocks on a snag somewhere nearby, in search of bark beetles, carpenter ants, insect larvae, or other tasty snacks.

The varying states of decay in snags and blowdowns (trees that have been uprooted by high winds) here provide a constant reminder of the only constant in the rain forest: change. Around these parts, most change comes courtesy of coastal storms blowing in off the

An old western red cedar snag is surrounded by the remains of its upper reaches. As this wood breaks down on the forest floor, it nurtures the growth of new plants and trees.

Pacific, mostly in winter. Besides lots and lots of rain, such storms often pack wind gusts topping out at 50 miles per hour or more. Evidence from tree rings and other sources shows there have been at least 10 storms off the Pacific coast with hurricane-force winds (74 miles per hour and higher) over the last 200 years.

Extreme winds can also strike almost out of the blue on and around Lake Quinault. This is thanks both to its location in a valley between two steep ridges and the fact that warm air blowing in over the top of cooler surface air can lead to some extreme turbulence at ground level. To wit, one night in January 2018, "a rotor circulation associated with a strong mountain lee wave"—in the words of University of Washington climatologist Cliff Mass—blew down more than 100 old-growth giants on the north shore of Lake Quinault, across the lake from the Rain Forest Nature Trail.

According to the National Park Service, some 80 percent of the downed trees in the Quinault rain forest were victims of wind storms. (Old age, disease, and fire account for most other tree fatalities.) This constant change is one way the forest stays so diverse;

different sections grow up at different times and successional patterns vary from valley to valley.

Knitting this jumble of living and dead wood together is the green carpet of mosses, lichens, and fungi we affectionately call "the padded realm." Around 90 different padded species jockey for space on or near the forest floor throughout the major river drainages of the Olympic Peninsula. Chances are you're walking by many of them along this trail.

▲ Old man's beard, one of several epiphytic air plants in the Quinault rain forest, drapes itself over a hidden tree bough.

One that literally sticks out is old man's beard (also known as Spanish moss), which looks like a wispy green beard as it hangs on just about every bigleaf maple branch in the temperate rain forest. Like many mosses and lichens, old man's beard is an epiphyte, meaning it grows on the surface of other plants and derives everything it needs to survive (including nitrogen, calcium, and magnesium) from passing breezes and drops of moisture. It doesn't need a bed of soil as a substrate for growth. And although epiphytes rely on other plants for physical support, they don't affect their hosts negatively like parasites would.

Old man's beard is just one of many in the epiphytic community of the Olympic rain forest. Keep an eye out for the long, draping fronds of Oregon spikemoss, which looks more like a small hanging fern than a mossy beard. Cat-tail moss forms narrowly tapered strands of white-green hairlike clumps. Higher up in the canopy, hanging moss looks like green feathers dangling from tree limbs. Oregon lungwort, a leaflike lichen that grows in thick clusters, also prefers the refined living higher up in the canopy, and harbors colonies of bacteria that account for some 20 percent of the nitrogen fixing (that is, converting molecular nitrogen in the air into ammonia or related compounds in the soil below) that keeps the ecosystem of the temperate rain forest in balance.

According to natural historian Tim McNulty, dozens of other mosses as well as lichens, liverworts, and licorice ferns add up to a collective dry weight of more than a ton per tree. Moss mats have more than twice the biomass of the understory plants that grow on the forest floor and are typically four times heavier than a tree's own foliage. Researchers at Evergreen State College were amazed to discover a symbiotic relationship between these epiphytes and the trees that host them. It turns out that the bigleaf maples and vine maples that epiphytes prefer shoot out additional root structures into the hanging mosses and lichens to extend their own networks and suck nutrients from the epiphytes themselves. It's a give-and-take relationship: the trees and epiphytes are symbiotic.

There's also a lot going on below the surface as well, with fungi dominating the temperate rain forest underworld. Less than 20 percent of the biomass in the temperate rain forest is located below ground, yet this unseen part of the ecosystem uses more than half of the photosynthetic energy produced by leaves and needles above ground. An important part of the proper functioning of this netherworld is a healthy fungi population. Dozens of different mycorrhizal fungi species, such as the yellow chanterelle, form microscopic root-like networks that redistribute nutrients and moisture to nearby tree roots, where they are needed most. In exchange, the fungi get the sugars and proteins from trees that they need to survive, closing the loop on yet another great symbiotic relationship in nature.

Red-backed voles, rodents about the size of little mice, dine almost exclusively on underground fruiting fungi called truffles. Attracted by the fragrance and flavor of the truffles, these voles have coevolved to become important spore spreaders for these and other species of underground fruiting fungi. The voles aren't the only ones hot for truffles. Don't be surprised to find Douglas squirrels, Townsend's chipmunks, deer mice, and northern flying squirrels—not to mention elk and deer—giving voles some healthy competition, foraging in the soils of the old-growth forest on the hunt for truffles.

Meanwhile, other mammals avail themselves of different sorts of rain forest delicacies. River otters, with their high metabolism, have to eat frequently—and the buffet of Willaby Creek is open 24/7. These semiaquatic mammals have thick protective fur that keeps them warm when they are swimming in cold water—as are all the rivers of the Olympic Peninsula, which are glacially fed. The river otters' short legs and webbed feet allow them to move quickly on land or through the water, and they use their long whiskers to detect prey—crayfish, frogs, turtles—in dark or cloudy water. River otters' ability to turn quickly and reposition is key to their success fishing—and their evolutionary success.

Another mammalian denizen of the temperate rain forest is the usually nocturnal raccoon, one of the most adaptable species in the Northern Hemisphere, partly because it is omnivorous. Raccoons are likely to be plying the banks of Willaby Creek looking for a midnight snack of crayfish, frogs, salamanders, fish, or other water-bound critters that can't get away in the sometimes narrow and shallow stream. On an especially good night, a raccoon might snag a coastal cutthroat trout. Two subspecies of this threatened fish inhabit the creek. One stays within the stream's freshwater system year round while the other ventures out into the ocean (like its anadromous salmon cousins) in late winter or spring, returning home to its natal stream to feed, seek refuge, and, in some cases, spawn out. While fishing raccoons don't tend to be too choosy, the anadromous trout come back from their travels bigger and bulkier than their stream-bound cousins.

A raccoon stalking trout in the shallows looks a lot like a miniature version of a bear fishing for salmon—no surprise, given that raccoons and bears are close relatives. (Along with pandas, the three species are grouped within the same order—Carnivora—under Linnaeus's system of classification.) Black bears, while not as common as their raccoon relatives, also visit the temperate rain forest in their never-ending quest for roots, berries, insects and, where there's a stream involved, fish. Early to midsummer is a likely time to see these behemoths in the forest, given that's when the flat red berries of devil's club, one of their favorite delicacies, ripen.

Bears may love devil's club, but humans not so much. Although attractive with its gargantuan palmate leaves that are 4 to 5 times the size of a human hand, the low-lying plant has been the scourge of hikers since time immemorial because of the little pricking thorns sticking out of its beefy stalks that just love to drape themselves in the way of the path. But given the widespread distribution of the plant—many of its seeds are spread through bear scat—hikers may be hard pressed to find a woodland trail anywhere from Southeast Alaska down to Northern California that hasn't been colonized by this pesky plant. That said, devil's club plays an important role in

Devil's club sports some midsummer red berries.

the ecosystem; it stabilizes soils and helps the forest recover from both natural disturbances such as landslides or blowdowns and human incursions like logging. Native communities made extensive use of devil's club for everything from fish hooks and lures, to medicine for arthritis and tuberculosis, to deodorant, to lice treatment. It's highly likely that this relative of the American ginseng plant has other, yet-untapped medicinal properties.

After the trail edges you out onto an overlook of the creek's gorge (at almost 0.2 miles into the hike), a nearby bench makes for a great lunch or snack spot. Next, head south; Willaby Creek runs downhill to the east as views open up into the verdant, multilayered forest. The bigger conifers dominate the cluttered landscape, but there is plenty of room in the midlayer of the canopy for a collection of deciduous trees to strut their stuff as well. Bigleaf maples, which typically grow to about 50 feet tall but spread their branches out equally as wide, comingle with their smaller cousins, vine maples, which top out at only about 15 feet tall on average. These trees are beautiful throughout the year, but they put on a real show in the autumn, when their chlorophyll breaks down and the green drains from their leaves, exposing underlying colors—reds, yellows, oranges—before they finally wilt to brown, make their break, and float to the forest floor. There they become part of the humus (the organic component of soil, formed by the microorganism-aided decomposition of leaves and other plant material), supporting the next generation of flora as it springs from the shallow soils of the rain forest floor. Epiphytes drape from just about every branch, and the occasional stand of red alder and a lone black cottonwood here and there complete this iconic temperate rain forest scene.

At about a third of a mile into the hike, look deep into the forest to the east to spot a little waterfall, where Willaby Creek cascades over a cliff through the canopy. If you're into birds, this is a nice vantage point to listen and look for them (especially first thing in the morning when they wake up and initiate their dawn chorus). Bald

eagles and osprey frequent these woods in search of tasty rodents, or fish from Willaby Creek. In spring and summer, marbled murrelets take up seasonal residence in mossy nests on large horizontal branches in old-growth trees. This mottled, brown and white bird may be small—only about 9.5 inches long and less than 9 ounces—but it's hardy, spending most of the winter out at sea foraging for the small fish and marine invertebrates that make up the majority of its diet. The bird uses its short, stout wings to help it swim as deep as 300 feet below the ocean's surface to source prey.

The marbled murrelet is the only member of the family Alcidae (auks and puffins) that nests in large trees. Its preferred perches are 200 feet above the forest floor, so the big conifers of the Quinault rain forest are perfect for the birds to be able to nest and still access the saltwater coast to catch the small fish and marine invertebrates they feed their young. In the fall and winter marbled murrelets head out to sea, making occasional trips inland for unknown reasons. They have been listed as threatened under the U.S. Endangered Species Act since 1992 and gained further protection in 1994,

▲ Look through the trees and you can spot Willaby Creek cascading over a small ledge on its way down to nearby Lake Quinault.

▲ The young leaves and berries of salal were a staple food of Native communities throughout the Northwest, but today they are consumed more by blacktail deer, Douglas squirrels, black bears, and other temperate rain forest wildlife.

▲ Fungus takes over the end of a cut old-growth log that was blocking the trail, while western sword fern capitalizes on the open space.

thanks to the Northwest Forest Plan, which limited logging on old-growth forests of the region.

Keep your eyes peeled and ears open for other birds such as Swainson's thrushes, western tanagers, and evening grosbeaks. But perhaps the most famous avian denizen here is the northern spotted owl, a medium-sized dark brown bird weighing about a pound and change and growing up to 19 inches tall, with a wingspan of approximately 42 inches. This owl is only at home in the old-growth forests of Oregon, Washington, and British Columbia. As such, its population was decimated by the industrial logging of the latter half of the 20th century, when Pacific Northwest forests provided most of the wood for the nation and beyond. Biologists consider the northern spotted owl an indicator species for the health of the temperate rain forest, and it is also listed as threatened by the U.S. Fish and Wildlife Service under the Endangered Species Act. While 1994's Northwest Forest Plan curtailed much of the logging on public lands that was eliminating spotted owl habitat, the bird's population continues to decline (at a rate of about 2.9 percent per year, according to the American Bird Conservancy) as a result of continued logging on private land and competition from the barred owl. A cousin of the northern spotted owl, the barred owl is both more adaptable and more aggressive, and has started taking over spotted owl habitat in old-growth forests.

Back on the trail, Oregon oxalis, salmonberry, thimbleberry, salal, maidenhair fern, lady fern, and western sword fern mingle

• The roots of a thriving western hemlock tree envelop a massive old-growth western red cedar stump.

with tall, lopey stands of devil's club, competing for whatever light and moisture the bigger trees allow through the canopy. Fungi— chicken mushrooms and red-belted polypores—battle to fill the spaces in between. Each small section of this thick understory carpet of plants, fungi, and mosses filters gallons and gallons of Olympic precipitation every year, capturing nutrients and reducing soil erosion in the process.

Soon after spotting the waterfall through the trees to the left, look for a small game trail to the right that leads 100 feet into the forest and deposits you at the foot of a 10-foot-tall old-growth cedar stump. You'll find old-time loggers' springboard notches carved into the sides of the stump and the roots of a medium-sized hemlock tree draped around it; the hemlock is currently around 100 feet tall as it grows toward the sky.

WHAT'S A SPRINGBOARD?

Back in the days before chainsaws and mechanized logging, a lumberjack used a springboard. This was a tapered wooden plank with an angled iron spike on one end that could be attached to a notch cut by the logger above the flared base of the biggest old-growth trees—typically those 6 feet in diameter or larger. Above the fray of the forest floor, two loggers could team up to cut down a big tree by dragging a "misery whip" or "Swedish fiddle" (loggerspeak for a long, flexible saw) back and forth between them as they each stood on their respective springboards.

In this photo from early logging days, the two men standing above the others are on springboards. •

At a signed junction with the Quinault Loop Trail, stay right on the Rain Forest Nature Trail and loop around another few hundred feet to find a huge fallen Douglas fir that you can climb atop and walk for some 200 feet into the heart of the forest. The unique vantage point from this odd perspective—elevated 10 feet above the ground—yields a fresh perspective on how everything in the forest is connected.

Back down on the main trail, you'll soon get to a stretch that follows alongside another huge fallen Douglas fir—trail makers had to go around this mammoth as it was too big to cut through. The trail makes its final bend to the north and soon enough you are back where you started, at the trailhead.

HURRICANE RIDGE

*A rare UNESCO Biosphere Reserve
and World Heritage Site*

DIFFICULTY
Moderate

LENGTH
1 mile

LOCATION
near Port Angeles, Washington

Hundred-mile views aren't uncommon from
Hurricane Ridge on even a partly cloudy day.

If you're the kind of nature lover who likes extremes, Hurricane Ridge—tucked amid glaciers and alpine meadows at the top of the world in the middle of Washington's Olympic Peninsula—might be just your cup of Dirty Chai Latte. From 5200 feet elevation, you can see for miles in every direction, but the view down at your feet of hardy, elevation-adapted flora—especially the stunted conifers everywhere and the wildflowers adding so much color to the scene in summer—may be just as captivating. Hurricane Ridge is special not just because of its natural beauty and alpine location in the mountainous heart of Olympic National Park, but also because of the endemic flora and fauna it supports and the waning high-elevation glaciers surrounding it.

Getting up there is certainly a little out of the way—you have to detour off U.S. Highway 101, then drive a two-lane mountain road up and up and up for 17 miles to reach Hurricane Ridge. But before you complain too much, remember that this well-maintained, paved road delivers you from sea level to true alpine country faster and easier than anywhere else in the contiguous United States.

The views from the parking lot are fabulous, but stretch your legs a little along any of the short trails originating from here and you'll reap the benefits, with hundred-mile vistas from forested bluffs of glaciated peaks and wildflower-festooned meadows. The 1-mile loop combining the Cirque Rim and High Ridge Trails is a great introduction to the high country and although you won't be alone, you'll be away from the throngs in the parking lot and visitor center. While Hurricane Ridge Road is open year round (Friday–Sundays and holiday Mondays in winter, weather-permitting), the vast majority of visitors make the trip in summer when (1) you can be outside in shirtsleeves, (2) some of the snow is melted, and (3) dozens of different high-altitude wildflower species are in bloom. If you visit during the July–August high season, you won't be disappointed.

Pick up the Cirque Rim Trail as it rises to the north from the far end of the Hurricane Ridge parking lot. The trail is paved, but has a steep grade here, so those in wheelchairs will need assistance. Follow it up for 0.1 miles until it dead-ends at the top on a small ridge with the parking area behind you. Looking back, you can't help but feel small. Several of the park's glaciers are on full display as you pan

△ Moisture off the Pacific Ocean, in the form of clouds, fills in the valleys of the Olympic high country.

around to the south, including Blue Glacier, the park's biggest, on the flanks of Mount Olympus 15 miles to the south.

Given how much snow and ice is in your view even in midsummer, you wouldn't think climate change would be a big problem up here. But how wrong you would be! The U.S. National Park Service conducted comprehensive surveys of the park's glaciers in 1982 and then again in 2009, and found an overall 34 percent loss of glacial surface area in the intervening three decades. In 1982, the park had 266 glaciers; by 2009, 82 of them were gone altogether and the rest were markedly smaller and thinner.

Less ice in the high country isn't just bad for the ice worms that eke out a living in glaciers, it also has ripple effects throughout

many "downstream" ecosystems. As the glaciers recede, there is less water for wildflower meadows just below and for the streams and rivers where five threatened species of salmon (Chinook, coho, chum, sockeye, and pink), as well as steelhead and bull trout, spawn. Because these fish are born in fresh water up in the highlands and then migrate down to the ocean, losing glacial ice has a direct impact on the biodiversity of the ocean.

At the top of the rise, go left and explore the dead-end part of the Cirque Rim Trail as it leads to a forested overlook that faces west. If you like conifers, you've come to the right place. Indeed, you'd be hard-pressed to find a deciduous tree that can survive the long, harsh winters at this alpine elevation, where 5 feet of snow covering the ground for half the year marks a normal winter.

▲ Olympic National Park has lost about a third of its year-round snow and ice over the last three decades alone.

▲ Fog shrouds the Strait of Juan de Fuca.

Even without deciduous species, the Hurricane Ridge area supports a wide diversity of trees. Mountain hemlock, silver fir, western hemlock, Pacific yew, Alaska cedar, western white pine, western red cedar, lodgepole pine, Sitka spruce, and Douglas fir are all represented up here, but the dominant tree at this elevation is the subalpine fir. Part of the way these tree-line huggers ensure success in this stratospheric realm is through the layering of their lower branches into the snow in a circle around the tree. Come spring, these branches will have made it down into the soil and will start rooting new trees right there on the spot. This phenomena explains why subalpine firs tend to grow in a circle.

If you think the conifers up here look a tad small, you're not crazy. The harsh conditions and exposure at this elevation—gale force winds, blowing snow, and occasional avalanches are the norm during the long, cold winter—force the trees to grow more stout than their lowland cousins. Some of these trees are half the height of others of the same species just a few miles downhill.

Along sections of the trail, you'll notice lots of yellow-green, hairy goatsbeard lichen hanging off tree branches. This air plant does well living off the gifts of the breeze. It's a favorite browse for the Columbian black-tailed deer that make themselves at home up here.

Another wildlife species known to snack on goatsbeard is the Olympic marmot. This endemic herbivore thrives in the rocky high ground around Hurricane Ridge and other parts of the Olympic peninsula above 4000 feet.

Columbian black-tailed deer on Hurricane Ridge aren't afraid of humans—but don't feed them as it's healthier for them to forage for their own wild foods.

Drink in the sublime scene, then turn around and backtrack to the previous junction, this time continuing straight (east) along the ridge, past the turnoff down to the parking area. The views open up to the north, and herbaceous plants and small shrubs vie for space in the teeming understory behind you. If it's summer, it's wildflower season in these meadows and throughout the Olympic high country. See how many types of blooms you can spot, and which colors of the rainbow you can check off.

WHAT IS ENDEMISM?

Endemic species are organisms whose evolutionary path has branched off from that of their ancestors, usually as a result of a physical barrier interrupting gene flow. Different species of the same plant or animal presumably start out genetically identical, but their divergent physical paths lead to the development of slightly different physical characteristics—and enough genetic disparity for biologists to be able to tell them apart. Many examples of plant and wildlife endemism exist on the Olympic Peninsula, which was separated from the continental mainland by impenetrable ice sheets during the last ice age. Some of the species west of this geographic divide adapted to fill specific environmental niches not found on the mainland, and as such, evolved into separate species.

> You can find several endemic plant species at Hurricane Ridge, including (top to bottom) lesser-bladder milkvetch, Piper's bellflower, and Flett's violet.

While there are plenty of common wildflowers around—Indian paintbrush, fireweed, broadleaf lupine—you'll also see more obscure blooms, some of which are endemic to the Olympic highlands. Keep an eye out for Piper's bellflower, which has a pretty star shape with light blue petals surrounding long, white, fuzzy anthers. Another endemic beauty you may well see here is Flett's violet, which sports a quintet of lobed purple-pink petals with a yellow smudge in the middle. Meanwhile, lesser-bladder milkvetch sends up crowns of a dozen or so small pink and white flowers. Other rare Olympic high country endemics you may stumble upon include Flett's fleabane, Henderson's rock spirea, Olympic Mountain groundsel, Olympic Mountain synthyris, Olympic aster, lanceleaf springbeauty, bracted lousewort, and Tisch's saxifrage.

Of course, most of the plants you can see up here are natives and not endemic—but that doesn't make those natives any less important ecologically. Narrow-sepaled phacelia blooms into a crown of small white flowers as it clings to the side of rocky slopes on which most other plants wouldn't dare set roots. White rhododendrons spread out their glossy green leaves on shady slopes. Meanwhile, showy sedge sends nodding heads of tiny off-white or yellow flowers beyond the tops of its spindly, dark red stems. And sickle-top lousewort sports a beak-like upper lip dressed in white or purple or yellow and produces a

Winter never completely leaves the high country of Olympic National Park, as evidenced by patches of snow lingering into late summer.

capsule-sized fruit which, contrary to what ranchers used to believe, don't actually give lice to ungulates (hooved animals) who eat it.

Up here at tree line, non-native plant species are less likely to survive, given the harsh conditions they haven't evolved to endure. That said, park biologists are keeping an eye on Canada thistle, a purple mop-topped invasive of Eurasian origin first introduced to Canada as an ornamental. Its subsequent spread across North America and displacement of native species along the way have been both dramatic and damaging. The plant's signature purple blooms have been spotted alongside the lower reaches of the Hurricane Ridge Road in recent years, and rangers warn it's only a matter of time before the plant's hardy seeds make it up to Hurricane Ridge itself. Once there, it could start displacing endemic and otherwise sensitive native plant species with nowhere to go but extinct.

Himalayan blackberry, English ivy, and English holly, among other invasives, are already wreaking havoc in Olympic National Park's lowland and coastal sections. It would be a shame for the unique alpine and subalpine reaches of the park to become overrun with pesky interlopers at the expense of the beautiful native flowers we can still witness today.

Keep moving forward, ignoring the right-hand turn onto the Big Meadow Trail which leads back down to the parking lot—you'll come back this way later anyway if you need to alleviate any FOMO (fear

∗ Looking toward Port Angeles, 5 miles away and 5000 vertical feet below.

of missing out). Soon enough the Cirque Rim Trail dead-ends at a junction with the High Ridge Trail. If you've had enough, you can turn right and stay on the paved Cirque Rim Trail, which leads back to the parking lot, making for a solid 0.5-mile loop.

If you instead want to go farther, hang a left onto the High Ridge Trail and ascend past the lift gear for the Hurricane Ridge ski area (open on weekends in the winter) into a grassy alpine meadow filled with red, yellow, purple, and blue wildflowers in mid- to late summer.

Keep hiking up and go left at the next junction, toward Sunrise Point, a narrow outcropping leading to a small overlook of the deep, shady valleys below and serrated, snowcapped ridges all around. It's one of those transcendent scenes that make you feel small and part of something much larger than yourself at the same time.

If and when you're ready to pull yourself away, retrace your steps back down from Sunrise Point and go left at the fork to round out the rest of the High Ridge Trail and get back to the parking lot. There is a lot more to see and do on the Olympic Peninsula, but at least now you can check Hurricane Ridge off your bucket list. While it's a little off the beaten path, no one has ever said they regretted the detour.

WEST BEACH SAND DUNES

Dunes backed by gnarled trees; driftwood bigger than boats

DIFFICULTY
Easy

LOCATION
Deception Pass State Park, Oak Harbor, Washington

LENGTH
1 mile

Deception Pass State Park can be a mystical place early in the morning, before the fog lifts.

Given the mild climate of Western Washington and the low-elevation setting (sea level, actually), this unique and dynamic coastal ecosystem is well worth a visit any time of the year. Summer is by far the most popular season here; besides strolling the beach in the sun, you can jump in a freshwater lake to cool off and even hike deep into the coastal forest to sit under the canopy of giant conifers. Winter is less popular but more rewarding if you like to see wildlife in action, as shorebirds flock to coastline waters, feasting on the fish and aquatic invertebrates that are flushed out of Deception Pass twice a day during ebb tides.

The sandy trail starts from the south end of the parking lot. Follow it through the picnic area to a small visitor center building—if you need a restroom, there are a couple located on the north side of the building.

Passing the building, you enter another world as the dunes ecosystem opens up before you. The trail becomes paved at this point and is essentially wheelchair accessible. At the fork, go straight (not left) to do the 1-mile loop hike counterclockwise so you can see the dunes and shoreline first, before looping back through the interior forest on the way back.

As you continue straight, you'll notice lots of American dunegrass springing up from the beds of sand on both sides of the trail. The occasional Sitka spruce tree pops up. Some of them are small and only a few years old and others are bigger and spread out into a more bushy shape than one usually expects from the species. The windswept nature of this site is no doubt to blame, but the trees don't seem to mind; even the bigger varieties out here on the coast are essentially dwarf versions of the trees farther inland, some of which can grow to heights over 200 feet tall.

The few open spaces remaining in the sandy pockets here and there are filled with American dunegrass, blue bunchgrass, field sagewort, common

Blue bunch-grass is one of the dominant herbaceous species you'll see growing within—and helping to stabilize—the dunes.

yarrow, European searocket, silver bur ragweed and Puget Sound gumweed, among other sand-tolerant ground covers.

▲ Silver bur ragweed wallpapers the sand in small sections of the dunes at West Beach.

Make sure to take a detour out onto the beach itself, just over the dunes on your right. Follow others' footsteps in the sand to find a good access point, then indulge in the westward Pacific Ocean views. You can't help but marvel at the sheer size of the driftwood logs that have washed up and lodged themselves on the upper beach and at the base of the dunes.

Many of these driftwood logs were huge fallen trees that washed out from the coastline or even river drainages, while others washed in from the sea and could be from points far, far away. Likewise, some of them are wedged into place and will probably be there for dozens if not hundreds of years, while others

▲ Puget Sound gumweed is endemic to this region.

with less secure footing might shake loose during the next big winter storm and move on to another destination somewhere up or down the coast. Regardless, they are all bleached practically white from their exposure in the ocean and to the sun and elements on the beach. The particularly immovable ones are coated in barnacles and lichens.

Even these long-dead logs provide lots of environmental services to the surrounding ecosystem. For starters, they protect the dunes from crashing waves and heavy winds while trapping sand behind them. They also help define and retain the border between beach and dune and provide cover for a wide variety of birds and mammals populating this unique intertidal zone. Over time, the driftwood breaks down and slowly releases its nutrients into the sand, where other plant species can benefit from them.

Part of what makes visiting these dunes so much fun is that they are a rare commodity in this part of the world. A robust assortment of symbiotic coastal plants are able to thrive in the wind-whipped,

▲ Deception Pass is often shrouded in fog during the early morning.

sun-exposed, salt-caked setting of Deception Pass. Deep-rooted plants like American dunegrass, blue bunchgrass, field sagewort, western snowberry, and Nootka rose help stabilize sand below the surface, which in turn helps anchor the dunes in place.

Meanwhile, the leaves and stems of ground huggers like sand verbena, red fescue, and coastal gumweed block the sand from blowing away above the surface, also important to keeping the dunes generally in place, shifty as they may be. These low growers have thick, waxy leaves which help protect them from the constant barrage of coastal elements here.

About 500 feet past the beginning of the loop junction, look for a sandy side trail to the left that leads to a viewpoint overlooking a gnarled Douglas fir that has grown up in a much different fashion from its brothers up the hill and farther inland. Normally the Douglas Fir is one of the tallest and straightest trees in the forest. In this case, because of its location along the windswept and storm-battered coast, this tree has grown

• European searocket, with its pretty little lavender flowers, colonizes open spots, usually small hollows in which it can set seed and flourish on its own without much competition.

more like an overgrown juniper, complete with low-lying, snaking branches. Rangers estimate this particular Douglas fir to be around 850 years old. An interpretive sign warns not to climb on it, tempting as it may be, in deference to its advanced age. Indeed, Mother Nature didn't intend it to be a jungle gym for humans large and small. After you've oohed and ahhed enough at this special Douglas fir, head back out to the main trail and continue south for another 500 feet or so. At this point, the main trail hooks left to start its way back through the forest.

Take the opportunity and cut out to the beach, where you may find clams and mussels. Oysters are less common here than in other more estuarine locales. One thing is for sure: where there are clams and mussels for the taking, there are gulls—lots of them. If you know which is which, you'll be able to tell a ring-billed from a western from an Olympic gull, but otherwise just enjoy seeing these scrappy denizens of the coast sail on wind gusts above the tideline, occasionally swooping down for a shellfish snack.

Many other types of birds besides gulls call this stretch of coast home, staying put year round to feast on a wide variety of leaves, berries, insects, and aquatic invertebrates. Belted kingfishers, northern flickers, spotted towhees, black oystercatchers, yellow-rumped

*It's hard to believe this gnarled specimen is an 850-year-old Douglas fir.

warblers, marbled murrelets, red crossbills, and great blue herons are just a few of the locals you may spot plying the dunes, beach, or surf for a little sustenance.

Many more birds that aren't permanent residents make appearances twice a year on their way up and down the Pacific Flyway between South America and Alaska. If you are visiting in a shoulder season, you may be lucky enough to spy any number of long-distance migrants, including orange-crowned warblers, barn swallows, Savannah sparrows, rufous hummingbirds, Anna's hummingbirds, and dark-eyed juncos coming up from Mexico or points farther south.

Meanwhile, another group of often-sighted migratory birds here are short-hop commuters. Trumpeter swans, American robins, varied thrushes, American goldfinches, Brandt's cormorants, pigeon guillemots, red-breasted mergansers, and three species of loons are among the many birds that summer and breed in Alaska and then fly south to overwinter on the ice-free lakes and nutrient-rich ocean beaches and bays of the Pacific Northwest.

In the winter, Deception Pass is like an open buffet for a wide range of diving birds. From mid-November to early April, red-throated loons gather by the hundreds twice a day—floating up en masse just offshore of Deception Pass about an hour before the ebb tide flushes out untold numbers of cod, herring, shrimp, and other favorite treats of these divers. When the tide starts to rip, the birds fly upstream, diving from on high into the roiling current, only to surface hundreds of feet downstream, ideally with fish in their craw. Despite these huge aggregations, red-throated loon population numbers have been dropping in recent years, and conservationists worry we could lose the species within decades if we can't figure out what's causing the decline and how to stem it.

Red-throated loons aren't the only birds working Deception Pass's winter tidal rip. Pacific loons and common loons join their cousins, albeit not in aggregations as large. Meanwhile, cormorants, ducks, gulls, and even some shorebirds employ similar fishing techniques when the getting is good—which is typically all winter long.

▲ Field sagewort, with its resilient green leaves and red stems, helps the dunes retain their sand and structure thanks to its deep roots.

▲ Sitka spruce's scaly bark hosts yellow lichens.

▲ It's always fun to look straight down at the ground whenever you are in a location as dynamic as a seashore with tidal variations—where a new retinue of eye candy comes in with every high tide.

▲ A curious harbor seal surfaces to check out the scene.

▲ Watching red-throated loons come together to fish the ebb tide out of Deception Pass is one of the great wildlife spectacles of the Pacific Northwest.

Birds are only part of the wildlife story on this wild coastline. Harbor seals loll on rocky outcrops, awkwardly sliding their smooth and slippery bodies into the nearby water if you walk (or wade or swim or paddle or motor) too close. Harbor seals, the most common marine mammals in the region, stick close to home, not usually straying more than 50 miles from where they were born. Their native habitat—where they rest, pup, nurse, and molt—is the rocky shoreline and the small sea-bound rock outcrops and islets dotting the coast. Favorite meals include rockfish, cod, herring, flounder, and salmon, but seals aren't too choosy and won't pass up an occasional bottom feeder or small pelagic fish.

Other marine mammals you could encounter here or nearby include California sea lions and Steller sea lions. If either species is anywhere nearby, you'll know it. They are imposing, elephantine beasts that snort and jockey for position in fearsome displays of aggression that rarely lead to injury but are highly effective at establishing a pecking order of dominance. This is especially true with regard to which males get to mate with a harem of females when breeding season is in full swing, typically in late June.

Less likely to be on the beach but no doubt hanging out just offshore are harbor porpoises and Dall's porpoises. And while you are

▴ As you loop back through the forest, Pacific yews and a coterie of other flora encroach on the trail.

▴ Sitka spruce's sprightly green needles are a constant companion as you loop back through the forest.

on the beach, keep your eyes trained on the sea and you might spot a whale or at least its spout. Some orcas live all year in these waters, while others migrate far and wide seasonally. Grays and humpbacks can be seen spouting offshore on their 5000 mile migrations.

When you've had your fill of beach combing and whale spotting, head back to the main trail, which now turns inland and hooks around to the left. As you leave the dunes behind, it feels like you are entering a semitropical wonderland; all the foliage starts to close in along both sides of the trail.

Indeed, the floral landscape is much denser on this side of the loop. There is still plenty of Sitka spruce, as well as Douglas fir, lodgepole pine, and Pacific madrone trees, but salal, ocean spray, red-flowering currant, and bracken fern fill in the gaps. Pacific yew trees become more prevalent the farther you get from the beach, here flanked by overlapping curtains of old man's beard lichens hanging from spindly lateral branches. This slow-growing conifer spreads out in the midcanopy under 50 feet tall.

A century ago, Pacific yews used to be much more common throughout the Pacific Northwest. But loggers eager to get at bigger cash crop trees like Douglas firs cleared whatever stands of Pacific yew they could, decimating the species throughout its range from Northern California up through British Columbia. General forest succession dynamics also favor taller trees over the long haul—another

▴ Old man's beard lichen hangs off a branch, dressing up the forest.

▴ Lodgepole pines have distinctive needles and cones.

factor that has led to this lesser conifer's recent diminishment.

An extract from the yew tree's bark called taxol, first discovered by National Cancer Institute researchers in the 1960s, has since become an important weapon in the pharmaceutical arsenal of doctors working to slow or stop the spread of aggressive cancer cells. This drug has proven to be a particularly effective chemotherapy treatment for breast and ovarian cancers, among others. These days, taxol is synthesized in the lab from extracts of cultivated yews so as not to further stress already flagging populations of the tree. Nevertheless, the lifesaving utility of this naturally occurring, bark-based chemical is reason enough to preserve not only yew trees but all of Mother Nature's creation. You never know where the next cancer-killing drug might come from.

Keep moving through the forest and soon enough you'll be back at the original trail junction where you started hiking. There is a lot more to see at Deception Pass if you have the time and inclination. But if you're too tired or it's too late to squeeze in another hike, rest assured you've seen some of the best sights and sounds the region has to offer along the West Beach Sand Dunes and its surrounding ecosystem.

TIDELAND ECOLOGY TRAIL

Intertidal zone along one of the only fjords in the Lower 48

DIFFICULTY
Easy

LOCATION
Quilcene, Washington

LENGTH
0.3 miles

This foray showcases a temperate rain forest and saltwater beaches commingling in all the right ways. Huge tree boughs hang over the beach, partially shading the myriad oyster shells, fallen leaves, and multicolored beach rocks. Just upland, a continuation of the trail showcases how Indigenous peoples used local plants to subsist on the bounty of the forest.

The 0.3 mile trail section of this hike is about as easy as it gets. Down at the beach, watch your step as you pick your way around driftwood logs, loose or slippery rocks, and errant leaves along the shoreline—but it's no more difficult than walking any other beach in the Northwest. The best time of year to visit is summer, but given the low elevation and mild marine climate, any time of year is usually fine. Note that Seal Rock Campground, its gated access road, parking area, trails, and beach access are only open April through September, so plan accordingly. If you decide to venture forth during the off-season, park outside of—but not blocking—the locked gate and walk in. Chances are you'll have the entire park to yourself.

The road off Highway 101 leading into the Seal Cove Campground bottoms out at the trailhead, where a kiosk provides campers with self-check-in instructions as well as a map of the trails around the beach and campground, a tide chart, and bear-safe information.

Follow the Salal-lined trail along the camp road to the left and marvel at the variety of plant life crowding the shoreline. Douglas firs, western red cedars, and bigleaf maples are the big boys on

⏴ Stair steps lead down to the beach and intertidal bounty of the Hood Canal.

the block, some growing upward of 100 feet tall as they stretch up and arch out toward the open light to the west. Pink honeysuckle, salmonberry, evergreen huckleberry, and Cascade barberry crowd the understory, providing delicious treats for birds, bears, and deer. Red alders and the occasional swooping, peely barked Pacific madrone fill in the gaps. The latter is colloquially referred to by Americans as "madrona" and by British Columbians—where the tree also thrives in similar wild, rocky environments—as "arbutus."

Whatever you call it, the Pacific madrone is universally acknowledged to be one beautiful species of tree, with its reddish outer bark that inevitably peels away in green snippets to expose a smooth, coppery inner bark, and long, oval, glossy evergreen leaves. In late March (give or take a week), small white, urn-shaped flowers come out. Later in the spring, madrones produce small, round, red-orange "warty" berries that can persist on the limb into late fall, lasting for months beyond the other berries of the forest. The late-season availability of madrone berries makes them an important source of nutrition for birds, deer, and small mammals otherwise prepping for a long, cold, hungry winter.

▴ Pink honeysuckle

▴ Evergreen huckleberry

▴ Western red cedar leaves

▴ Cascade barberry

Another reason to love seeing Pacific madrones in the wild is that they're famously hard to tame. Indeed, many a city slicker has tried to plant one in the backyard to no avail. The trees thrive in poor, fast-draining, rocky soils—such as you might find on a cliffside along the shoreline of Hood Canal—where they help provide stability and stave off erosion. Given the tree's independent disposition—and the fact that habitat destruction has greatly reduced the madrone's range—it's especially satisfying to see such hardy, healthy shoreline volunteers thriving in a natural environment, providing a nice pop of green and reddish brown color.

After about 1000 feet, turn around and return to the trailhead kiosk, then head down the rough-hewn stairsteps to the beach below. As you descend, the briny scent of the sea fills the air. Why do we love this smell so much? Maybe it's a subconscious reminder of our

Pacific madrone bark detail.

An intertidal still life with a fallen bigleaf maple leaf and a Pacific oyster shell.

primordial roots eons ago as sea creatures. Or maybe we just love the ocean, and the pleasant childhood memories it conjures when the olfactory senses are triggered. Near the bottom of the steps, a large Douglas fir bough, with deep striations of brown and gray in its bark, swoops over the pathway, beckoning to the beach below.

Down the last few stairsteps and onto the sand, Hood Canal—one of only two true fjords in the contiguous United States—spreads out before you. Geologically speaking, a fjord is defined as a long, narrow inlet with steep sides or cliffs. It is created by a glacier. This is exactly what happened here during the Late Pleistocene epoch some 13,000 years ago, when the Cordilleran Ice Sheet retreated, excavating the channel that British explorer George Vancouver later named "Hood's Channel" in honor of a British admiral who never set foot in the New World. The Cordilleran's retreat is also responsible for carving out Puget Sound itself (the other true fjord in the contiguous U.S.), as well as Lake Washington and several other long, straight valleys in the region.

Pick your way over driftwood logs, algae-covered rocks, and irregularly shaped, ridged white Pacific oyster shells. The shells' fleshy invertebrate insides were long ago swallowed up by hungry gulls, crabs, starfish, or maybe humans. These bivalve mollusks thrive in the estuarine environment where fresh water meets salt water; Hood Canal, an ocean inlet with an abundance of creeks emptying into it, makes for ideal oyster habitat.

The life cycle of an oyster provides an illuminating lesson in marine biology and ecology. In Hood Canal, Pacific oysters typically begin the spawning process in summer, when the water temperature warms above 64 degrees F. Males take this environmental cue

A big old Pacific madrone tree guards the beach along the Tideland Ecology Trail.

and expel sperm clusters that disintegrate into billions and billions of individual sperm cells. Meanwhile, nearby female oysters, filter feeding as usual, draw these expelled sperm cells into their own mantle cavities where their eggs are stored—and fertilization begins. Females then release small clouds of 50–200 million fertilized eggs in the form of planktonic larvae into the water column 5–6 times per minute for several minutes during every spawning event. These larvae bob in the water column for 20–30 days before settling and attaching to a suitable substrate, such as the surface of a rock, another oyster's shell, or just about any free surface in the intertidal zone, hard or soft, natural or man made. When it lands, each settling oyster secretes a natural glue to help it adhere so it can commence making a living—that is, filtering phytoplankton and other nutrients from the seawater.

As the ultimate couch potatoes, oysters sit back, glued to their rocks, and let the food come to them. Water flows in, and the oyster's gills extract oxygen and give back carbon dioxide and uric acid, while also capturing small particles of food in the form of free-floating phytoplankton.

Big oyster populations can collectively filter huge volumes of seawater every day, which not only helps reduce turbidity (caused by algae, pollution, and other gunk), but also stabilizes the nutrient balance in the water column. While oysters can't clean up our coastal waters on their own, they can be part of the solution, so it's in everyone's best interest to encourage their growth by devoting more habitat in the wild to nurture them.

The oyster shells underfoot high up on this beach are Pacifics, a non-native species introduced from Japan in 1902 and soon thereafter posed as an alternative to dwindling stocks of native Olympia oysters. The smaller and more sensitive Olympias ("Olys" for short), plentiful across intertidal reaches and an essential part of Indigenous diets up and down the Northwest coast for millennia, were losing their battle against pollution—especially all the unregulated,

• Pacific oyster shells are in abundance along the shoreline here.

*Just another day at the beach.

chlorine-based toxic effluents released by paper mills into Puget Sound during the first half of the 20th century. The larger Pacifics, with their thick, rough shells growing to about 10 inches in length, could better withstand the pollution, and the nascent oyster-farming industry coalesced around these non-natives.

By the 1960s, Olys were all but gone from their usual stomping grounds, but ecologists like Betsy Peabody of the nonprofit Puget Sound Restoration Fund refused to give up on the region's only native oyster. The Johnny Appleseed of Oly oysters, Peabody began hunting for the increasingly scarce bivalves around deep, protected inlets and other estuarine backwaters far from the effluent pipes of the offending paper mills. Lo and behold, she uncovered remnant patches of the once-abundant little white oysters—Olys only grow to a maximum of about 3 inches long, a third the size of Pacifics—and began seeding them far and wide in their native habitats in an effort to bring them back from the brink of extinction.

Improved water quality and stricter rules on harvest limits in recent decades have made the Olys' comeback a little easier. But continued development around shorelines—introducing silt into the water column, and making it difficult for these filter feeders to eat—as well as the construction and maintenance of bulk-heads and dikes that can scour beaches where Olys might otherwise congregate mean it's still an uphill battle for this small but mighty Northwest bivalve. Increased interest in Olys among foodies who love them for their sweet, metallic, celery-tinged taste—look for them at the Oyster Bar in Grand Central Station next time you're in New York City—is helping environmentalists' case for protecting the threatened oysters' habitat around Hood Canal and greater Puget Sound.

Naturally, there's a lot more going on in the intertidal zone than a few oysters filter feeding, but much of it we can't see as it takes place just below the tide line in the offshore eelgrass beds. Dungeness crabs, ghost shrimp, heart cockles, striped sun stars, aggregating anemones, and sunflower sea stars jockey for position and prey. Shiner perch, with their vertical silver bars, dart in and out of eelgrass beds in search of copepods, while summer brings runs of steelhead trout, coho, and Chinook salmon, as well as summer-run chum, a salmon subspecies unique to Hood Canal.

▲ Fried eggs are among the jellyfish species frequently spotted in Hood Canal.

Offshore, jellyfish employ their own form of jet propulsion to move themselves through the water column. These amazing primitive marine invertebrates are composed of three layers (an outer epidermis, a middle jellylike mesoglea, and an inner gastrodermis) and a "nerve net" that allows them to smell, detect light, and respond to stimuli. Their simple digestive cavity is both stomach and intestine, with one opening serving as both mouth and anus. Like their Cnidaria cousins the sea anemone, sea whip, and coral, the body parts of a jellyfish radiate out from a central axis, allowing it to detect and respond to stimuli—be it something to eat (phytoplankton, zooplankton, larvae) or something that might eat it—from any direction. Its primary offensive and defensive mechanism is the sting of its tentacles, which leaves thousands of tiny venom-producing barbs (nematocysts) in the skin of victims. Luckily for the saltwater swimmers among us, most jellyfish stings aren't strong enough to cause anything but some minor discomfort in most humans. Some of the most common jellyfish in Hood Canal include moon, lion's mane, and fried egg. The last, with big white translucent bells and yellow internal organs (thus, the name) are the easiest to identify, but seeing any jellyfish slip and slide through the water column is a treat.

Pick your way over the driftwood on the beach and climb the stairsteps back up to the trailhead kiosk and parking area. It's hard to leave the intertidal zone, with so much to discover under every rock, and a seemingly magnetic pull to the saltwater. Time to plan your next visit to the Tideland Ecology Trail on Hood Canal.

TOUCH OF NATURE INTERPRETIVE TRAIL

Possible sightings of bald eagles and 3-foot clams

DIFFICULTY
Easy

LOCATION
Penrose Point State Park, Lakebay, Washington

LENGTH
0.25 miles

This trail at Penrose State Park introduces visitors to a quintessential lowland forest ecosystem populated with some of the most iconic plants and trees of the Pacific Northwest. It is also a wonderful shoreline setting along South Puget Sound's Carr Inlet.

The trail was built in 1982 by local Eagle Scouts, then updated in 1991 by another generation of the same troop. Numbered sign-posts along the way correspond to a paper guide you can get at the trailhead; the guide includes explanations of the flora you'll encounter on the 0.25-mile loop. Penrose State Park is open year round but gets most visitors during the summer months. That said, if you go in the off-season, you just may have the sights, sounds, and smells of the intimate ecosystem to yourself.

Look for Touch of Nature Trail signs to the west of the park's main parking area and follow the trail as it quickly dips into the woods. Like most forested areas of Western Washington, Douglas firs dominate here, but plenty of other flora prevail in the moist soil. Western red cedar trees with swollen trunks love the soggy bottom of this stretch of land. Bigleaf maples spread a layer of deciduous, broad-leaved boughs across the midcanopy, with epiphytes along for the ride collecting nutrients and moisture off the passing breezes. Big, thriving evergreen huckleberry bushes spread out in the understory—in some cases, even climbing tree bark for an extra lift above the fray.

Stands of red alder grow thin and straight, fixing nitrogen in the soil which other plants then use as fertilizer. Western sword ferns pop up here and there, large fronds radiating from their centers, while salal creeps into the gaps with its leathery green leaves that turn a striking marbled red late in their season. In late spring, look for western trillium's showy white and purple flowers dotting the trailside.

▲ This western hemlock's roots grew around an old stump.

▲ Beaked hazelnut forms a dense canopy of overlapping oval leaves.

One common tree here that you don't see on every hike west of the Cascades is Oregon ash. It flourishes in the open habitat that often follows floods, windstorms, and other disturbances, but doesn't do as well when conifers get a head start on it and steal its sunlight. Thanks to its shallow but wide-spreading root system, Oregon ash is particularly well adapted to soggy ground (like the swampland on which the Touch of Nature Trail was built), withstanding wind storms and flooding much better than many other native trees in the region. Squirrels, songbirds, rodents, rabbits, ducks, and geese love Oregon ash seeds, while deer and elk graze on its leaves.

The trail cuts through the forest and then curves around and leads along Carr Inlet. The shimmery green leaves of a 15-foot-tall Oregon crabapple tree hang over the shoreline, anchored by a gnarled trunk and root system that help stabilize the thin-soiled shoreline. A huge old western hemlock that must have grown up around an old cedar stump sports

Western red cedars and evergreen huckleberry
hug the Touch of Nature Interpretive Trail.

roots standing 4 feet off the ground—a typical sight in the true temperate rain forest. Another relatively uncommon Northwest native that loves this type of marine shoreline setting is the Pacific madrone in all of its red, peely barked, leathery green-leaved glory. Canadian milkvetch mingles with stands of giant horsetail.

Another increasingly sparse plant that thrives in the moist environment here is beaked hazelnut, famous as the earliest native shrub to bloom. A harbinger of spring, the plant's long yellow catkins come out as early as February; its serrated oval green leaves are soon to follow. As soon as its twin nuts (also known as filberts or hazelnuts) ripen in their horned double husk—thus the name "beaked"—they are sure to be whisked away and eaten or cached by enterprising squirrels and Steller's jays.

The latter bird is a half-black, half-blue corvid, part of the lineage that includes ravens and crows—some of the smartest and most adaptable birds around. It's known to be loud and aggressive, chasing other birds off potential food sources and roosting sites. While the Steller's jay's aggressive demeanor and territorial nature doesn't sit well with some birdwatchers, it cuts a striking figure as it darts through the forest noisily warding birds, squirrels, and other competitors away from where it wants to be.

Another bird that loves this coastal ecosystem is the bald eagle, not only a symbol of the nation's founding but also of how modern-day Americans' resolve and collective effort can bring back wildlife from the brink of extinction. Biologists estimate there were as many as 100,000 bald eagles nesting across the country when the United States adopted the bird as its national symbol, back in 1782. By 1963, there were less than 1000 of the birds left in the contiguous United States.

Several factors contributed to the bald eagle's decline, but the almost-final straw was the proliferation of the pesticide DDT after World War II. This noxious synthetic chemical was sprayed indiscriminately to fight mosquitoes and keep pests away from agricultural operations. Its residue washed into waterways, where it contaminated not only aquatic plants but also fish. When a bald eagle ate contaminated fish, DDT entered the bird's bloodstream, interfering with its body's ability to produce strong eggshells—and a generation of bald eagles was decimated. (Populations of peregrine

falcons and brown pelicans also fell precipitously during the same timeframe, again as a result of widespread DDT contamination.)

In response to the problem, the federal government banned DDT in 1972, and 6 years later further protected the bald eagle's future by putting it on the Endangered Species List. These efforts paid off, and nowadays as many as 30,000 bald eagles live in the contiguous U.S. Many are in the Pacific Northwest, which is prime habitat for them. If you stare at the tall shoreline conifers of Penrose State Park long enough, you'll likely spy one or two of these majestic brown-and-white birds either at roost or on the wing.

Another plant you'll see at Penrose Point is Himalayan black-berry. This non-native invasive has been frustrating land managers across the Pacific Northwest for decades, given how fast it can spread and how hard it is to remove. On the bright side, late summer can be a great time to visit Penrose Point if you like to gorge yourself on the fruit, free for the reaching. (Long sleeves might save you from pricks by the thorny stems.)

Loop back on the short, well-marked trail and return to the trailhead. While the Touch of Nature Interpretive Trail is educational and stimulating, it is just *so* short! Since you're already parked, you might as well wander down to the beach between Penrose Point and the small spit to the northwest. The Washington Department of Fish and Wildlife has "enhanced" it with non-native (but delicious) Manila clams and Pacific oysters, making it a hot spot for local harvesters during the legal season, from late fall to early spring. But plenty of native species likewise prevail in these rich intertidal waters. Native littleneck, butter, horse, and softshell clams commingle freely, burrowed into the sand, typically at or below the ever-shifting water line. Occasional patches of rare native Olympia oysters, much coveted on dinner plates from Beijing to Manhattan, can also be found here in their ideal habitat.

⌐ Thorny, fast spreading, and hard to remove, non-native Himalayan blackberry plants are a problem all over the Pacific Northwest—but their yummy late-summer berries make them easier to tolerate.

Even more exciting is the occasional Pacific geoduck sighting. Only viewable at a very low (minus) tide as they are burrowed deep in the sand at the low-water line, these oblong monstrosities of the intertidal zone can grow to more than 3 feet long in a fleshy gray-white-yellow extrusion ("neck") that sticks out of a much smaller (around 8 inches across) shell. They dig deep into submersed mud or sediment, anchoring their shells and using their long necks to siphon clean seawater down to their dug-in shells. These wonders of the Northwest coast reach maturity before their 5th birthdays if not before, and some specimens have been known to live to 160 years old. Scientists have even started to examine trace elements in their shells to track climate change over long stretches of recent history.

• The beach along Carr Inlet at Penrose Point.

If it's a clear day, raise your eyes off the tidal flats and look toward the east-southeast. You may be lucky enough to see Mount Rainier looming large, appearing to float on thin air, almost close enough to reach out and touch. Actually, you would need pretty long arms: Washington's tallest peak is 55 miles away as the crow flies. But seeing it from this sandy perch, with Puget Sound in the foreground, is the icing on the cake.

NISQUALLY VISTA TRAIL

Subalpine forest, wildflower meadows, and up-close glacier views

DIFFICULTY
Easy

LOCATION
Mount Rainier National Park, Paradise, Washington

LENGTH
1.1 miles

The Nisqually Vista Trail leads through high-elevation forests and subalpine meadows to an overlook of the Nisqually Glacier and Mount Rainier's summit.

For an easy introduction to the highlights of Mount Rainier, without the pesky summit climb, try the Nisqually Vista Trail. This 1.1-mile paved trail starts near the Henry M. Jackson Visitor Center at Paradise and winds its way to views of Nisqually glacier and the peak of Mount Rainier. The hike is within Mount Rainier National Park, which requires a $30 entrance fee that's good for 7 consecutive days oo consider spending more time and visiting other attractions nearby, including Myrtle Falls and the Reflection Lakes, among many others.

The best time of year to visit is midsummer, when abundant wildflower displays carpet the trail edges and fill the meadows. The whole trail is paved, so you can leave your hiking boots in the car (it's not wheelchair accessible, however, with stairs at the beginning). That said, the Nisqually Vista Trail is also great for snowshoeing if you want to visit in winter—just follow the bright orange flags and poles, because the trail will be buried in several feet of snow. If you can time your visit for sunrise or sunset and the weather is clear, you'll get to see alpenglow on top of Washington's tallest peak.

Start out at the well-marked trailhead at the west end of Paradise's Lower Parking Lot and ascend the stone stairway. At the top, turn left, then go straight at the next junction to do the loop counterclockwise, so you can gently descend and save the best viewpoint for last.

At just over 5200 feet in elevation, you're a mile high and smack dab in the middle of the transition zone between high-elevation forests and sub-alpine meadows. Dense stands of conifers open up into rolling meadows filled with wildflower blooms during summer, when the prodigious amount of snow blanketing the mountain's flanks finally melts.

Gradually ascend the wide, paved trail through this forest dominated by subalpine fir trees. Heartleaf arnica, vanillaleaf, cloudberry, green false hellebore, garden valerian, thinleaf huckleberry, western pearly everlasting, and dewberry poke out of the understory in varying proportions. Dewberry, a native blackberry variant, spreads quickly over disturbed sites—such as areas where storms have blown down trees—pulling more than its weight in reducing soil water loss due to evaporation. This little, green, insect-pollinated plant flowers earlier in spring than other fruiting plants and is an important food source for insects, rodents, birds, and bears.

▲ Thinleaf huckleberry

While Pacific silver firs, Sitka spruces, Alaska cedars, Douglas firs, mountain hemlocks, and Sitka mountain ashes mingle in the forest around you, it's the subalpine firs that steal the show as they move to higher elevations and displace wildflower-filled subalpine meadows. At such a high elevation, these slow-growing trees don't get much taller than 80 feet, but lower down in the forest they can grow to almost double that height. The tree's slender, spire-shaped form with its splayed skirt of branches toward the base is a classic Christmas tree shape if there ever was one—just another marvel of biological evolution out here on the flanks of Mount Rainier. The upper branches are too short

▲ Cloudberry

to be weighed down and snapped off under the weight of snow they typically bear from November to June. Meanwhile, the long lower branches are splayed out and pressed to the ground by the heavy snowpack in a wide radius around the trunk, growing new roots where they meet the soil. This layering approach is an adaptation that allows the tree to create mats of branches from which new trees will sprout and grow, producing islands of subalpine firs at similar elevations here along the Nisqually Vista Trail and elsewhere around Mount Rainier and the Cascades. While subalpine firs are right at home here in Washington's upper reaches, you can also find them at tree line up into Alaska, down through the Rocky Mountains, and as far south as Arizona.

As climate change exerts more and more pressure on ecosystems everywhere, subalpine firs are just one of many tree species scrambling to maintain their territory. The temperature increases we have already experienced over the last few decades have pushed many of them higher into formerly wide-open alpine meadows, displacing habitat for wildflowers and other herbaceous understory

▲ Subalpine fir trees are encroaching on the meadows of Mount Rainier's flanks because of the onset of climate change and years of fire suppression.

▲ A small subalpine fir tree sprouts in the meadows off the Nisqually Vista Trail.

plants. Meanwhile, the trees are losing ground at lower elevations as things heat up. While this may seem like a fair trade, it's not. Given the fact that Mount Rainier is conical, there is more land available at lower elevations on and around its flanks than higher up around tree line.

Another reason these subalpine firs are encroaching on Mount Rainier's meadows is the success of our fire suppression efforts over the last 100 years. These ecosystems burned periodically prior to Euro-American settlement. Many of the fires were sparked by lightning; others were intentionally set by Indigenous peoples inhabiting the area for at least the last 13,000 years. They would burn the subalpine meadows—if a lightning strike didn't do it for them—to boost berry harvests, herd game, improve sightlines for hunting, and clear their favorite trails. Whether set by lightning or man, these fires every few years curbed the establishment of seedlings in meadows and prevented upslope tree-line creep.

With the establishment of Mount Rainier National Park in 1899 (and the concomitant displacement of Native populations from the henceforth "public" parkland), humans stopped intentionally setting fires here and got good at putting out the ones sparked by Mother Nature. Without these periodic burns, subalpine firs and other tree-line specialists were afforded the time to set seed and take root. As soon as these trees got a few feet tall, they started outcompeting herbaceous meadow plants for sunlight and soil moisture. As a result, the subalpine meadows before you are shrinking. They have nowhere to go uphill, given how inhospitable the terrain gets at the foot of glaciers, so the meadows are simply retreating. Like Mount Rainier's glaciers, these subalpine meadows may not be long for this world, so get a good look while you can.

Actually, it's hard not to get a good look, especially if you are lucky enough to visit in midsummer, when wildflowers are at their peak. As the trail curves to the left, cross the footbridge over the creek and wonder at the meadows opening up to the right. Broadleaf lupine blooms early—look for its purple-blue leaflets surrounding erect, 1- to 3-foot-tall inflorescences (flower heads) in June as the snow melts out (although stragglers can be found through the sum-mer, especially at higher elevations) These hardy beauties also "fix" nitrogen (the process of converting airborne nitrogen to a solid form, ammonia, with the help of symbiotic bacteria) in the surrounding

◦ Pink mountain-heather

soil, where other plants can make use of it as a natural fertilizer. Lupines are also a favorite browse for the abundant Columbian black-tailed deer and Roosevelt elk that patrol the park's high country.

Typically by the 4th of July, the real wildflower fireworks start to explode across the meadows. Cascade asters stick up 2 feet high and sport 6–8 pale purple "ray" flowers (elongated petals) with yellow disk flower crowns (in the middle) on each stem. Bunches of 1-foot-tall Indian paintbrush lend splashes of pink-red to the land-scape, while fringes of pink mountain-heather—each stem carrying a dozen or so tiny, bell-shaped, pink-purple flowers—hang on the hillside. Depending on the timing of your visit, some of the other colorful wildflower blooms you'll likely encounter in these meadows include shrubby cinquefoil, Gray's lovage, Parry's catchfly, short-beaked agoseris, alpine speedwell, Menzies' penstemon, and alpine buckwheat.

The wildflower-filled subalpine meadows of Mount Rainier are highly popular attractions, drawing some 2 million visitors to the national park every year. But all that love has been hazardous to the health of the fragile ecosystem over the last century, mostly as a result of off-trail hiking and camping. While the fragile plants of these meadows must endure intense competition for limited resources and long, harsh winters buried under dozens of feet of snow, humans remain their biggest threat. Subalpine soils are easily worn, especially by trampling that can pack them too dense to support plant life.

A massive meadow restoration effort started in the 1980s contin-ues today in the subalpine areas of Mount Rainier. The National Park Service has gone to great lengths to build out and maintain an excel-lent trail system, designed to optimize access to nature and views while keeping people off the fragile meadows. But it's up to each of us to do our best to stay on the trail and leave no trace of our visit.

At 0.5 miles in, you'll get to the far end of the loop at the Nisqually Glacier Overlook, marked by an interpretive sign and a spectacular view of the shrinking glacier leading up to Mount Rainier's summit. Nisqually Glacier has retreated 1.5 miles since the 1850s. About 12 percent of that retreat has taken place since 1970, during which time annual average temperatures in the national park have increased by 2.7 degrees F while precipitation has decreased more than 20 percent. Not only has there been less precipitation, but

The glacier in 1910.

The glacier today.

▴ The Nisqually Glacier has retreated 1.5 miles since the end of the Little Ice Age in the 1850s—a consequence of global warming.

the ratio of it has shifted to more rain and less snow, which has led to increased summer melting and decreased winter ice accumulation—a double whammy for the glaciers here.

The Nisqually Glacier isn't alone. Mount Rainier National Park has lost some 40 percent of its glacial and perennial ice surface since 1896. Two of the mountain's 29 major glaciers have already disappeared completely, and the rest could be gone within decades unless we can turn around our profligate use of fossil fuels.

This great melt-out isn't just bad for tourists visiting Mount Rainier National Park. As increasingly less water comes off these glaciers each year (because more of the annual precipitation is rain), the distribution and extent of plants in the meadows directly below is decreased. This in turn negatively affects populations of butterflies, salmon, and other wildlife that have evolved over the eons to be here. Meanwhile, millions of people across the region depend on glacier-fed rivers spilling off Mount Rainier for drinking water, crop irrigation, and hydroelectric power.

Drink in the picture-perfect view of the still-glacier-clad mountain and then continue on, leaving the wildflower meadows behind and descending through yet more stands of subalpine fir, to complete the loop back to the parking lot. It's not every day you can immerse yourself in nature and indulge in sights so magnificent. Likewise, it's not every day you can view such sobering effects of climate change on the landscape around you. A hike on the Nisqually Vista Trail affords both opportunities—perhaps turning even the most apathetic into environmental protection crusaders.

MAGNUSON PARK WETLANDS

Once a U.S. Navy airfield, now prime wildlife habitat

DIFFICULTY
Easy

LOCATION
Sand Point, Seattle, Washington

LENGTH
Up to 3 miles

L ocated on the Sand Point peninsula in the northeast section of Seattle that juts out into Lake Washington, 350-acre Magnuson Park occupies a large chunk of the former site of Naval Air Station Seattle at Sand Point, where a small fleet of naval planes was based between the mid-1920s and 1970. When the station was decommissioned, a small portion of the former base was given to the National Oceanic and Atmospheric Administration (NOAA) to serve as that agency's Western Research Center, and the rest ended up in the city of Seattle's hands.

Since opening day in 1977, Magnuson Park has been a year-round magnet for Seattleites interested in open space, outdoor recreation, and access to Lake Washington. The park's mile-long freshwater shoreline offers quiet beaches, boat launches, lifeguarded swim areas, and shoreline clearings that are perfect for picnicking—all accessible by foot, auto, or public transportation.

But it was a civic desire to bring more wildlife and ecological integrity to one of Seattle's flagship parks that led to a major overhaul of a 40-acre swath in the center of the park that had been covered in tarmac for almost a century. The re-creation of an important habitat setting was finished in 2009.

The lush, rolling wetlands at Magnuson Park were created from a former naval air station.

▴ Gravel trails were laid down before the plants started to fill in around them in the late 2000s, making the new landscape feel like it's been there much longer.

▴ This young Sitka spruce tree stands a good chance of growing to full height (approximately 200 feet) and living out its 500-year life expectancy, given that it's protected as part of Magnuson Park's $18 million wetlands restoration.

The resulting wetlands are a true mix of art and science. Preexisting landscape features (trees, boulders) were combined with thousands of greenhouse-cultivated native plants across a cascading network of more than 60 shallow, interconnected ponds. It couldn't look more natural if it had always been that way.

The centerpiece of the design is a collection of five distinct yet interconnected naturalistic wetland systems, each feeding the next hydrologically, until whatever is left of the stormwater running off the playfields drains into Lake Washington—filtered by the very wetlands it has just passed through. The runoff that had been piped under the concrete airfield since the late 1920s was brought back to the surface of the land—and the once-flat site was regraded to direct water flow from west to east, through the ponds and surrounding marshy soils.

Summer is definitely the busy season at Magnuson Park, when warm temperatures and sunny skies are the norm. Nature lovers may appreciate the setting more in the spring, when the plants of the wetlands bloom and wildlife activity reaches its annual zenith. Fall and winter bring cooler temperatures and gray skies, but provide more solitude.

Find the well-marked trailhead for the Frog Pond Trail at the northeast corner of the park's NE 65th Street parking lot. A sign there demarcates the area you are entering as a "Federally Protected Wetland" and warns to stay on the gravel trails and keep dogs on leash, plus no bikes allowed. As you proceed into the wetlands, Oregon white oak (also known as Garry oak) branches drape over the trail and stems from thorny Nootka rose stems and dainty Pacific ninebark leaf out in the midstory alongside copious numbers of common snowberry plants.

In 100 feet, go right at the first junction and into the wetlands themselves. The hillside to your left is awash with native vegetation. Sitka spruce and Douglas fir saplings scattered throughout the site have years to go before they mature, but in the meantime, a wide variety of successional deciduous trees—black cottonwood, common hawthorn, bigleaf maple, red alder, Hooker's willow, western crabapple, red-osier dogwood—fill in where they can. These upper stretches, the emergent wetlands, are the first spongy stop for stormwater moving downhill from the playfields above.

• Nootka rose and common snowberry compete for sunlight under the forest canopy.

If it's spring, assorted wildflower blooms crop up trailside. Look for wood forget-me-nots, common columbines, large-leaved lupines, twinberry honey-suckles, bloody crane's-bills, American brooklimes, Douglas asters, oxeye daisies, and yellow irises, among dozens of other blooms. Queen Anne's lace sends

• Oxeye daisy

Common hawthorn trees, in all their bushy glory, dot the northern and eastern perimeter of the wetlands.

up its large heads with dozens of tiny white flowerlets, while curly dock and broadleaf cattail plants crowd each other to gain more space in the riparian zones along the pond edges.

In stark contrast to these natural beauties, salvaged industrial materials from the site's naval air base past—utility pipes, tunnel liner weirs, chunks of repurposed tarmac—have been strategically placed around the wetlands as sculptural elements, and, in some cases, water conveyance structures. Planners incorporated these man-made objects into the design as a reminder to visitors that these wetlands sprung from a working industrial site.

In another 100 feet or so, go left onto a smaller trail that winds north, then west, past many of the smaller ponds in the middle of the stormwater run to the lake. This is a great spot to stop, look, and listen for wildlife, as you're now really in the thick of the wetlands.

If it's late spring or summer, scan the surface of the ponds in front of you for dragonflies. For the planners and landscape architects behind the wetlands design and construction, the profusion of dragonflies here—an indication of a healthy, naturally functioning wetland ecosystem if there ever was one—is reward enough for their efforts. Sporting different shades of red, green, and blue in various combinations, five species of dragonfly (green darners, cardinal meadowhawks, western pondhawks, blue dashers, and eight-spotted skimmers) can be seen around the Magnuson Park wetlands in July and August, although they often show up earlier to feed on newly hatched insects.

A true wonder of nature, the dragonfly has been around for some 325 million years. The ability to manipulate each of its four mostly translucent wings independently gives it all kinds of flight path and hovering options. It hunts mosquitoes, butterflies, and other smaller insects lurking on or just below the water's surface by holding its six legs together like a basket and scooping upward into its jaws. Its giant eyes afford 360-degree vision, which gives the dragonfly the best eyesight in the insect world.

These wetlands attract a lot more than insects, important as they may be to the habitat's healthy functioning. Some 185 different bird species have been spotted in Magnuson Park. Waterfowl are the most common. Diving ducks include greater and lesser scaups, common goldeneyes, and buffleheads, which dive for bivalves on the bottom of Lake Washington and return to the wetlands to roost. Other divers here include common mergansers; harlequin, canvasback, and red-head ducks; and pied-billed, horned, red-necked, and western grebes. American wigeons, gadwalls, mallards, and American coots are the primary dabblers working the wetlands and lakeshore here, although northern shovelers, green-winged teals, and wood ducks aren't uncommon, either.

Other bird species frequenting Magnuson Park and often spotted in and around the wetlands include cedar waxwings, belted king-fishers, willow flycatchers, common yellowthroats, northern flickers, downy woodpeckers, Bullock's orioles, Anna's hummingbirds, black-capped chickadees, Bewick's wrens, bushtits, killdeers, American rob-ins, spotted towhees, song sparrows, and red-winged blackbirds. Tree and violet-green swallows fly in from their cliffside and under-roof

‹ A retreating Queen Anne's lace.

‹ Himalayan blackberry is a noxious invasive weed, but those berries taste so good!

nests on the hunt for flies, beetles, and flying ants. Dowitchers, least sandpipers, and greater and lesser yellowlegs stop by on their migrations twice a year, poking into the mud at the edge of the wetlands ponds for insects and aquatic invertebrates.

California quail, house finches, and golden-crowned sparrows thrive in and around the prodigious thickets of Himalayan blackberry that have taken over parts of Magnuson Park. Seattleites have a love-hate relationship with this pesky, invasive trailing shrub. On one hand, it crowds out native plants with its fast-growing, thorny stems; on the other, its late-summer fruit is delicious. This hard-to-remove plant has been making inroads into the wetlands, despite efforts by park staff to keep it at bay.

Meanwhile, great blue herons, the official bird of Seattle per decree of the city council in 2003, stalk the shallows, patiently in search of small fish and occasionally spearing one for a quick meal. The green heron, a cousin of the great blue, is less likely to be out and about during the day—it's primarily a nocturnal hunter—but you will occasionally see one perched in the thickets alongside the trails in the wetlands. This small, greenish black bird is famous for dropping insects and other items onto the surface of the water as bait to attract small fish to the surface, where it can nab them. Although they prefer fish, green herons aren't picky when it comes to meal time: insects, spiders, crustaceans, snails, rodents, reptiles, and amphibians should all be worried when these aquatic hunters are on the prowl.

Speaking of amphibians, another iconic wildlife species of the Magnuson Park wetlands is the Pacific chorus frog (also commonly known as the Pacific tree frog). The tiny little green or brown frogs have dark, spotty markings on their backs and can adjust their coloration to better blend in with their surroundings. Sticky round toe pads allow them to climb and cling to just about any surface. These highly adaptable, 2-inch-long creatures are found everywhere from coastal rain forests near sea level to subalpine environments high in the mountains—but their preferred habitats are freshwater wetlands just like these at Magnuson Park.

The signature repeated *ribbit* croaking of Pacific chorus frogs is actually a mating call used by males to attract females. You can hear the signature croaking of individual frogs any time of day, but you'll

typically only hear the large, namesake choruses of them after dark. When one male starts croaking, others often join and create a choir of frogs. Because Pacific chorus frogs are the most common frogs on the West Coast, their sound is famous worldwide, thanks to its extensive use by Hollywood sound engineers as a nighttime aural backdrop—even if the production's proposed setting is far away. While other North American amphibians continue to lose ground in terms of population numbers, Pacific chorus frogs seem to be hanging on just fine, which is a testament to their adaptability. Time will tell if they can keep adapting as climate change dries up more and more of their traditional habitat. But the more wildlife-friendly habitat we can add, the more we can ensure they keep doing well. It's encouraging that their population numbers around Magnuson Park have increased threefold since the new wetlands went in.

As for reptiles, if you look closely you may be able to spot a northern alligator lizard, a common slider turtle, or a common or northwestern garter snake making its way across the trail, either on the hunt for its next meal or just escaping your impending footfalls.

Mammals also make their presence known throughout the wetlands. American beavers colonized the new wetlands soon after they were complete, and helped reengineer some of the ponds

▲ Pacific chorus frogs can take on varying shades of green or brown, but they all share the signature eye-line stripe.

▴ Bull thistle is classified as a noxious weed by Washington State because it can outcompete native plants, but here in the wetlands it's just another herbaceous plant doing its best to defend the small territory it has staked out.

▴ It's sometimes hard to believe you're inside the borders of a major city when trudging through the wetlands at Magnuson Park.

by damming up outlets with their lodge-building activity. Muskrats have also moved in, building nests with underwater entrances burrowed into the banks of the larger downstream ponds. You could even see a North American river otter lolling in this urban backwater. Raccoons, eastern cottontail rabbits, Virginia opossums, and long-tailed weasels make it a party, with an occasional cameo by marauding coyotes.

Of course, you may not see many or even any of these wildlife species, which typically make themselves scarce at the sight, sound, or smell of humans (and some are just nocturnal). But if you have some knowledge of their behavior patterns and are willing to stay put for long periods of time by the side of a wetlands pond, your chance of a sighting will go way up.

After a couple of zigs and zags, you'll come to a junction with the main Frog Pond Trail that you left earlier to dally in the wetlands. Go right and walk another 200 feet or so on the nicely maintained gravel path before taking a trail to the right, off into the upper reaches of the wetlands. Pick your way through some of the spongy upland marsh that serves as the primary filter to extract contaminants from any stormwater overflowing from the playfields above.

You'll eventually find your way to the north shore of more wetlands ponds. Look for a side trail heading out to Lake Shore Drive NE (one of the main park roads). Cross over and find the continuation of the trail into the woods adjacent to the lowest and perhaps biggest of the

The dark clouds that hang over Seattle all winter deliver plenty of precipitation to help nurture these wetlands.

wetland ponds. This pond has a mouth-of-the-creek feel and represents the last stop for any remaining stormwater before it ends up in Lake Washington, as pure and filtered as any wetland can make it.

Follow the trail another 500 feet out to the lakeshore and dip your toes (or more) in the water if it's warm out and you're so inclined. Even if wading isn't in the cards, stare out at the water and consider that some of it traveled the same route you just did—from 17 feet higher, down through a maze of ponds and marshes, into the lake here at your feet. Chances are a few mallards will be around to keep you company; make sure not to feed them, as it actually hurts wildlife species' chances for survival when they take human handouts.

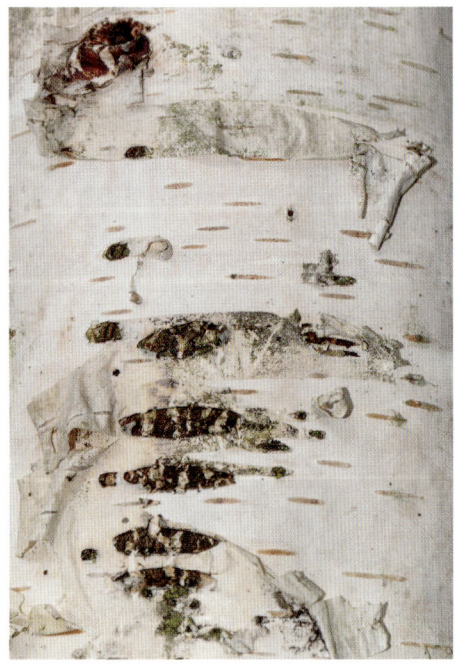

▲ There's a surprising diversity of flora here in the wetlands—such as this paper birch tree not normally associated with the greater Seattle area.

When you've blissed out enough lakeside, retrace your steps along the lower pond. After crossing back over Lake Shore Drive NE, go left along the southern edge of the ponds to get a different perspective on the marshy wetlands. Follow this trail around to the right, where it eventually delivers you back to the beginning of the loop and out to the NE 65th St. parking lot.

While there have always been reasons for locals to go to Magnuson Park over the years, now nature lovers from far and wide are flocking there to see what's causing all the fuss among Seattle's leading-edge ecology community. The fact that Seattle Parks and Recreation was able to take a flattened, paved-over airfield and turn it into a topographically complex, hydrologically functioning and wildlife-rich ecosystem should give us all hope that humanity knows how to work with nature—not just against it. Wherever we live, we should all advocate for similar types of restoration projects.

TRADITIONAL KNOWLEDGE TRAIL

Trail identifying native plants used by Indigenous communities

DIFFICULTY
Moderate

LENGTH
0.5 miles

LOCATION
Snoqualmie Valley, near North Bend, Washington

Home to Indigenous peoples for millennia, the Snoqualmie Valley is rich in natural resources and ecosystems.

The Snoqualmie Tribe created the Traditional Knowledge Trail in 2013 on a small, forested tract of land along a tiny creek in the center of their reservation, to showcase the native plants they have depended on for food, materials, and medicine since time immemorial. The 0.5-mile jaunt into the gnarled forest, tucked between a residential neighborhood and the sprawling Snoqualmie Casino complex, makes for an educational if concise outing. Two dozen interpretive signs along the way display plants (identified by their names in both English and the Snoqualmie's traditional *Lushootseed* dialect) along with photos, drawings, and other info related to the Snoqualmies' traditional use of flora.

While the trail may be short, it is rocky, rutted, muddy, and generally unmaintained, so bring some good sneakers or hiking shoes that you don't mind getting dirty. The out-and-back routing means the first (downhill) half is easy. But save some energy for the 0.25-mile return trip, when you'll have to make up for the initial modest elevation loss. Also, beware of stinging nettles along some sections of the trail; wear pants or socks you can yank up to your knees to avoid the itchy tingling that can come from an unprotected hike through these parts. The hike is on tribal land managed by the Snoqualmie Tribe Environmental and Natural Resources Department; visitors should be respectful by packing out any garbage and not removing any rocks, leaves, branches, or other elements from this sacred tribal land.

If the sign at the trailhead isn't enough, the mammoth 200-year-old Douglas fir tree adorning the break in the forest where the Traditional Knowledge Trail begins ensures you're at the right place. No tree could be more emblematic of this place—the ancestral stomping ground of the Snoqualmie Tribe specifically, and the wet and wild west side of the Cascade Mountains in general. Well adapted to the moist and mild climate of the region, the Douglas fir has been the dominant tree of forests on the west side of the Cascades from Oregon into British Columbia for the last 7000 years, following the retreat of the last ice age glaciers.

While Scottish botanist David Douglas was the first European to identify the tree for science during his landmark survey of the region beginning in 1825, Indigenous peoples have been using its wood for

▲ The signature furrowed bark of the Douglas fir is an easy identifier.

▲ The flat sprays of needles of the western red cedar—the only cypress conifer native to the Northwest—make it easy to distinguish from all the other (pine-style, cylindrical-needled) conifers of the region, such as Douglas fir, western hemlock, and Sitka spruce.

a lot longer as fuel for heat and cooking, and as a raw material for making house poles, spear handles, harpoon shafts, spoons, dipnet polls, fire tongs, harpoon barbs, salmon weirs, caskets, and fish hooks, among other necessities.

So as not to waste any part of nature, Native communities also traditionally made use of the Douglas fir's sticky pitch to seal joints on harpoon heads, fishing rods and hooks, as well as to caulk their canoes and other watercraft. This pitch—rich in minerals, enzymes, and antioxidants—was also the active ingredient in the Snoqualmies' medicinal salve to treat irritations and disinfect wounds. Natives also chewed on the Douglas fir's bud tips to relieve sore throat symptoms and heal cold sores.

Moving along, the trail quickly ducks into the forest, passing by a healthy and huge western red cedar, another iconic tree of the west side of the Cascades. The Snoqualmies, like all American Indians of the region, made full use of this cedar's practical advantages, including its natural rot resistance and ease of shaping. Lumber was used for plank houses and canoes, while the inner bark went into baskets, clothing, and hats. Rope was made out of the tree's branches and roots, and its larger boughs were used as ceremonial decorations.

While Douglas firs and western red cedars may be the kings of this forest, many other types of plants round out the scene. The mottled, ashy gray bark of the red alder—often colonized by white lichen and moss—is a frequent sight in the midcanopy. The name derives from the bright, rusty red color that develops in bruised or scraped bark. Red alders can grow to more than 90 feet tall, grabbing remnants of sunlight streaming through the Douglas fir and western red cedar branches above. The Snoqualmies made use of red alder hardwood to carve bowls, ladles, and masks, while using the bark to make a reddish dye to stain other woods. And to this day, tribal members smoke salmon on alder planks.

Vine maple boughs swing gracefully across the middle canopy layer, plastering their big, deciduous, 9-lobed, palmate leaves across the view. Come autumn, these leaves lose their chlorophyll and green pigmentation, turning the forest into a kaleidoscope of fall colors against the ever-present backdrop of green. Epiphytes hang in the balance off every light-exposed branch. This scene, including the fall color display, is exaggerated higher up in the canopy as bigleaf maples carry on a similar life cycle. The Snoqualmies used the wood from these large-limbed trees to make canoe paddles, mallets, and spindle whorls.

Make your way through the gauntlet of the overgrown trail as it winds its way down into a little creek valley. Western beaked hazelnut trees, in round-topped thickets, spread their leggy branches and

▲ When the nuts of the western beaked hazelnut tree start to ripen in September, jays, squirrels, and chipmunks get to work collecting and caching them.

▲ Ripe salmonberries in early summer are a favorite snack of humans, bears, and birds alike.

dark green leaves far and wide throughout the forest, dropping tasty filberts—also known as hazelnuts and beloved not only by humans but also seed-eating birds such as woodpeckers and jays—in the early fall. These nuts were a staple food for the Snoqualmies, who kept them in huge pits by the cooking fire for easy snacking access.

One of the filbert's main floral competitors in the understory is salmonberry, which grows to a similar height (a maximum of 12 feet) and spreads out into sinewy thickets. Salmonberry's alternating dark green leaves are made up of sharply toothed leaflets, and in late spring its prized yellow-pink (salmon-colored) berries start to pop out, attracting not only humans but bears, birds, and other

▴ Salal is an evergreen shrub but some of its small, leathery leaves turn orange and brown in the winter.

▴ Highly adaptable western sword fern is a common sight around the forests of Western Washington.

lovers of nature's treats. According to Snoqualmie lore, Swainson's thrush, a small migratory songbird that breeds in northern latitudes but migrates through the Pacific Northwest, "sings" the salmonberries ripe when it shows up each May on its way north for the summer breeding season.

Another big presence alongside the trail is salal, an evergreen shrub which can grow up to 5 feet tall in thickets. Its signature leaves are a shiny dark green. In spring, these tough little shrubs bloom out with small, white, urn-shaped flowers; late summer brings mealy but edible dark blue berries. Loaded with vitamins and antioxidants, these berries were a staple food of Northwest Indigenous communities, and the Snoqualmies were no exception. Besides being abundant and nutritious, salal berries contain natural preservatives, and were often formed into cakes and dried on cedar boards or skunk cabbage leaves for eating months later. Salal jam continues to be a popular item for Snoqualmie families in the region to this day.

Elsewhere in the understory, western sword ferns jockey for territory with heart-shaped wild lily-of-the-valley, while the occasional western starflower creeps out where it can. Bleeding heart, cascara, vanillaleaf, western trillium, bracken fern, wild ginger, devil's club, horsetail, dewberry, and dull Oregon grape are just some of the other native plants along the Traditional Knowledge Trail. Tribal members made full use of each part of these plants, deriving most of the food, medicine, tools, and utensils they needed from the land and resources around them.

The trail bottoms out as the creek you've been hearing along the hike—a tinkling tributary of nearby Coal Creek—finally makes an appearance. Pick your way across the water on rocks and fallen logs and explore the bottomlands around you. Dull Oregon grape loves the terrain at this juncture, with just enough dappled sunlight getting through the Douglas fir canopy to fuel the development of its slightly shiny, toothed-edge evergreen leaves. These plants bear small but fragrant yellow flowers (beloved by bees and other pollinators) in spring, followed by purple-blue berries (beloved by birds and browsing mammals) in late summer. Its low-growing, evergreen leaves provide plenty of foliage cover for small animals plying the forest floor in the stark winter months. The Snoqualmies made use of the plant not only by dining on its flowers, tart berries, and young leaves, but also by using the bark and roots as an antimicrobial medicine.

Vanillaleaf, a Northwest native named for the vanilla smell of its dried leaves in winter, spreads by underground rhizomes into a dense understory ground cover.

Overlapping bracken ferns dress up the forest floor in lacy finery.

At this point, turn around and head back to the trailhead, which unfortunately is mostly uphill. Wind your way back up the gully—reveling in your newfound knowledge of the plant life around you. As you are almost done, avoid a shortcut on the right leading back up to the road near the trailhead. This trail is less maintained than the main route, and is ripe with American stinging nettles. The low-growing nettles love the moisture of riparian zones and are often associated with stands of red alder in the Northwest.

Foresters and gardeners know the presence of stinging nettles indicates high soil fertility, so it's no wonder to find it at home here in this undisturbed pocket of second-growth forest primeval along the Traditional Knowledge Trail. It is one of the rare Northwest plants that fixes nitrogen—that is, converts airborne nitrogen gas into terrestrial ammonia which other plants use as natural fertilizer. Foraging chefs love cooking with the plant as it's a good substitute (both in flavor and consistency) for spinach when boiled. It's also high in nutritional value, with healthy doses of protein, fiber, silicon, potassium, and vitamins A, K, and C in each serving.

Stinging nettles were another important food source for the Snoquamies, but in addition they used its dried stalks to make fiber for spinning into twine for rope and fishing nets. They also took advantage of its medicinal qualities to treat back pain and arthritis.

These days, doctors recognize the usefulness of compounds in nettles (some synthesized by biotech and others not as of yet) for reducing inflammation and lowering blood pressure, as well as for controlling enlarged prostates. And recent studies have confirmed that consumption of nettles over a long period can alleviate lung, stomach, urinary tract, and anemia issues.

Nettles are the bane of many hikers' existence because the hairs on their stems irritate the skin where shins or calves graze against them trailside, literally leaving skin stinging for hours. If you don't have any anti-itch cream on hand, bruise up a bracken fern or sword fern—there are plenty around—to expose the tiny spores on the underside of its blades and rub it over the affected area. The sori, a natural chemical produced by the fern's spores, can alleviate the itchy sensation, at least temporarily.

Hopefully you'll get back to the trailhead without tingling calves and with a newfound appreciation of the bounty of the forest and how people once lived within nature's means.

LAYSER CAVE

A rare woodland native and a cave
occupied for thousands of years

DIFFICULTY
Moderate

LOCATION
Randle, Washington

LENGTH
0.5 miles

Layser Cave is the kind of spot where we picture our cave-dwelling ancestors holing up to avoid the elements and the wild creatures of the world. Fittingly, it's in a snug location deep in the primeval Gifford Pinchot National Forest—beyond the reach of cell service. The woodland scenery alone is beautiful enough to justify a trip, but the rich archeological site at trail's end sets the experience apart from thousands of other purely scenic forest hikes in the region.

While the trail into Layser Cave may be short—it's only 0.25 miles in—good sneakers or hiking footwear are recommended, given the profusion of roots, rocks, and other obstructions along the way. While the hiking is not strenuous, there are a fair amount of ups and downs along the way. Summer or early fall are the best seasons to visit Layser Cave; the entire area can be socked in by snow in winter.

If you are tired of crowded hikes, the trail to Layser Cave might be just right for you. Most hikers visiting the region will head to Mount Rainier National Park, leaving many of the excellent hiking trails of the nearby Gifford Pinchot National Forest— like this one—free and clear. But beware if you are hiking alone; there likely won't be other hikers around to help if you turn an ankle or worse.

Start off by ducking down into the forest via a couple dozen stairsteps built into the trail just after the succinct "Trail" sign at the trailhead, across from a small parking turnout by a big curve

▲ Descending into classic second-growth Northwest forest along the Layser Cave Trail.

in Forest Road 83. Soon enough, you're immersed in the world of native plants. Invasive species, often tracked into forests on the soles of visiting hikers, are seldom seen on this infrequently visited trail. Instead, western sword fern, Douglas fir, vine maple, western hemlock, and red alder—all natives evolved to be right here—grace just about every view along the way.

The trail then traverses a particularly rich vein of Cascade forest diversity, thanks to its location at the northern edge of many plants' and trees' ranges. Keep your eyes peeled for cameos from dull Oregon grape, ocean spray, black oak, red huckleberry, salal, vanillaleaf, western bracken fern, white fir, Sitka spruce, black locust, green false hellebore, Alaskan cedar, thinleaf huckleberry, subalpine fir, heartleaf arnica, western pearly everlasting, Pacific dogwood, American trailplant, common snowberry, rhodora, and Pacific blackberry.

BLACKBERRY WARS: HIMALAYANS VS. PACIFICS

The Pacific blackberry, also known as dewberry or California blackberry, is the only truly native blackberry on the West Coast of the United States. And it is especially gratifying to see it in the wild, given how it has been eclipsed over most of its range by the non-native invasive Himalayan blackberry. Infamous for shading out other understory plants and invading any available open space, Himalayans are a scourge on wild spaces across the Pacific Northwest. If left unchecked, Himalayan blackberry's thorny canes, which grow upward of 15 feet tall and spread for some 40 feet across the ground, can take over hillsides and clog rivers and streams, potentially wreaking havoc during flood events. The hardy invasive long ago took over the prime habitat of the Pacific blackberry where it could (and then some), so it's always reassuring to see the native plant surviving in the wild somewhere. Keep an eye out because one of those rare sightings is along the hike to Layser Cave.

Any available substrate seems to be fair game for colonization by an active crew of lichens. These dual organisms are part fungus and part alga or cyanobacterium (or both), combining efforts—and their different techniques of obtaining energy—to maximize growth. Lichens are one of the most widespread and adaptable species on the planet because of their hybrid nature and general resilience to weather and temperature extremes. In fact, there are some 17,000 different types of lichen; 3000 and counting in the United States alone.

Besides being beautiful to look at, with their radiating patterns and varied colors, lichens play an important role in their ecosystems. For starters, given their algal component, they are champs at converting atmospheric carbon dioxide into oxygen through photosynthesis—which helps keep carbon dioxide out of the atmosphere (where it does the most harm in terms of climate change) and also provides us with fresh, clean air to breathe. As well, scientists can monitor atmospheric levels of all kinds of pollution by analyzing the region's lichens, because they filter and retain traces of everything that passes their way, including airborne heavy metals and other noxious pollutants.

Lichens abound along the trail to Layser Cave. Light green, stringy old man's beard hangs from tree limbs. Flaky lobaria lichen splays out from the crevices in Douglas fir bark. Rounded amoeba-like blotches of lichen in the

↟ Native Pacific blackberry is rare, but it can be found along the Layser Cave trail.

↟ Common snowberry is a native deciduous shrub found all over the wet west side of the Cascades.

↟ *Lobaria* lichen on Douglas fir bark.

▴ Dozens of bird and mammal species, as well as uncountable insects, make use of standing dead tree snags (like what remains of this western red cedar) for foraging, nesting, denning, roosting, and resting.

▴ A modern-day rock firepit and log bench inside Layser Cave.

family Lecanoraceae make big white and light green spots on boulders. You see a lot of these three, but many other colorful lichens are also on display.

At 0.3 miles in, go right at a fork in the trail, the most direct route to Layser Cave. In another 400 feet, a huge cliff on the right hints that the cave is getting near. Follow the trail for another few hundred feet as it curves around to the right and you'll notice a rough-hewn railing on the left. A few more steps and the opening to Layser Cave comes into view on the right, wedged under the very cliff you just walked around.

It's a little creepy to venture into the dark cave, which measures approximately 60 feet by 40 feet inside, but well worth it. You'll have to duck to enter, but the ceiling height improves to about 10 feet as you move into the middle of the cave. Beyond that, the ceiling sinks again in the farthest reaches of the cave's interior, probably a good place to store dried fruit and protect game caches from marauding wild animals.

The cave was not discovered by modern-era humans until 1982, when U.S. Forest Service employee Tim Layser happened upon it while surveying the area for an upcoming timber sale. Since then, archaeologists have uncovered evidence of human habitation there— perhaps the ancestors of the modern day Cowlitz and Yakama communities— dating as far back as 7000 years and ending about 3500 years ago, around the time a huge volcanic eruption at nearby Mount Saint Helens rocked the region. Presumably the destruction from the

eruption as well as the ensuing ashfall made the region uninhabitable
for years if not longer—and the cave seems to have been forgotten by
Indigenous peoples in the process.

▴ Looking out to the
forest from inside
Layser Cave.

After its 1982 rediscovery, archaeologists uncovered upward of
10,000 artifacts at the site, making it one of the most significant digs
in the American West. Part of what made the cave such a good find
is the fact that over the eons, the alkaline calcium carbonate in the
cave's ceiling dripped onto and into the soil of the floor below, naturally preserving the tools, animal remains, arrowheads, plants scraps,
and other items scattered around the interior.

One interesting item uncovered in the cave was an atlatl, a throwing device which launched stone-tipped darts. This primitive but
effective weapon was used by Indigenous communities in the region
for thousands of years to hunt deer and elk, prior to the ascendancy
of the bow and arrow. Hunters would drive their ungulate (animal
with hooves) prey into a box canyon, then slaughter them with an
atlatl and short thrusting spears. More than 100 deer were butchered
inside the cave, based on the archaeological record. Remains of elk,

Calcium carbonate marbling covers the walls and ceiling inside Layser Cave.

mountain sheep, grouse, rabbit, and even salmon from the nearby Cowlitz River were also found inside Layser Cave.

Another interesting find: the oldest dated specimen of huckleberry ever discovered, although curiously, it wasn't the montane variety that grew locally, but rather a coastal species, indicating that the cave's inhabitants were part of a trading network radiating hundreds of miles in each direction. Other items found inside the cave that support the trading network hypothesis include beads made from ocean shells and arrow tips crafted from obsidian that is only found in Oregon.

Once you've explored the cave, follow the lower trail below its entrance instead of the way you came. This lower trail leads to a short detour with an outlook where you can see the top of Mount Adams, roughly 20 miles to the southeast, as the eagle flies. Complete the detour loop and then either retrace your steps back to the trailhead, or, if you're feeling adventurous, take the trail to the left up onto the top of the massive cliff formation above Layser Cave. (Watch your step, as this uneven path isn't maintained.) You'll see many of the cameo species listed above as you scramble up the cliffside. Once you're on top, take in the sweeping view through the tree branches from Layser Cave's roof deck, then find your way down to the main trail and follow it back to its commencement at Forest Road 83. You'll have a lot to think about on the drive out, from the crazy diversity of the forest to thousands of years of human history.

BILLY FRANK JR. NISQUALLY NATIONAL WILDLIFE REFUGE

Flyway wonders plus a celebration of native plants and Indigenous rights

DIFFICULTY
Easy

LOCATION
between Olympia and DuPont, Washington

LENGTH
2 to 4 miles

A pied-bill grebe scouts the shallows among water lilies.

If you love birds, fresh air, and nature, a walk around the Billy Frank Jr. Nisqually National Wildlife Refuge along the Nisqually River Delta at the southern end of Puget Sound is sure to delight. The refuge contains some 8 square miles of wetlands, and sits squarely on the Pacific Flyway—a major north–south route for migratory birds—so it naturally attracts a wide variety of wildlife species, and the people who like to see them. Visitors are free to explore for an hour or a day via a 6-mile network of boardwalks, trails, and dikes, which provides close-up views of birdlife in Puget Sound.

The entire complex is easy to access. It's all wheelchair and stroller accessible; the section surfaces are paved, gravel, and boardwalk (take care, the wood can be slippery when wet). The network of interconnected paths is generally flat throughout the complex (less than 5 percent grade). A profusion of wildlife means any time of year is good for a visit to the refuge, but the wetlands are typically fully flooded by January—which also happens to be peak chum salmon season in the Nisqually River—so look for waterfowl and raptors aplenty then.

Unlike many of the other hikes highlighted in this book, the Billy Frank Jr. Nisqually National Wildlife Refuge is truly for the birds. The refuge, an estuarine vein in the midst of one of the busiest metropolitan areas in the country, was created in 1974 to protect habitat

and nesting areas for waterfowl and other birds. With open grassland, riparian woodland, freshwater marsh, open mudflat, salt marsh, and estuary, there's truly something for everyone at the refuge.

◂ Common snowberry's white berries reportedly have a delicious wintergreen zing, but don't eat them! They contain saponins, a mildly toxic natural compound that the plant sends out into surrounding soils to inhibit the growth of neighboring plants.

Some 180 species of birds either pass through or live year round on refuge grounds, making it one of the best birding spots in the region. You may get closer to birds than you ever have before—especially if you are there just after sunrise. Bring binoculars to maximize your potential sightings.

A REFUGE FOR WILDLIFE— AND PEOPLE

The Billy Frank Jr. Nisqually National Wildlife Refuge is the site of the signing of the first treaty between the nascent government of the Washington Territory and Native communities—the so-called Treaty of Medicine Creek—back in December 1854. Governor Isaac Stevens made the treaty law with the blessing of representatives of the Nisqually and eight other Indigenous communities from around Puget Sound. The tribes granted more than 2 million acres of land to the United States in exchange for the establishment of three reservations, recognition of traditional Native fishing and hunting rights, and cash payments over 20 years.

But White settlers (and government officials) largely ignored the terms of the treaty, essentially barring Nisqually tribal members and other American Indians from accessing their own traditional fishing grounds—even though they had been guaranteed that access. It went on this way for a century, until the 1960s, when a disenfranchised Nisqually fisherman named Billy Frank Jr. had had enough. He started a grassroots campaign to get the federal government to recognize the rights granted at the Treaty of Medicine Creek, getting arrested more than 50 times for exercising what he considered his right to fish in the Nisqually River using traditional Indian methods, as guaranteed in the 1854 treaty. Frank's civil disobedience forced the issue to the courts, and a 1974 ruling by U.S. District Court Judge George H. Boldt (later reinforced by the U.S. Supreme Court) reestablished Native fishing rights as originally delineated by the treaty.

▴ Billy Frank Jr. was arrested more than 50 times before he won tribal rights that had been guaranteed but denied for more than a century.

Unfortunately, the salmon runs aren't what they used to be, largely due to overzealous development during the same 100-year period. The upshot for Native communities is that their so-called share isn't anything close to what it once was, and fishing isn't the source of sustenance or financial independence that it could have been for Indigenous communities in the 21st century and beyond.

In 2015, President Barack Obama signed the Billy Frank Jr. Tell Your Story Act into law, redesignating the refuge in honor of the Nisqually treaty rights activist (he had died the year before) and establishing a national memorial at the former Douglas fir grove within the refuge where Governor Stevens and the nine communities signed the original Treaty of Medicine Creek in 1854.

From the parking lot, pick up the Twin Barns Loop to the right of the Norm Dicks Visitor Center as the loop heads east into the most upland section of the refuge, the riparian forest along the verdant banks of the Nisqually River. Treat yourself to the short spur trail to the Riparian Forest Overlook for a better view of the Nisqually River. Here it curves through a surge plain, where storm-fueled flood tides overflowing the refuge's dikes have forced a course change in the river's path. After a tumultuous run from its namesake glacier on the flanks of Mount Rainier (some 75 miles away as the eagle flies), the Nisqually bottoms out as it enters refuge grounds and percolates its way through one last, big S curve for its last 2 miles before it meets the Pacific Ocean at Nisqually Reach. The forest here looks more typical of other upland sites around Puget Sound, with scattered Douglas firs and western red cedars mixed in among red alders and bigleaf maples.

Along the edges of the boardwalk, cayenne-red sprigs of red-osier dogwood spread out widely in the riparian landscape. This fast-growing, drought-tolerant, native deciduous shrub is an excellent soil stabilizer; look for it along the banks in riparian zones like this one, where it helps keep the land from eroding into the river. In springtime, this dogwood sprouts delicate, creamy white flowers that pollinators love.

▲ Red-osier dogwood lines the Twin Ponds Loop boardwalk.

Another environmental service performed by red-osier dogwood is nitrogen fixing. All plants use nitrogen from the soil as a fertilizer to produce chlorophyll, the green pigment that traps light energy from the sun. Chlorophyll, in turn, is an essential component in photosynthesis, the process by which plants combine water and atmospheric carbon dioxide to produce their own "food," the sugars essential to their survival and growth. Most plants are purely takers when it comes to nitrogen, but a select few—alders, lupines, dogwoods, and others—convert atmospheric nitrogen into a terrestrial form (ammonia) that other nearby plants can make use of as a natural fertilizer. This is accomplished through a symbiotic relationship with bacterial partners.

THE GREEN REVOLUTION?

Given nitrogen's essential role as a fertilizer to growing plants, farmers have long supplemented their soils with natural forms of nitrogen (such as manure and compost). But the widespread transition to synthetic fertilizers and pesticides around the world in the 1950s (dubbed the "Green Revolution," a misnomer if ever there was one) has wreaked havoc on ecosystems everywhere. These chemicals filter through soil, poisoning terrestrial ecosystems, and seep into waterways, causing algae blooms and oxygen-deprived "dead zones"—which marine wildlife cannot tolerate—in the water column. Yes, we all have more food to eat, but at what cost?

Another native deciduous shrub you'll see is Pacific ninebark, which thrives in just this kind of wetland habitat. While birds and herbivores browse on its red seed pods, this twiggy shrub shines as a draw for pollinators: its enticing white flower clusters harbor abundant nectar for many types of insects, especially bees. And with western honey bee populations falling by some 30 percent a year on average over the last decade, we can use all the Pacific ninebark we can get. The dwindling of western honey bee populations has huge implications not just for our own food systems, but also for the health of ecosystems everywhere.

Why are the bees dying? Many factors are at play, but the short answer is starvation. The bees simply can't find enough nectar to survive, let alone thrive, as we pave over every last parcel of private land where their preferred food sources grow, planting much of the rest with monocultural crops that do them no good. As pollinator numbers continue to plummet in the Pacific Northwest and around the world, providing space and opportunity for native nectar-bearing plants should be a priority for land planners and managers.

Bees are far from the only creatures on the wing you'll likely see at this refuge. The signature white head and black body of the bald eagle is a frequent sight in the treetops, where they have a great vantage point for spotting and grabbing prey, be it surf or turf. Upward of 25 bald eagles make their home at the refuge year round, while many more

Pacific ninebark attracts bees as well as many other pollinators.

◄ Nootka wild rose
produces hips after
flowering.

come and go on their wanderings up and down the West Coast. The largest congregation of bald eagles here occurs every January, when the birds come to this fully flooded estuarine buffet to fatten up for breeding.

While you may not see one, keep your ears tuned for the *hoo-hoo-hoo, hoo-hoo* of great horned owls. Their relatively large size (they grow up to 2 feet tall, with wingspans maxing out at 5 feet), strong talons, and finely tuned senses of sight and hearing make them a major predatory force in the meadow. They roost in the upland riparian forest by day, saving energy to come out and hunt under the cover of night. If you see one resting on a branch, you'll know it's a great horned by its sharply pointed gray-brown ear tufts for which it is named. The soft-feathered wings of the great horned owl keep the sound of its rapid approach nearly silent, helping it ambush prey from above.

These owls' diverse taste in prey and overall adaptability to extreme environments make them one of the most widely distributed birds in the Western Hemisphere, ranging from the arctic tundra of Alaska down to the tropical rain forest of Brazil. They'll eat whatever they can get their huge, powerful talons wrapped around, despite being smaller than some of their prey. Around these parts, raccoons, rabbits, squirrels, mice, voles, and even other birds—including falcons and other owls—are all fair game for this stealthy carnivore. And thanks to a particularly poorly developed sense of smell, great horned owls will even go after the one animal that most other predators avoid: skunk.

After 0.5 miles of walking on the Twin Barns Loop boardwalk, you'll come to a fork in the trail. If you choose left, you'll follow the other side of the loop (with views out across the meadow) back to the parking lot—making for a 1-mile walk. But if you've still got the energy and desire to see more, continue right toward the Nisqually River Overlook, where an observation deck and mounted spotting scope afford closer views of the nearby Nisqually River. After checking out the overlook, double back and hang a right onto the Nisqually Estuary Trail, a 0.5-mile gravel path atop a dike constructed in the 19th century to reduce saltwater intrusion into the former farm's crop fields. The result has been an informal separation between the refuge's freshwater and tidal wetlands, and the Nisqually Estuary

▲ Broadleaf cattails hug the shore of the Nisqually River.

Trail puts you squarely in between the two, with great views from the slightly elevated perspective in both directions.

Looking to the south, Nootka rose sprigs and broadleaf cattails line the edge of the dike and views of the freshwater wetlands open up. Great blue herons, perhaps the most commonly sighted bird at the refuge and a fixture throughout Western Washington, stalk the shallows on the hunt for frogs, crustaceans, and small fish.

Standing nearly 4 feet tall, with wingspans of 6 feet or more, great blue herons are stately birds. It's hard to believe such a large organism weighs only 5 or 6 pounds, but, like all birds, their bones are hollow, which saves weight and facilitates flight. Their frizzy blue, gray, and white chest feathers grow and fray continually, and the great blues comb through this "powder down" with fringed claws to remove fish slime and other oils from their feathers as they preen. They can hunt day or night thanks to lots of rod-type photoreceptors in their eyes that give them better night vision than most birds.

It's fascinating to watch one of these large, stately birds gingerly tiptoe on its stilt-like legs, exhibiting what seems to be infinite patience, waiting for its chance to strike. When the bird does attack, it's like a bolt of lightning striking just below the surface of the water as its beak clamps down on its unwitting prey. The specially shaped neck vertebrae of great blue herons are crucial to their ability

• A boardwalk leads visitors deep into the Billy Frank Jr. Nisqually National Wildlife Refuge.

to strike quickly from a distance, which is in turn crucial to their survival. Luckily for those of us who love them, great blue heron populations are stable across the United States. But the more we chip away at our remaining wetlands in general, the more we chip away at habitat for great blue herons and other wildlife dependent on healthy hydrological systems.

Another bird to watch for on the freshwater meadows is the northern harrier. These lean and long raptors, also known as marsh hawks, like to soar low over marshes, their long, rounded wings pointed upward to maintain cruising altitude as they scan the surface below with intense yellow and black eyes for their next meal, preferably a cricket, frog, or small bird. These long-distance hunters travel as far as a 100 miles a day in search of prey. Other raptors frequenting the refuge include red-tailed hawks and peregrine falcons as well as the aforementioned bald eagles and great horned owls.

If you see a small golden streak flitting across the meadows, it's probably an American goldfinch, the official state bird of Washington (as well as New Jersey and Iowa). These small yellow songbirds clean seeds off plants to sustain themselves, so there is plenty to keep them busy here at the refuge. From lowly oxeye daisy wildflowers to 80-foot-tall red alders, there is a wide variety of seed-bearing flora at hand. Goldfinches also indulge in grasses and weeds, the sap of bigleaf maples and vine maples, and the occasional insect treat—none of which is hard to source within the borders of the refuge. In summer, these striking birds' plumage turns bright yellow, contrasting sharply against its black caps and wings (they turn a subtler brown in winter).

Even if you don't see any of the previously mentioned birds during your visit to the refuge, you'll be certain to come across some waterfowl. Canada geese have become ubiquitous in natural settings across the region, and you can count on seeing some here. Cackling geese are also common in winter. As for dabbling ducks, all nine present in Washington State make appearances here, but the most frequently reported are mallards, American wigeons, green-winged teals, and northern pintails. Also, keep an eye out for beautiful multi-colored wood ducks as well as easily spooked pied-bill grebes in the freshwater shallows.

▴ Red alder, like this one with lichen growing on its bark, used to be considered a scourge on the landscape before ecologists realized its important role in fertilizing surrounding soils and nurturing other tree species, while providing wildlife habitat.

▴ Eastern cottontail rabbits aren't native here, but have been on the West Coast for more than a century now, fitting right in to suburban and agricultural landscapes.

Plenty of other wildlife makes its home here as well. Winter salmon runs attract harbor seals and California sea lions into the Nisqually's delta. Meanwhile, some 50 different species of mammals make their home at or near the refuge, including Columbian black-tailed deer, western gray squirrel, North American river otter, long-tailed weasel, American mink, and eastern cottontail rabbit.

When you've reached the other end of the dike trail, check out an even higher viewpoint from the observation tower, where you'll get a 360-degree, bird's-eye view of the refuge lands spread out in every direction. At this point, depending on time and energy, you can either retrace your steps back to the parking lot (for an approximately 2-mile round trip) or continue your exploration of the tidal salt marsh ecosystem via the tantalizing Nisqually Estuary Boardwalk Trail, which extends via wooden decking on pilings for another mile out into the salt marsh. If you venture this way, don't miss the bird blind and two more viewing platforms, one over McAllister Creek's wetlands as it merges into Puget Sound and the final one overlooking the southern end of Puget Sound by Nisqually Reach. (Note: the last 700 feet of the boardwalk, including the final viewing platform, is closed to foot traffic October–January to keep visitors out of harm's way during waterfowl hunting season.) If you are planning to hike all the way to the trail system's terminus at the final viewing platform overlooking Nisqually Reach, budget enough time for a 4-mile hike, and keep in mind that refuge staff lock the gates just after sunset.

DECEPTION FALLS
NATURE TRAIL

Geology, volcanism, ecology—and ouzels

DIFFICULTY
Moderate

LOCATION
near Skykomish, Washington

LENGTH
0.5 miles

Upper Deception Falls offers a beautiful view of the cascading water.

This short gorge hike through pristine old-growth forest right alongside Highway 2 leads to close waterfall views at various spots along the Tye River. The way the landscape looks and works around Deception Falls is equal parts geology, volcanism, and ecology—the perfect Cascades hollow. Throw in plenty of negative ions—those free-floating oxygen atoms abundant around waterfalls are thought to contribute to good health and good mood—and you have a recipe for a great short hike, either on its own or as a leg stretch during a Highway 2 road trip.

The trail is well maintained and well loved, but it still has plenty of obstacles and roots, so leave the flip-flops at home. Most people have no problem making it around the fairly level terrain, although there are some instances of stairsteps built into the trail. Keep small kids at hand and pets on a leash as it's a long way down into that waterfall gorge.

The Deception Falls Nature Trail starts innocently enough as a paved trail before quickly suggesting a left hand turn for the loop that sends hikers into a series of rooted rough trail switchbacks down and to the left. Once the switchbacks end, you're riverside, and the sounds of rushing water finally start to drown out the traffic on the Highway 2 bridge above. Epiphytes drip off maple boughs while stately conifers tower above it all. This is quintessential old-growth forest, with lots of huge trees, snags, nurse logs, and a peaty, mossy carpet of green everywhere but the center of the trail.

Rocks and fallen logs can be slippery, so: hiker beware. The stream is rocky up above but meanders down to a more sandy edged vibe visible 500 feet downstream if you care to explore *off-piste*—but the trail continues on in the other direction.

A grove of huge red alders, some still thriving in place but others fallen and sideways, hosts a colony of beard moss that's as temperate rain forest as it gets. Douglas firs dominate, but girthy

• You'll see a wide variety of ferns on the way to Deception Falls, including elegant little spreading wood ferns.

One tree grows from the old decrepit stump of another.

▴ Time will tell if biologists can help western white pine make a comeback after destruction by blister rust.

▴ Glacial erratic boulders (left by melting glaciers) are strewn willy-nilly through the forest and provide a great substrate for lichens and mosses.

western red cedars, stout and scaly Sitka spruces, spindly but tall western hemlocks and wide-spreading bigleaf maples are also common trees here in this classic west-side Cascades forest.

One tree species that used to be abundant here and elsewhere on the wet west side of the Cascades is white pine. A fungus called white pine blister rust, accidentally introduced from Asia more than a century ago, has decimated white pine populations across the country Hardest hit are high elevation white pine stands on the west side of the Cascades, such as those found right here along the banks of the Tye River. Forest Service data shows white pines have lost 90 percent of their coverage on the west side of the Cascades due to blister rust.

A small number of individual white pines are genetically immune to this fungal incursion. Biologists are trying to get to the bottom of how these particular trees are able to avoid blister rust's terminal wrath. The Forest Service has been locating and breeding individual rust-resistant white pine trees and planting the resulting seedlings around forests like these, where the trees would normally thrive. Time will tell if this program succeeds in bringing the tree—considered "near threatened" by conservationists due to its declining population—back from the brink.

Continue hiking, and take a short side trail that bottoms out into a veritable rock grotto. It looks like the Tye River here has had its course altered a time or two as a result of violent weather felling trees and loosening boulders.

Cupping some water down at the river's edge, it's hard not to be taken aback by how clean and clear it runs here. Most of it started as snow not too far above, but gravity also has something to do with it. As the water hurtles down, there is little time for it to "gather moss"—but there is more to the story. The granite rocks below are high in silica, a hard mineral that doesn't leach much into the water. This lack of nutrients combined with relatively sparse sunlight means algae doesn't have much to feed on in such running mountain rivers and streams. But just because it looks cleans and seems safe doesn't mean you should drink straight from the river—or any natural body of water—given the risks of giardia and other waterborne illnesses.

Return to the main trail and look around at all the decay on display. Fallen logs crisscross the forest floor. Some are empty inside except for the roots of new trees using them as a growth substrate. Straight lines of trees that look like they were planted by a landscaper are really lined up as a result of growing on top of the same fallen nurse log.

Beetles bore into dead logs, ushering bacteria and fungi inside to help decompose the wood. Spongy deadwood all around the forest

▴ This massive, decaying downed tree trunk will likely serve as a nurse log in decades to come.

▲ Twistedstalk is one of many understory plants making cameo appearances along the trail to Deception Falls.

▲ Just about all of the creatures of the forest can appreciate oval-leaf blueberry.

floor retains and then drip-feeds moisture and other nutrients into the soil, where other plants can make use of it. As an interpretive sign along the trail points out, a tree can live here for 500 years and then feed the forest for 500 more.

Wherever the tree trunks, logs, and boulders yield a little territory, a wide variety of understory plants jockey for territory, colonizing the thin but spongy soils of the forest. Salal, Schreber's big red stem moss, California spikenard, twistedstalk, and deer fern, among other greenery, vie for coverage of the forest floor.

Carpets of medium green oval-leaf blueberry leaves provide nutritious winter forage for deer and elk, not to mention delicious tart blue fruit in late summer that appeals to raccoons, bears, squirrels, chipmunks, and lots and lots of birds. Licorice fern sends up sprigs of eager volunteers stretching for the light. Tiny starlets of bright green juniper haircap moss cover patches of once-bare soil. Occasional clusters of small, triangular spreading wood fern dress things up like nature's perfect fashion accessory.

Amid this apparent chaos, dozens of species of wildflower blooms appear, typically in May and June, adding some much-needed variety to the otherwise green, gray, and brown color palette of the forest. Western trillium's big flowers with white petals are anchored by big, fuzzy, pollen-caked anthers; the blooms turn a beautiful violet hue as they age. The flowers of bride's bonnet have similar coloration but are smaller. Coralroot orchid has violet stalks and yellow blooms

▴ Licorice fern fronds reach for the light from their lowly perch on the forest floor.

▴ Tiger lily is always a welcome sight in the forest.

on the tips of its violet stem bracts. It is often mistaken for a fungus, thanks to its funky coloration with no green anywhere in sight. And if you get the chance to see a tiger lily, count yourself lucky as this drooping, brown-freckled, orange lily is one of the prettiest flowers in the forest.

Meanwhile, salmonberry and thimbleberry try to out-thicket one another with their enveloping, floppy green leaf stalks up at shoulder height—perfect for seeing their brightly colored berries (yellow and red, respectively) in late spring and early summer. Devil's club sneaks in between where it can, its thorny stalks providing a layer of defense against human berry pickers looking to go deep.

In hollow stretches where the river overflows its banks occasionally, skunk cabbage prevails. The signature stinky flowers in March herald the beginning of spring in the Cascades. A greenish stalk, tiny flowers, and a yellow leaflike bract—the reason for skunk cabbage's other common nickname, swamp lantern—are visible above lingering patches of snow. Later in spring, the plant's true green leaves emerge, continuing to grow all summer; by August they can each stretch 3 or more feet long by a foot wide. The plant's fetid smell attracts pollinators like flies and beetles, while its short, fleshy underground stem is a favorite delicacy of rooting black bears and Roosevelt elk. Alongside similarly oversized devil's club, the mature leaves of skunk

Lower Deception Falls: equally as scenic as the upper falls.

cabbage—the longest of any native plant in the region—can make one feel Lilliputian.

Back on the main loop, look for a short spur 0.5 miles in. This leads to a viewing platform above lower Deception Falls, where the Tye River falls over a ledge and takes a 90-degree turn immediately at the bottom. No one knows for sure how this waterfall got such an odd shape, but remnants of an old streambed hint that it once ran straight through this spot. One theory says that a massive pile of logs leftover from an ancient flood forced the river to turn. Another holds that the Tye is following a layer of soft rock that runs at right angles to the stream's original course. Yet another idea is that the river turns right to flow along a fault line—rocks along faults erode first because they are typically damaged when the earth moves.

Take in this unusual sight and continue hiking back upstream, stopping at two more wooden viewing platforms at different scenic spots along the Tye's rocky course. Listen for the flute-like song of the American dipper, a stout ouzel that lives at the edges of rapids like these and lays its eggs in the rocks beside or behind waterfalls, out of the reach of potential egg snatchers. These robin-sized, blue-gray forest birds with long, pinkish legs feed underwater, stepping along gingerly in the rocky shallows with their heads down and beaks probing for aquatic insects and worms as well as small fish and their eggs. These ouzels should be familiar to anyone well versed in the writings of John Muir, who waxed poetic about watching them go about their business. American dippers are also known to "fly" to the bottom of deeper pools and walk around the bottom, immersed, until they find something edible that was worth the trouble. While population numbers for dippers are holding steady, these birds depend on clear, unpolluted streams for survival and are

particularly sensitive to human development along or near their nesting habitat.

Keep moving beyond the final
viewing platform and soon you'll find
yourself back at the beginning of the
loop—but your hike isn't quite over yet.
Now it's time to follow the other path to
the "Upper Falls View," which leads to a
footbridge over the river and a staircase
up and underneath Highway 2, to a small
overlook of the stately upper Deception
Falls, which tumbles down 20 feet.
Technically, the upper falls can be seen
by passing cars heading east on Highway
2, but it goes by quickly in a car traveling at 60 miles per hour. You are much
better off seeing it on foot via the trail
and drinking in both its beauty and the
negative ions floating on the mists above
the falling water for as long as you like.

▲ Bracket polypore fungus and beard moss adorn whatever tree trunks will have them.

Some American Indians believed
that the mists emanating from waterfalls
like this one were sacred and carried
their prayers up to heaven. While we'll never know for sure whether
this is true, we do know that negative ions—oxygen atoms that have
picked up an extra electron and are thus negatively charged—coming off falling water can help lighten the mood of depressed people
and may even help the rest of us stay grounded. Proponents claim
exposure to negative ions can neutralize free radicals, revitalize cell
metabolism, enhance immune function, purify the blood, and balance the autonomic nervous system, while encouraging deep sleep
and healthy digestion. Is any of this true? A visit to Deception Falls
may hold the answer for you.

FIRE AND ICE TRAIL

From volcanoes to glaciers in a short alpine hike

DIFFICULTY
Easy

LENGTH
0.5 miles

LOCATION
near Glacier, Washington

Hikers of all ages will enjoy close proximity to a volcanic ("fire") and glacier-carved ("ice") landscape here. The Fire and Ice Trail is the primary interpretive trail among several world-class hikes radiating from the Heather Meadows and Artist Point areas at the end of Washington State Route 542.

You'll encounter alpine meadows filled with wildflowers, a glacial tarn and stream, and a number of wild plants and animals native to this rugged high-elevation ecosystem. Unless you're a skier or snowboarder, the best time to visit the high elevation area is summer. (Some of the deepest snows in the contiguous United States take hold in winter.) Wildflowers start to bloom in late June, but the best shows come later in summer, which is also when all of the tasty berries start to ripen.

From the Heather Meadows Visitors Center parking lot adjacent to the Austin Pass Picnic Area, the well-marked, wheelchair-accessible trail (made of loose gravel) quickly descends into a canyon of pillared andesite rocks. The ground below your feet is made of age-old rock that formed as flowing lava cooled and shrank, cracking into 5- or 6-sided parallel columns that then eroded over time.

But this valley before you wasn't fully baked at that point. More recently,

▴ Cascade bilberries make any late summer or early fall hike in the high country near Mount Baker a delicious experience.

some 15,000 years ago, an ice age gripped the planet and glacial ice covered everything from Vancouver Island to the Cascades to Eastern Washington, filling river valleys and surging over mountain ridges. As glaciers slowly moved downhill, they scraped and scoured the bedrock below them, forever altering landscapes in their wake.

As the planet started to warm, this high mountain basin was one of the last in the area to lose its ice. Bagley Glacier melted away for good around 10,000 years ago, leaving this valley between Mount Herman and Table Mountain and a series of meltwater lakes in its wake.

Continue down the well-maintained trail as it crosses through meadows strewn with pink mountain-heather, Cascade bilberry, and thinleaf huckleberry. If it's midsummer, brace yourself for riotous wildflower shows. Some of the prettiest include alpine aster, Tolmie's saxifrage, avalanche lily, Sitka valerian, bleeding heart, round-leaved violet, false azalea, alpine speedwell, small-flowered paintbrush, slender bog orchid, glacier lily, and the oddly shaped but aptly named elephant's head.

Clusters of mountain hemlocks punctuate the scene. These conifers are well adapted to a heavy snowpack, and that's certainly what they get here, with

▴ Fireweed is a tenacious colonizer of disturbed sites such as fire-scarred or avalanche-scoured landscapes.

▴ Alpine aster

some 50 feet of snow falling on Mount Baker and its flanks every year. Down lower, these trees typically achieve heights of 60–100 feet tall, but up here at these wind- and snow-lashed high elevations, they are typically not much more than 10 feet tall, including some annual cropping off the top by snow and wind. As an adaptation to

Sitka mountain ash features red berries that are too bitter for most human palates.

Western bracken fern finds enough nutrients in this rock crevice.

these harsh subalpine conditions, the trees' new buds here every spring are stubbier and shorter than new growth on lower-elevation Mountain hemlocks, to avoid getting snapped off by heavy snow. Also, their flexible trunks allow them to bend under the weight of the winter snow, which can leave fairy shapes in the snow when the trees finally bounce back up straight.

Most of these trees, whether solitary or in clumps, grow on knolls that melt earlier than other spots. Dendrologists (scientists who study trees) have discovered that successive rounds of tree growth up here in the Mount Baker highlands are associated with specific periods of warming in the past. They can date the trees you see around you to a period 700–900 years ago and another era around 500 years ago. Two more recent surges in subalpine tree growth occurred 300 and then 150 years ago.

As you continue down the trail, thickets of Sitka mountain ash send up red, tannen-filled berries. Humans find them too bitter to eat, but birds, especially pine grosbeaks, love them. Other birds you may see up here in the high country include golden eagles, horned larks, mountain bluebirds, American pipits, Lapland longspurs, gray-crowned rosy-finches, and Vaux's and black swifts. If you came looking for white-tailed ptarmigan, you could get lucky here along the Fire and Ice Trail, but you'd have a better chance of success farther up on the flanks of Mount Baker—say, on nearby Ptarmigan Ridge, the beginning of the climbers' route for those looking to summit the peak.

This alpine high country attracts plenty of non-avian wildlife as well. Mountain goats, native to these Cascades, climb and scramble along the rocky cliffs above. Actually more closely related to antelopes than goats, these sure-footed, short-horned, white-coated

The view of Mount Shuksan, at 9131 feet elevation, is a highlight of the Fire and Ice Trail.

• You may catch a glimpse of a hoary marmot, one of many high-country residents.

• Pikas do an excellent job of blending in with their surroundings.

creatures are master grazers on what little herbaceous and shrubby plant matter they can find between crevices in the cliffs. They can be aggressive if approached, so give them plenty of space.

If you hear a high-pitched whistle that seems like it is coming from a rock nearby, it's probably a hoary marmot warning its peers of your presence. The largest members of the squirrel family, hoary marmots can weigh as much as 10 pounds and typically reach 30 inches in length. They feed on grasses, flowers, insects, and even the occasional bird egg. Hibernating for 7–8 months a year, they excavate burrows in the soil, typically under or among boulders. During hibernation, a hoary marmot's heart rate slows to only 8–10 beats per minute; body temperature drops to near freezing.

Another denizen of the high country you might see dashing for cover is the pika. While these round-eared, tailless fluffballs may look like rodents, they are actually the smallest members of the lagomorph family (hares and rabbits). They don't grow more than 8 inches long and live out their days foraging for grasses and wild-flowers among the rocks of these mountain slopes. Unlike marmots, they do not pass their winters hibernating, but instead hole up inside dens, surviving on grasses they have cached.

Another iconic species of the high country is the black bear, most often seen out and about in the late summer and early fall gorging on Cascade bilberries and thinleaf huckleberries. When a bear eats a berry right off the bush with its lips, it almost looks like it is kissing the plant. If you do see a bear, stay calm. Don't make any sudden movements or take off running—this could trigger its predator instinct. In most cases, the bear will run away as soon as it knows you're there, or, if it is in the middle of a berry-eating session, ignore you altogether. In any case, don't try to get closer for a photo, do look big (wave your arms and jacket above your head) and make noise (talk, sing, yell). Back away slowly to give it space for its own exit.

Of course, the larger, fiercer grizzly bear used to be common in these parts, but settlers with rifles extirpated them over the course of the 1800s. That said, some 15,000 grizzlies persist north of the border in Canada's British Columbia province. Sporadic unconfirmed

▲ The stream alongside the Fire and Ice Trail is one small link in the chain transporting large amounts of glacial meltwater to the lowlands.

sightings of grizzlies from this Canadian population straying down into American territory not far from Mount Baker means you may have a chance, though slight, of seeing one here.

Down you go and finally the trail bottoms out at a viewpoint of Upper Bagley Lake, giving you a good perspective on the combination of forces that formed this classic U-shaped glacial valley. At this point you can either turn around and follow the trail back to the

Check out the columnar andesite on the way down to Upper Bagley Lake.

A little self-reflection may be in order if you find yourself next to Terminal Lake. ▸

parking lot or continue on a more traditional and rugged hiking trail—not wheelchair accessible—as it hooks left and loops back along a small seasonal stream carrying some of the world's clearest water downstream to feed the thirsty wildflower meadows. Neither engineers nor farmers could have dreamed up a better irrigation system to keep the plants watered.

With the loop almost complete, revel in the serene waters of Terminal Lake, a summer-only tarn that marks the end of the glacier's extent as it carved out this valley some 10,000 years ago. A small wooden boardwalk makes it possible to get right up to the water's edge and see your reflection—as well as the reflection of jagged Mount Shuksan and neighboring peaks—in the clear calm below. The image of yourself surrounded by so much natural glory is one you won't soon forget. Even without a camera, this might be the selfie of a lifetime.

When your tarn-side meditations are over, finish the loop and head back to the parking lot, relishing your newfound, firsthand knowledge about some of the primal forces that have shaped and continue to work on landscapes all around us.

GINKGO PETRIFIED FOREST

Remnants of a swampy subtropical forest in the high desert

DIFFICULTY
Easy

LOCATION
Ginkgo Petrified Forest State Park, Vantage, Washington

LENGTH
Just over 1 mile

The Trees of Stone Interpretive Trail bisects quintessential sagebrush steppe habitat along the Columbia River uphill of Wanapum Dam.

For millions of years an ancient subtropical forest lay hidden below what we saw as just another stretch of Columbia plateau sagebrush steppe. It wasn't until the late 1920s, when road crews building Vantage Road along the Columbia River started unearthing huge pieces of petrified wood, that someone realized something special was going on down there. George Beck, a geology professor at nearby Washington State Normal School (now Central Washington University), noticed a worker hauling a huge piece of petrified wood down the hillside near the road and began investigating. He brought back a team of students armed with excavating tools and within a week they had unearthed dozens more pieces of wood that had been likewise fossilized and buried underground for eons.

Over the next few years, Beck and students continued to dig at the site while they lobbied public officials to protect it as a natural and cultural resource. In 1935 the State of Washington complied, establishing Ginkgo Petrified Forest State Park over approximately 11 square miles of desert where the majority of fossilized wood was found.

While Beck and his team were surprised to find petrified logs of tree species typically found in humid subtropical forests (such as the present-day southeastern United States), even more shocking was the discovery of petrified ginkgo trees, which had been extinct on this continent for millions of years. They took some samples to study and preserve, but left others where and how they found them so others could revel in the experience of *in situ* discovery.

Today, the best way to drink in all of this geologic time is to hike the Trees of Stone Interpretive Trail, a just-over-1-mile crushed gravel loop along the hillside above the Columbia River, where 21 of the petrified logs are on display right where Beck found them. Each of these ancient remaining logs is protected by heavy metal grates to ward off thieves and vandals, but just seeing them is inspiration for imagining how this land might have looked eons ago.

▴ A petrified ginkgo log along the Trees of Stone Interpretive Trail. Ginkgo trees have been extinct in North America for 7 million years, but George Beck found this 17-million-year-old petrified specimen sticking out of the desert floor in 1931.

Back then, during the Miocene epoch some 17 million years ago, the climate around these parts was wet and humid and dominated by boggy marshes, shallow lakes, and swamp cypress forests—definitely not what you would expect to encounter in the arid inland Northwest of today. Ancestral horses, dogs, bears, saber-toothed cats, beavers, and deer lived in this swampy forest alongside an array of long-extinct wildlife species only known to modern man thanks to the fossil record. (Signs of early humans wouldn't show up here for another 3–5 million years.)

A wide variety of deciduous hardwoods—ginkgo, sweetgum, elm, cottonwood, maple, walnut, oak, sycamore, and horse chestnut—flourished on the hillside while Douglas fir, hemlock, and spruce grew in thick stands at higher elevations. This is evidenced by where Beck and other paleontologists found specific petrified logs. The theory goes that these coniferous logs probably didn't come from this swampy hillside but instead were carried east on massive volcanic mudflows (lahars) from the newly forming and seismically active Cascade mountain range to the west. These mudflows would have jumbled all kinds of woody debris into the forests encountered on the way to the Columbia Gorge, explaining the combination of petrified wood types found near modern-day Vantage.

But Mother Nature wasn't yet done shaping these lands into how we know them today. The next Miocene-era assault on the forest below our feet was from massive volcanic fissures to the east that poured floods of molten lava west across the Columbia Plateau. These scorching flows leveled the landscape and buried everything in their path in thick layers of lava that eventually cooled into basalt rock. The lava flowed around those trees and logs that were already waterlogged and mud caked from earlier lahars, encasing them in pillow basalt, at which point they started petrifying.

▲ This petrified spruce log was likely washed down from the Cascades in a lahar around 17 million years ago, before settling here and (very gradually) turning to stone.

Usually if a log is buried underground, it will eventually decay, leaving little if any trace, as the erosional forces of oxygenation, soil compaction, and groundwater infiltration bear down on it. But if the log is encased in an oxygen-deprived basalt tomb and the groundwater filtering through is particularly silica-rich—as would be the case after an ash-spewing volcanic eruption—the wood fiber is slowly replaced by silica and other minerals that crystallize over millions of years, eventually turning the wood into rock. It's these log rocks (or rock logs) that are the main attraction here today.

THE CCC AND THE GINKGO PETRIFIED FOREST

Once the state of Washington committed to making Ginkgo Petrified Forest into a state park in 1935, George Beck enlisted the help of a Civilian Conservation Corps (CCC) crew stationed in nearby Vantage to help unearth and protect the huge and heavy petrified logs and to build out trails and other visitor facilities. The CCC, a federal program created by President Franklin Roosevelt as part of his New Deal to put Americans back to work and lift the country out of the Great Depression, employed nearly 3 million unmarried and otherwise jobless young men during its 9-year run beginning in 1933. Each CCC worker got food, shelter, clothing, and $30 per month, $25 of which had to be sent home to their families. It's unlikely that turning a desolate hillside above the Columbia River into a natural attraction capable of handling thousands of visitors a year would have been possible without the help of the CCC.

The Trees of Stone Interpretive Trail (along with the petrified log enclosures, Trailside Museum, and caretaker's cabin) is a great example of the kind of work the CCC did, but you can also see its imprint on dozens of other major public works projects in natural areas across the Pacific Northwest.

Start the Trees of Stone Interpretive Trail at the well-marked trailhead on the northeast side of the parking lot and follow it to the Trailside Museum, a small enclosed open-air room featuring information placards on the petrified forest and its discovery. This delightfully rustic structure, which includes a small caretaker's cabin behind the museum, was built in the mid-1930s by the Civilian Conservation Corps. It's worth a stop to learn more about the site and then continue on the trail. Go right at the fork where you'll immediately see the first of the 21 petrified logs on display.

This petrified maple, partially dug out of the soil surrounding it and covered with a metal grate, looks like a tree trunk made of rock—which is exactly what it is. The tree trunk's outer (bark) layer is a glossy black color, while the interior heartwood is striated with green-blue streaks, pink stripes, and orange smudges—a result of the infiltration of minerals including copper, manganese, iron, and chromium into the structure during the petrifaction process.

Next up, another 250 feet down the trail, is a big old Douglas fir trunk that looks like so many fallen logs you've seen on hiking trails of the Pacific Northwest—but this one is made of stone-cold rock.

▲ The Civilian Conservation Corps built out the facilities and trail network at Ginkgo Petrified Forest State Park, including the enclosures for the 21 petrified logs that connect the dots of the Trees of Stone Interpretive Trail.

⏶ Big sagebrush carpets the landscape as far as the eye can see, interspersed with a surprising array of other hardy desert plants.

⏶ Bastardsage turns pink in the fall, spicing up the color palette of the otherwise sand-beige and sage-green desert.

⏶ Cheatgrass, an invasive plant brought over from Europe by settlers long ago as feed for their grazing livestock, has become a scourge of the sagebrush steppe.

This must have been one of the logs that was transported to this location via lahar from the newly forming Cascades. It sports a lot of orange coloration—likely from iron infiltration during petrifaction—on the fossilized but otherwise iconic Douglas fir bark.

Backtrack past the petrified maple log and then fork right to head uphill and to the west, following the path suggested by occasional trail signs. Keep hiking up the slight grade and stop to check out the sweeping vistas. The blonde-beige color palette of the desert belies the present-day floral species diversity at your feet. Big sagebrush is the dominant shrub here and across the Columbia Plateau. Its light green branches perfume the air with the cleansing scent of sage when the wind blows (which is often in this part of the world, home to Washington's largest wind farm only 15 miles to the west). Flannel bush, Saskatoon serviceberry, bastardsage, prickly lettuce, big galleta, three-tip sagebrush, winterfat, brownplume wirelettuce, and wild buckwheat are other natives commonly seen here.

While these plants are doing fine here in their native habitat, especially in protected reserves like Ginkgo Petrified Forest State Park, certain invasives are claiming increasing amounts of territory across the Columbia Plateau. Cheatgrass may be the most worrisome to those concerned about the long-term health of the Northwest's vast inland desert and the native plants and wildlife that live here. One issue is its tendency to burn, substantially upping the brushfire risk across the desert. Native plants here are not evolved to handle such frequent burns (every 5–7 years on average lately) and each cheatgrass-fueled brushfire creates more colonization space for the weed, which feeds off the extra nitrogen fire brings to the soil.

Another problem is cheatgrass's hardiness in colonizing open and disturbed areas before native plants have a chance to get in and set seed. These factors conspire against greater sage-grouse, mule deer, pygmy rabbits, and other native wildlife dependent on native plants both for forage and cover. A monoculture of cheatgrass across the Columbia Plateau would mean the end of desert ecosystems as we know them.

That said, there is little we can actually do to effectively stop the spread of cheatgrass—it's already taken over some 50 million acres of sagebrush steppe across the American West. Herbicides have been effective at removing grown cheatgrass plants, but they do nothing to stop the already-rooted seeds, which mean new plants the following spring. Some researchers believe that employing all-natural soil microbes to inhibit growth of the cheatgrass root system below the surface shows promise as a potential solution. But it could be years before we know whether such treatment is feasible on the massive scale effective cheatgrass curtailment would require.

Don't let these plant issues weigh on your conscience for too long, though: you've got more petrified rocks to discover. Next up are fossilized examples of spruce, elm, sweetgum, and horse chestnut—each as out of place in the present-day high desert as the next—unearthed and protected behind a metal grate like others along the trail. Soon you'll encounter the only remains of a pre–ice age ginkgo tree you'll ever see on this continent—even if it is only a stone statue of its former self.

Ginkgo trees might be the ultimate old-timers, as the only survivors of a group of ancient plants that lived 190 million years ago, during the Jurassic period, when the supercontinent Pangaea split apart. Evidence of the tree disappeared from the fossil record in North America around 7 million years ago, and from Europe 3 million years later. While botanists assumed the tree was extinct worldwide in modern times, living examples were found in remote parts of Asia, where Buddhist monks had been nurturing them for hundreds of years in relative isolation.

Cut to the present, and ginkgo trees are once again widespread in North America and Europe, but this time around they are cultivated and planted as a non-native naturalized species—ironic, as they may in fact be the oldest native plant species on either continent.

Of course, ginkgos couldn't have made it this far without being survivors of the first order, which is part of what makes them so popular as landscaping elements in planned urban and suburban settings. The tree's natural ability to tolerate drought, air pollution, poor soil quality, inundation with pet waste, and the constant salting of roads gives them an advantage over other common landscaping trees. In fact, ginkgos are so tough that 6 of them remain today as the only flora that sprouted back to life within several square miles of 1945's atomic bomb blast in Hiroshima, Japan. The ginkgo will forever remain a symbol of resiliency. Indeed, this species never seems to give up.

Follow the crushed gravel interpretive trail as it loops around at its western extreme until you've seen all 21 petrified logs, then follow it back to the trailhead or take the optional dirt hiking trail farther up the hill for better views. This latter option also passes the only petrified redwood log on display here.

Looking around at the big sagebrush, the sandy desert floor, and the blue sky streaked with wispy clouds, it's still hard to imagine this spot as a lush subtropical swamp. But you cannot deny what's written in stone at the Ginkgo Petrified Forest.

DRY FALLS

A 5-square-mile oasis centered around a 400-foot ancient waterfall

LOCATION
near Coulee City, Washington

DIFFICULTY
Easy

LENGTH
0 to 15 miles

Looking out over the cliffs of Dry Falls and the Sun Lakes below them, it's easy to forget you're in the middle of the desolate and dry Channeled Scablands of eastern Washington's Columbia Plateau. This refuge in the desert was the site of a massive waterfall 13,000 years ago, during the last ice age. While the falls have long been dry, the pockmarked landscapes below them host a much wider array of soil types, plant life, and wildlife than the thousands of square miles of surrounding sagebrush steppe.

Fifteen miles of hiking trails wind their way around Dry Falls and through the state park that encompasses it, but you can also visit the highlights of this dramatic setting without straying far from the car. Keep an eye (and ear) out for rattlesnakes if you venture onto the canyon floor. The best seasons to visit are mid- to late spring, when desert flowers bloom and wildlife is most active, and of course summer, when temperatures soar and the area's abundant freshwater lakes invite toe dipping or more.

The best overview of this dramatic scene is from a roadside pull-out by the Dry Falls Visitor Center along State Route 17, on the northwest lip of Lenore Canyon, directly across from the massive cliff face. From this vantage point, the panoramic view to the southeast is dominated by Dry Falls' 400-foot-tall basalt precipice across the canyon and a series of lakes and wetlands below. These are bisected by Umatilla Rock, a blade of basalt that runs for almost a mile through the middle of Lenore Canyon.

It's hard to imagine what the scene spread out before you might have looked like 13,000 years ago, when the equivalent of tidal waves of water were pouring over the massive basalt wall and scouring out a

Common mullein grows out of a small crevice in the vertical cliff wall below the Dry Falls overlook on Washington State Route 17. ▸

new bottom for the canyon you are now looking across. What we see these days is a geological wonder and landscape view rivaling any in North America.

The Pleistocene-era waterfall—2.5 times higher and 5 times wider than Niagara Falls—came into existence when a glacier moved down into the present-day Okanogan Valley of north-central Washington, choking the Columbia River, mighty even back then, in the process. The roiling river rose behind the ice dam, eventually spilling over the lowest point in its south wall and carving a 30-mile-long canyon, today known as the Grand Coulee, ending at a broad basalt ledge—what we now call Dry Falls. The rerouted torrential tributary, moving at 65 miles an hour and with 10 times the flow of all the present-day rivers in the world combined, then tumbled over the wall and flowed south through Lenore Canyon before spreading out across the flats to the west and rejoining the main westward-flowing channel of the Columbia again.

The ice dam would then refreeze and rebreach periodically over the next 2000 years or so, its floods exacerbated by contributions from an even bigger ice dam breaching (and refreezing and rebreaching) farther north at Glacial Lake Missoula. These cataclysmic flushes put huge sections of the inland Pacific Northwest suddenly under hundreds of feet of water over the course of just

Looking over Lenore Canyon, Dry Falls Lake, Umatilla Rock, Green Alkali Lake, and last but definitely not least, Dry Falls.

a few days, significantly expanding the Grand Coulee and Lenore Canyon in a short amount of geological time. When the ice sheets finally melted for good, the Columbia River returned to its former course, leaving the Grand Coulee dry and exposing to the light of day the newly bare basalt cliffs of Dry Falls and the scoured canyon floor below.

* Netleaf hackberry leaves

Take your time wandering around this perch overlooking Dry Falls. Common mulleins spread out their green leaves from cracks in the cliffs below, while netleaf hackberry plants climb the fence and dress up the view with their green leaves and reddish brown berries in fall. White-throated swifts and chukars slice through the air from cliffside nests directly below you.

The paved and fenced viewing path meanders along the edge of Lenore Canyon to a covered lookout with a short, fenced catwalk out into the abyss. Looking down into the canyon, you'll notice sprawling Dry Falls Lake at the bottom of the canyon and little Green Alkali Lake a bit farther uphill into the base of the rock wall. These are among the plunge pools that formed where glacial floodwaters landed after topping Dry Falls. Also look across the canyon floor for dozens of pockmarked depressions called potholes, formed by "kolks" (whirlpools or underwater tornados) drilling into the basalt from above during these glacial floods.

You'll also notice a much greener color palette at the bottom of the canyon than on the tops of the mesas all around. This is thanks to a variety of factors, including the deposition of gravel in some areas and the buildup of loess, a silty and fecund sediment that accumulates from windblown dust, in other areas. All the scrapes carved and potholes drilled by the glacial floodwaters provide plenty of habitat for plants to grow among the rocks. It truly is an oasis within the harsh desert all around.

When you've fully taken in this ultrawide view, get back in the car and drive down into Lenore Canyon itself to poke around the trails between and around the talus slopes, lakes, potholes, crevices, and glacial erratic boulders at the foot of Dry Falls and Umatilla Rock.

You can drive right down to the edge of Dry Falls Lake, park the car, and set out on foot from there to explore firsthand the biologically diverse canyon bottom.

The diversity of flora in Lenore Canyon alone can be attributed to the commingling of so many different ecosystem pockets on the canyon floor in the wake of the glacial floods: fertile loess deposits in swales, potholes, and cracks in the basalt; rocky lithosols (thin-soiled basalt formations with poor water-holding capacity) below talus slopes at cliff bases; gravel beds from scoured bedrock; riparian wetlands surrounding lakes and creeks; and remnant glacial debris (rubble and erratic boulders).

Like elsewhere across the Channeled Scablands, big sagebrush, rigid sagebrush, bluebunch wheatgrass, three-tip sagebrush, yellow rabbitbrush, spiny hopsage, greasewood, antelope bitterbrush, needle-and-thread grass, Idaho fescue, winterfat, Indian ricegrass, snow buckwheat, and Sandberg bluegrass are found in abundance around Dry Falls. What makes this area special from a botanist's perspective

are the sheer number of vascular plant species (more than 400) that persevere on the canyon floor despite the hardscrabble conditions.

△ Yellow rabbit-brush offers cover and nesting habitat for the greater sage-grouse as well as small birds and rodents, and is a food source for black-tailed jack-rabbits and many butterflies.

If it's spring, scan the bottom of the talus slopes directly below the cliffs of Dry Falls and Umatilla Rock, where lithosols support the growth of colorful wildflower blooms through the spring and early summer. Look there for bitterroot, mariposa lily, threadleaf flea-bane, arrowleaf balsamroot, longleaf phlox, low larkspur, locoweed, Gairdner's penstemon, and Woods' rose, among others.

Black cottonwood and thinleaf alder trees stake out comple-mentary territory along the shorelines of the plunge pools and in the riparian areas along seasonal creeks and spring seepages. Red-osier dogwood, mock orange, yellow willow, and Great Basin wild rye fill in the gaps. The dampest areas support woolly sedge, small-flowered bulrush, and rare wildflowers such as shooting star, saxifrage, and common bistort.

Several plants that are seldom but sometimes seen around Dry Falls qualify for endangered or threatened species protection. If you see any purple milkvetch, porcupine sedge, annual Indian paintbrush, slender cryptantha, desert cryptantha, beaked spikerush, giant helle-borine, sagebrush stickseed, Suksdorf's monkeyflower, dwarf evening primrose, smooth cliffbrake, dwarf phacelia, Austin's knotweed, or wood sage, consider yourself lucky—and feel good that efforts to protect these liminal species are at least allowing them to hold steady in some of their habitat, dwindling as it may be.

Supporting all of this flora are the cryptobiotic soil crusts that serve as the interface between belowground and aboveground—and as such, regulate the flow of nutrients and moisture to and from plants' taproots. This top layer of lichens, mosses, and algae protects the bare ground below from the constant erosional forces at play in the desert, but also provides an ideal open substrate for invasives to establish themselves.

And invade, they do. An increasing number of non-native invasive plants are encroaching on the territory of long-standing natives. Cheatgrass has been especially troublesome here at Dry Falls as well as across the Columbia Plateau. Its long sprouting season, rapid growth in dense thickets, and ability to produce and disperse huge numbers of seeds give it a leg up on native bunchgrasses. Madwort, hoary cress, Russian knapweed, Canada thistle, and purple loosestrife are also aggressively expanding in the park, taking over large swaths of the canyon floor, especially in areas disturbed by weather events or frequently trampled by human foot traffic.

As for wildlife, there's plenty of that, too, circulating through the various ecological niches of Dry Falls and its surroundings. You might not see them, but bobcats, yellow-bellied marmots, American

▲ Lichens paint the rocks on the canyon floor.

▲ Black-tailed jackrabbit

badgers, muskrats, ground squirrels, coyotes, black-tailed jackrabbits, sagebrush lizards, and northern Pacific rattlesnakes are among the terrestrial species that live or spend lots of time around Dry Falls. Mule deer and Rocky Mountain elk often browse the lush foliage on the canyon floor as well.

Avian life here is also abundant, which isn't surprising given what an oasis of green this place is in the midst of the desert. Greater sage-grouse, with its spiky tail and beautiful white mane, is right in the heart of its native habitat. Peregrine falcons, prairie falcons, and golden eagles nest in depressions in the basalt cliffs and live large on a steady diet of mice, voles, and rabbits. Red-winged blackbirds chatter and sing, while goldfinches flitter incessantly amid the reeds around Dry Falls Lake. Great blue herons, black-crowned night herons, and great egrets stalk the shallows of the plunge pools and seasonal streams, on the hunt for frogs and small fish. Gray-crowned rosy-finches, canyon wrens, Bullock's orioles, Barrow's goldeneyes, loggerhead shrikes, Brewer's sparrows, sage thrashers, yellow-headed blackbirds, chukars, yellow-breasted chats, lark sparrows, lazuli buntings, and California quail are among the other bird species commonly sighted at Sun Lakes-Dry Falls State Park. Keep an eye on the sky for brown pelicans, sandhill cranes, trumpeter swans, and snow

• Gargantuan Lahontan cutthroat trout thrive in the alkaline water of the plunge pool lakes and connecting streams on the floor of Lenore Canyon at the foot of Dry Falls.

Mormon metal-
marks are big,
beautiful butterflies
with a predilection
for snow buckwheat
and yellow rabbit-
brush. ▸

geese, all of which migrate through twice a year and tend to stay a
while to feast on the buffet at the bottom of the canyon.

Aquatic species thrive in the lakes and wetlands here as well.
If it's springtime, look for Lahontan cutthroat trout—the largest
subspecies of cutthroats, with adults topping out at 39 inches long—
swarming up seasonal creeks to Green Alkali Lake. Lower down in
the canyon, Dry Falls Lake is flush with trout (rainbows, browns,
and tigers) that the Washington State Department of Natural
Resources stocks for the fly-fisherfolk who flock here from all over
the Pacific Northwest. (The rainbows here are reportedly the largest
in Washington.)

Butterfly enthusiasts will have plenty to get excited about.
Mormon metalmarks, with their distinctive, white-spotted orange
and black wings, feed on the snow buckwheat and yellow rabbitbrush that blooms in pockets on the canyon floor in the early fall.
They lay lavender-colored eggs on the stems of wild buckwheat and
snow buckwheat in the fall. The eggs then overwinter and hatch
the following spring. Mormon metalmarks are listed as "rare and
threatened" at the northern extent of their range in Western Canada
and conservationists would like to see similar action on the U.S. side
of the border, where habitat loss has also driven their population
numbers way down.

Sightings of dozens of other butterfly species abound. Look for Lorquin's admirals, spring azures, Boisduval's blues, sagebrush checkerspots, mourning cloaks, lilac-bordered coppers, western pine elfins, great spangled fritillaries, Sheridan's green hairstreaks, painted ladies, and common wood nymphs. Late summer and early fall are your best bets for butterfly spotting in this part of the world.

▲ A darkling beetle travels the desert floor in search of plant scraps.

The diversity of plants and habitat types around Dry Falls is the main draw for wildlife, rare and otherwise. But the fact that wildlife habitat everywhere has been shrinking as our human footprint expands means that places like Sun Lakes-Dry Falls State Park are that much more important, as bulwarks against the loss of biodiversity.

While glacial floods may have been the main driver of environmental change here eons ago, these days it's us. It's ironic that we marvel at the destructive and restorative forces of Mother Nature, but seem blind to our own environmentally destructive actions. Appreciating special places like Dry Falls and its environs—but not to the point of overuse—is key to understanding the importance of taking care of the environment, so it can continue to take care of us.

PINE LAKES LOOP TRAIL

Wildlife haven teeming with diversity and vitality

DIFFICULTY
Easy

LENGTH
1.25 miles

LOCATION
Turnbull National Wildlife Refuge, near Cheney, Washington

The Turnbull National Wildlife Refuge in Eastern Washington is one of a handful of oasis-like patches within the otherwise arid Channeled Scablands of the Columbia Plateau. Wetlands cover 20 percent of the 4.5-square-mile refuge, and three distinct but connected ecosystems—upland, swamp, and underwater—attract a wide range of fauna and flora. The 1.25-mile Pine Lakes Loop Trail offers an easy stroll on a mostly paved pathway through some of the refuge's highlights. You're bound to see some sort of wildlife—most likely waterfowl—partaking of the natural riches of the flood-prone landscape, and to feel restored by spending time in this dynamic outdoor setting.

The refuge is open year round, and gets the most human visitors in summer, when days are long and temperatures typically top 80 degrees F. But spring is the ideal season for stopping by, given the profusion of wildlife intent on finding mates and consummating their relationships as wildflowers and other plants send up colorful blooms to attract pollinators such as bees, birds, and bats. Winter is often cold, snowy, and bleak in Eastern Washington, but those looking for solitude should find plenty along Turnbull's trails then.

Park in the South Smith Road parking area and cross the street to the well-marked trailhead. Zigzag through a small patch of forest on the paved trail and stop at the overlook of Winslow Pool, the smaller of the two lakes you'll visit. Take a gander through the

anchored swiveling binoculars there to scan the lake surface and adjacent wetlands for waterfowl and other wildlife.

Yellow salsify, common storksbill, bull thistle, creeping thistle, and broadleaf cattail are the most common plants along this stretch of the trail, with Woods' rose, common snowberry, and common St. John's wort making occasional appearances. Bigbract verbena and Canadian horseweed spread out over remaining soil patches.

The paved path continues south past a junction with a dike trail to the left—ignore this for now, as you will be looping back later—and continue straight on the pavement, now with Middle Pine Lake to your left.

While these lakes are some of the larger wetlands in the refuge, smaller vernal pools, scoured by the ancient glacial floods that

▴ The Turnbull National Wildlife Refuge is a vibrant island of life in arid Eastern Washington.

created the Channeled Scablands and further eroded by thousands of years of exposure, fill up with water as the snow melts in the spring. This melt provides much-needed hydration for area wildlife as well as nearby plants eager to get on with the business of photosynthesis.

Out to the right, admire groves of white-barked quaking aspen trees. In the fall, their leaves turn gold and reflect light every which way as they shift in the wind. In an unusual but ultimately successful adaptation, these iconic trees of the Rockies and Intermountain West regenerate vegetatively by sending up suckers from long, lateral, underground rhizomatic roots; the resulting trees are essentially clones of the others in the network. They are quick to colonize burned-over lands because they can send up new shoots from their fire-safe rhizomes long before new conifer seeds can take root, giving them an advantage in the early stages of forest succession.

▴ Bigbract verbena

▴ St. John's wort

▴ Eastern Washington represents the far western edge of the range for quaking aspens and their signature trembling leaves.

▴ Hairy vetch's purple flowers add a dash of color to an otherwise beige scene.

In spring, look for a range of colorful wildflower blooms from the likes of arrowleaf balsamroot, common camas, prairie star, poet's narcissus, hairy vetch, small camas, great blanketflower, bitterroot, western blue flag, large-leaved lupine, showy milkweed, sticky geranium, yellow fritillary, sagebrush buttercup, and nineleaf biscuitroot. Saskatoon serviceberry's blue-black berries look to be glowing dark red on the inside, and are a favorite of birds. Red-osier dogwood's stiff stems take up the midstory where they can.

▲ Butter-and-eggs may be nice to look at, but it's an invasive weed at Turnbull National Wildlife Refuge, out-competing native plants for precious real estate.

While these native plants fit right in here and are doing well thanks to the protections offered by being in the refuge, they are not immune from the dog-eat-dog nature of life. Following disturbances like big storms or floods, invasive plant species are colonizing habitat niches that would otherwise be filled by natives. Switchgrass and Canada goldenrod are among the worst offenders at Turnbull, but several others are troublesome as well.

One particular pesky (yet nevertheless attractive) invasive flowering plant that is cropping up all over the refuge is butter-and-eggs, so named for the yellow-on-yellow coloration of its blooms. This Mediterranean beauty was introduced to North America as an exotic ornamental in the 1800s and quickly jumped out of backyard flower beds and into the woods and wilds of our temperate latitudes. Today it's a constant struggle to keep the hardy herbaceous plant in check, especially because off-season flowering draws nectar-loving insects and birds. These pollinators in turn spread butter-and-eggs' pollen and seeds far and wide as they go on their way, ensuring that the plant continues to flourish despite the best efforts of refuge personnel.

All of this floral abundance is merely a backdrop for this refuge's reason for being: to protect wildlife, especially birds. Indeed, Turnbull is a birder's paradise, with more than 200 different avian species spotted here in any given year.

Waterfowl—ducks, geese, and swans with webbed feet and water-repellent feathers that facilitate floating and swimming—rule the roost at Turnbull, given the fact that so much of the refuge is either under water or waterlogged. Canada geese, gadwalls, American wigeons, northern shovelers, American coots, and blue-winged, green-winged, and cinnamon teals are year-round residents of the nutrient-rich wetlands here. White pelicans, tundra swans, hooded mergansers, goldeneyes, northern pintails, ring-necked ducks, canvasbacks, wood ducks, trumpeter swans, red-necked phalaropes, and redheads, along with dozens of other waterfowl species, come and go with the seasons.

DABBLERS OR DIVERS?

In case you hadn't noticed, all ducks can be divided into one of two camps: dabblers or divers, depending on how they feed and take off. Dabblers—teals, shovelers, pintails, gadwalls, mallards—tip their tails up in the water to feed upside down, and can spring directly into flight. Divers—canvasbacks, redheads, wigeons—go deep in search of food and have to run across the water's surface to gain enough speed to lift off. Geese and swans are also technically dabblers, but the terminology is generally reserved for ducks proper.

There's plenty of other birdlife here besides waterfowl. The ponderosa pine–dominated forest on the west side of the refuge is prime woodpecker habitat. The white-headed woodpecker is the most common here, but downy, hairy, and pileated woodpeckers as well as red-naped sapsuckers and northern flickers make a comfortable living poaching insects out of tree cavities.

Meanwhile, look skyward for patrolling raptors—peregrine falcons, American kestrels, red-tailed hawks, and northern harriers—as they hunt for American red and Columbian ground squirrels as well as yellow-pine and least chipmunks. At night, great horned owls and northern pygmy owls take over the hunt.

Fish are also fair game, although these Columbia Plateau lakes and ponds don't grow them big. Redside shiners, measuring 7 inches long, are the kingfish of these wetlands, but they are far outnumbered by smaller pumpkinseeds and brook sticklebacks, topping out at 4 and 2.5 inches long, respectively. The 3-inch speckled dace also schools up in these teeming wetland waters.

▸ Ponderosa pines are the dominant trees of the landscape.

Piles of sticks at one end of Middle Pine Lake are surely the work of industrious American beavers maintaining an underwater lodge. Northern river otters and long-tailed weasels can also be spotted. Rocky mountain elk, Columbian white-tailed deer, cougar, coyote, and American badger, along with 11 species of bats, are among the other mammals busy at work in and around the refuge.

Yet another mammal—this one truly "charismatic megafauna" and not normally associated with the Pacific Northwest but habituated here at Turnbull nevertheless—is moose. Some 5000 of the animals, smaller than their cousins to the north in Canada and Alaska but still standing 6 feet at the shoulders and weighing between 600 and 1100 pounds, roam the eastern side of Washington and the Idaho panhandle, preferring the forested habitat with lakes and marshes and wetlands they find here at Turnbull. These herbivores can stomach even the harshest roughage but it's hard for them to bend low, so they end up eating a lot of twigs and bark off the middle and upper trunks of quaking aspens, black cottonwoods, and other trees and tall shrubs. Their dwindling numbers here mean state wildlife biologists now consider Washington's moose to be a Priority Species, and have initiated collaborative efforts with private landowners and public land managers to ensure there is enough nutrient-rich habitat for them to wander in and out, unmolested by hunters and other controllable threats.

Keep moving north and look off to the right for a smaller water source called the Ice Pond, surrounded by reed canary grass and broadleaf cattails against a backdrop of stately ponderosa pines.

▲ The Ice Pond and ponderosa pines, with broadleaf cattails in the foreground.

Before the days of refrigerators and freezers, this is where local farmers—and perhaps Indigenous peoples including the Coeur d'Alene, Palus, Spokan(e), and Yakama long before them—sourced ice during the winter.

Just beyond, you can't miss a basalt rock outcropping on the side of the trail that looks like a dilapidated, man-made, aggregate wall. This waist-high feature is actually a remnant of the lava flows that in part formed this landscape some 6 or more million years ago. More ponderosa pines gather behind the wall. Examine the rock face of the wall and you'll find a wide assortment of lichens clinging to the rough and tumble surface, including the wispy green, beard-like shield lichen of the class Lecanoromycetes and brown-and-olive-spotted lichenized fungi from the family Umbilicariaceae.

When you're done ogling at rocks and lichen, keep walking. When you get to the northeast corner of Middle Pine Lake, take the trail to the left, which crosses via an old farm dike back to the junction point you previously passed. Along the way, common mullein pokes its velvety, light green leaves out of the rock crevices in the

side of the dike, with the yellow flower clusters of common yarrow providing a nice color contrast.

    This is one of the few remaining dikes constructed by farmers during the late 1800s in an attempt to tame the wild wetlands for farming. It is a reminder that the grounds we see today weren't always so wild, or so friendly to wildlife. Enterprising non-Native settlers cut down trees, introduced exotic ornamental and crop plants, drained marshes to grow crops and graze livestock, and suppressed wildfires, which had always been a natural part of the ecosystem. But in the end, all of their work was for naught, as the flood-prone land was just too swampy to sustain successful crop and livestock production. By the late 1920s they had all bolted, leaving a messy, cutover patchwork of land dotted with ill-conceived dikes, run-down structures, and overgrown fields and orchards. Only remnants of a few of the original wetlands remained.

    Land managers had their work cut out for them in restoring the terrain to a semblance of its former natural glory when it became a wildlife refuge in 1937. Initial projects involved massive earthmoving

▲ This ancient aggregate basalt wall looks like a crumbling work of man but has been here for a lot longer than humans.

to eliminate some of the man-made ditches and dikes and recreate a more natural wetlands. In the intervening years, refuge workers have been concentrating on optimizing various habitat niches for native flora and fauna, including removing invasive species that might creep in. They also educate the public on how important the naturally functioning ecosystems here are—both for the plants and animals that call the refuge home and as a step toward becoming more environmentally attuned.

There's still a lot of work to be done on all of these fronts around the refuge, with new challenges brought on by the ascendancy of climate change and its effects on where plants and wildlife can live. Luckily, the local community—including duck hunters who are able to hunt in the refuge by permit during a special season, and a consortium of nonprofits such as Ducks Unlimited and the Inland Northwest Land Trust—have banded together to help fund the refuge's restoration efforts and maintenance backlog. Hopefully with this help, the Turnbull National Wildlife Refuge will remain healthy and vibrant for all.

STEPTOE BUTTE

Volcanism, glaciation, and massive floods—with a spectacular view

DIFFICULTY
Easy, driving

LOCATION
near Steptoe, Washington

LENGTH
4-mile drive

The rolling hills of the Palouse turn different colors as the seasons change and farmers work their crops.

While Steptoe Butte, in the middle of Eastern Washington's Palouse country, is an interesting geological anomaly in its own right, what's even more special is the expansive 360-degree view it affords of the colorful, rolling, loess-covered hills all around it. Jutting up through several other layers of geological time, Steptoe Butte is essentially a quartzite island floating in a sea of basalt. You can drive right up and get a bird's eye view of this stunning landscape that, thanks to its rich geological history, features some of the most fertile soils in North America.

Given that you can drive to the top—and there isn't really a hiking alternative, anyway—Steptoe Butte is something everyone can enjoy, even from behind a windshield. But the best experiences come with getting out, walking around, and truly immersing yourself in this odd, almost aerial setting. The best time of year to visit Steptoe Butte is spring, when local farmers' wheat and other crops are at their most colorful. That said, the view is also great in summer and fall, although the surrounding fields are less colorful. (Winter views from Steptoe Butte tend to be predominantly white, thanks to abundant snowfall in the area—and local roads are often dangerously covered with black ice.)

From the entrance to Steptoe Butte State Park, off Hume Road on the outskirts of the sleepy little town of Steptoe in rural Whitman County, drive around and around and around in increasingly tighter concentric circles until the road dead-ends 4 road miles later (it's only 1.25 miles as the eagle flies) at the summit of Steptoe Butte, elevation 3612 feet—approximately 1000 feet higher than everything else around it.

The view spread out around you in every direction is otherworldly. If you're lucky enough to be there in spring, an undulating patchwork of green, mauve, beige, and ochre stretches as far as the eye can see: local fields planted with wheat, lentil, barley, chickpea, and canola, among other crops.

• Yarrow is one of the more common plants on the hardscrabble Columbia Plateau. It's almost as pretty in the fall as it is in spring bloom.

The rolling farm fields look like multi-hued sand dunes, reflecting the sun's light in different ways. Shade slowly moves up and down hills at the edges of the day. In fact, the fields are a form of dunes, but they are made from slightly more stable loess instead of sand.

Thanks to this fine loess, the Palouse is one of the most productive agricultural areas per acre of any region in the world. Its fertile soils are complemented by a climate hospitable for crops like these that favor grassland ecosystems. In fact,

▲ Curlycup gumweed flowers later in the season than many other herbaceous plants of the Palouse.

these rolling hills spread out before you have made Whitman County the top wheat-producing county in the United States every year running since 1978.

It's not just the skill of local farmers that makes the Palouse so productive. The root of these hills' fecundity lies in a combination of factors. Volcanic eruptions some 15 million years ago sent wave after wave of lava over the prehistoric, mostly quartzite, landscape. When the lava stopped flowing and cooled, it eventually petrified into basalt rock, which underlies more of Earth's surface than any other type of rock.

It's what happened next, in geologic time, that makes the soils of the Palouse so fertile today. During the beginning of the end of the last ice age—about 13,000 years ago—most of modern-day western Montana lay beneath a huge, 2000-foot-deep lake. Glacial Lake Missoula, as geologists now call it, formed when the Cordilleran Ice Sheet dammed the Clark Fork River just as it crossed the modern-day border with Idaho. The lake rose and rose behind this dam, eventually bursting through in a cataclysmic flood of water, boulders, icebergs, and mud that raced at 60 miles an hour across huge swaths of Idaho, Oregon, and Washington on its way to the Pacific. The floodwaters traveled via the channel of the Columbia River, which it carved much deeper into the gorge we now know. As the climate warmed, there were some warmer years and some colder years, so the ice dam built up and was broken through some 60 more times

Bunchgrass and Pacific poison oak on Steptoe Butte in late summer; Palouse wheat fields lie below.

over a 2000-year stretch, reinforcing the earth-shaping forces of the massive initial flood.

The wave action of the glacial floods scraped and carved the underlying basalt into the rolling topography we see today. Subsequently, over thousands more years, the hills and valleys of the region filled up with sediment known as loess, composed primarily of windblown dust and silt. The resulting soils, a combination of loess and eroded volcanic basalt, are not only rich in nutrients but are also well irrigated by winter precipitation and the drip-feed of snow melt from far-off higher elevations to the north.

Steptoe Butte claims many distinctions. It is the highest landmass around for dozens of miles in any direction. It is also the oldest rock across the Pacific Northwest. *And,* it marks the westernmost edge of the original North American continent.

While the basalt that underlies the 19,000-square-mile Palouse ranges from 7–15 million years old, the quartzite of Steptoe Butte is closer to 400 million years old. While this isn't the oldest stone in North America—some ancient rocks in Canada that stretch down into New York, Wyoming, and Minnesota date back 2–3 billion years—it's no spring chicken, either.

Steptoe Butte is named after a U.S. Army lieutenant colonel, Edward Steptoe, who was well known locally for orchestrating a successful retreat of his 164-man battalion from a group of 1000 or more marauding American Indians 15 miles to the north in 1858. While Lt. Colonel Steptoe's tail-turning exploits may have been impressive, his name has become famous around the world—at least among English-speaking geologists and geology enthusiasts—to describe similar types of isolated rock protrusions within lava flows, often at the summit of hills or mountains.

▲ Lichens populate just about every inch of exposed rock around Steptoe Butte.

Of course, such a protrusion, exposed to so much hot, direct sun and buffeted as it is by high winds, is heavier on rock and lighter on flora than more lowland sites. But that hardly means it's devoid of life. Even the copious rock faces host a plenitude of life in the form of lichens. Verrucous varieties crust up into warty relief, while areolate lichens look like old, cracked paint. Meanwhile, sub-squamulose lichens flake off, peeling up at their edges, and squamulose ones take on a look of overlapping scales. Lecanoromycete lichens hang off rock faces like wavy

▲ A ladybug alights on a velvetleaf huckleberry plant.

▲ Missouri goldenrod, well known throughout the grassland prairies of the Upper Midwest, is at the western extent of its range here in the Palouse.

green beards, jockeying with brown-and-olive-spotted lichen from the family Umbilicariaceae and light green species of the genus *Acarospora* for rock face real estate.

Plenty of plants make their home on Steptoe Butte as well. One of the dominant floral species in the park is black hawthorn, a brushy, thorny shrub-tree that American Indians used extensively for making baskets and other essentials as well as for medicine. This drought-tolerant plant can grow as tall as 13 feet high, but tends to be more of a horizontal spreader out here in the desert, dominating understory patches where it can. You'll know it by its straight, strong thorns that grow as long as 1 inch, off the plant's main stems. The plant's tiny white flower clusters in spring yield to big, dark red berries in the late summer that linger into early winter. It used to be much more prevalent here until so much of the land was converted for agricultural use and planted with cash crops. You can still see plenty of black hawthorn along the flanks of Steptoe Butte, but it no longer covers every hillside as far as the eye can see.

Other plants you'll likely encounter as you look around this quartzite summit include velvetleaf huckleberry, common yarrow, sideoats grama, Missouri goldenrod, pink alumroot, Saskatoon serviceberry, curlycup gumweed, smooth sumac, and three-tip sagebrush. Beware of Pacific poison oak, a cousin of the poison ivy so familiar to East Coasters, which can cause a rash that will keep you scratching for a couple of days. Lower down on the flanks and extending out over the few remaining wild patches of Palouse prairie grassland are Idaho fescue, bluebunch wheatgrass, junegrass, Sandberg bluegrass, cow parsnip, common chokecherry, Palouse thistle, Douglas spirea, common elderberry, basin wildrye, common snowberry, and sweetbriar rose, among others.

While trees aren't a dominant landscape feature of the region, small patches of forest persist across the Palouse—large, dark green spots on the landscape could be copses of ponderosa pine, Douglas fir, lodgepole pine, grand fir, western larch, Engelmann spruce, western hemlock, or western red cedar—a classic Pacific Northwest lineup. But because this is also the Intermountain West, you'll see some quaking aspen groves, as well as an occasional Lemmon's willow, especially in riparian areas and meadows, scarce though they may be in these generally high and dry parts. The Palouse typically gets only 10–20 inches of rain per year.

Just because the grassland prairie is now mostly cultivated farmland doesn't mean the wildlife has gone away. Mule deer, Columbian white-tailed deer, coyote, bobcat, raccoon, badger, porcupine, beaver, muskrat, black-tailed jackrabbit, eastern cottontail rabbit, Columbian ground squirrel, black bear, and cougar are among the species doing just fine throughout the Palouse.

As for birds, northern harriers, red-tailed hawks, Swainson's hawks, and short-eared owls dine on a wide assortment of smaller fauna such as rodents and rabbits. Vesper sparrows, Savannah sparrows, and western meadowlarks eat the seeds and fresh sprouts of herbaceous plants; they have thrived on crops and agricultural waste throughout the region as farms proliferated. Less common since the major conversion to agriculture in the 1940s but still hanging on are ferruginous hawks, sharp-tailed grouse, long-billed curlews, upland sandpipers, and loggerhead shrikes.

Up here above it all, chukars and rock wrens dart around in the rarified airspace surrounding Steptoe Butte. These two cliff-dwelling bird species love heights, making Steptoe Butte's 1000-foot knob a perfect habitat for them.

▲ Steptoe Butte rises approximately 1000 feet above the surrounding grassland prairie of the Palouse, providing a great perch for chukar and rock wrens, not to mention a launch for human paragliders.

Of course, these birds, like most wildlife, are more active around the edges of the day. This also happens to be the best time to visit Steptoe Butte, as low-angled rays of sun bathe the hills in a reddish gold, almost-Martian aura. There might not be a better spot in Eastern Washington to watch the sun go down.

PALOUSE FALLS

DIFFICULTY
Easy to
moderate

LENGTH
0.5 to 1.25
miles

LOCATION
near Perry, Washington

*River drops nearly 200 feet into
stunning flood-carved canyon*

If you enjoy off-the-beaten-path destinations, Palouse Falls may be perfect for you, given it is truly in the middle of nowhere (half an hour's drive from the nearest human settlement, the small town of Hooper, population 54). Walking around the trails at Palouse Falls State Park is easy; the main overlooks are paved and the trails between them are sandy, flat, and free of obstructions. You will have no problem checking out the falls and the Palouse River Canyon below them from each of the strategically placed vantage points. Most people visit in the summer when the weather is most accommodating, but spring is the best time to see the waterfall running at its fullest and most spectacular.

While the fences are well maintained and do a good job of keeping visitors from falling into the gorge, keep a close eye on kids and pets and be careful. Watch out for rattlesnakes, which may be seeking

▲ Watch out for locals like this northern Pacific rattlesnake on the trails at Palouse Falls State Park.

shade under a bush or rock. Don't reach or step into any dark crevices, and when hiking around, step on top of big rocks or logs rather than over them, as a snake could be tucked under the other side where your foot might land. If you do see a rattlesnake or hear its warning buzz, calmly back away in the direction you came—that's what the snake's warning is telling you to do.

One other rattling hazard worth noting is the last 2.4 miles of the driving

approach. Once you turn off State Route 261 (at the marked entrance to Palouse Falls State Park), brace yourself for a bumpy ride on a washboard dirt road that will have you and your vehicle shaking. Batten down the hatches and take it slow, because you'll be out of cellular range and there's nary a tow truck for many miles.

⸱ Sculpted by the Missoula Floods, the plunge pool of Palouse Falls is a punchbowl of columnar basalt.

Given the last stretch of bumpy road, you'll be glad to finally pull into the parking area by the falls overlook. Park in one of the two dozen parking spots where the road dead-ends and walk down the paved trail to the main viewing area. Majestic Palouse Falls will come into view.

Picture-perfect Palouse Falls is a gorgeous sight as it bisects the columnar basalt walls of the canyon surrounding it. An upper section, Squaw Falls, drops 20 feet before sending the river down a shallower grade to the south for another 1000 feet before doglegging

The high desert plateau of Eastern Washington is a good place to find tumbleweed and other plant life that looks like it's right out of a Roadrunner cartoon. ▸

right and then plunging over the lip of Palouse Falls and dropping down to the canyon floor, 186 feet below. At the bottom, the river emerges out of its large plunge pool and continues flowing south to its confluence with the mighty Snake River 6 miles downstream, at the site of present-day Lyons Ferry State Park.

The Palouse River certainly has a large amount of flow, but there's no way it was ever strong enough to have carved out the huge, amphitheatrical gorge around it. That was the work of the Missoula Floods during the last ice age. An ice dam in what is now western Montana breached repeatedly between 15,000 and 13,000 years ago as the climate warmed, sending thundering torrents of water, icebergs, and mud at speeds topping 60 miles an hour across the present-day eastern side of Washington, through parts of Idaho and Oregon, down the Columbia River Gorge, and on to the Pacific Ocean.

At the top of the falls directly across from you, the ancient flood-waters ran several hundred feet deep, so think about the force exerted on the ground at the bottom of the plunge and you'll understand why it looks almost like a huge bomb crater. As soon as the floodwaters carved the canyon a new bottom, the raging torrent filled it to the brim and kept moving on its path of destruction.

The canyon walls that the waterfall bisects, let alone most of the bedrock underlying the 15,000-square-mile Channeled Scablands, are

Looking south over the Palouse
River Canyon.

Washingtonians love Palouse Falls so much, the State Legislature made it the official State Waterfall back in 2014 thanks to petitioning from local middle schoolers.

composed of columnar basalt created by magma oozing out of the ground through volcanic fissures in Earth's crust around 15 million years ago. As the magma cooled, contraction led to the formation of cracks at the surface which worked their way down through the hardening underlayers, forming the columnar appearance we see today.

It's hard to take your eyes off the waterfall, but another natural wonder may be vying for your attention. Listen for the click-whistle sound of yellow-bellied marmots who live in the rocks directly below the chain link fence. These 7- to 10-pound, around-20-inch-long rodents (some call them "giant ground squirrels") have grizzled gray fur on their faces and backs, yellow-white fur on their chests and bellies, and perky reddish tails trailing behind. Their signature call warns fellow marmots of threats nearby, such as the approach of humans (or coyotes or black bears). They live in burrows dug into the cliffside and connect with neighboring burrows via elaborate tunnel networks.

Biologists consider yellow-bellied marmots to be selective herbivores but that doesn't mean they're picky eaters ("selective" refers to the fact that they reject the toxic parts of plants while eating the rest, underscoring their adaptability). On the contrary, they feed on a wide range of plants, including whatever grasses, flowers, and forbs they can find, and liberally indulge their taste for seeds come late summer. During the coldest stretches of winter, they hibernate in their burrows, but otherwise are out and about on the cliffs.

Look for yellow-bellied marmots in the rocks below the main Palouse Falls overlook. ▸

Now that you've seen Palouse Falls in its full glory, check out the small trail network to the south which showcases some of the major plants of the Columbia Plateau shrub steppe ecosystem all around you. Big sagebrush, tumbleweed, yellow rabbitbrush, Idaho fescue, and antelope bitterbrush compete for the majority of real estate on the desert floor here (and beyond, throughout much of the Columbia Plateau). Western white clematis, seep monkeyflower, common yarrow, prairie goldenrod, pink alumroot, and Lewis mockorange lend a little color to the otherwise green and light brown scene. Saskatoon serviceberry, fragrant sumac, and sideoats grama grow along the canyon edge, with shoots sticking up here and there through the chain-link fence. Western juniper, boxelder, chokecherry, narrowleaf willow, and netleaf hackberry trees punctuate the landscape.

▴ Yellow rabbitbrush is one of the most common plants around Palouse Falls State Park.

Work your way south through this desert landscape to a higher overlook that offers a different perspective of the waterfall as well as additional views of the river's canyon course to the south. This more elaborate, covered upper overlook is named after the late Roald Fryxell, who was an anthropologist at nearby Washington State University in Pullman, Washington. Fryxell led excavation efforts back in the mid-1960s at one of the most significant archaeological finds in the country, the Marmes Rockshelter, just a few miles downstream from Palouse Falls.

▴ Big sagebrush sets off the spectacle of the waterfall.

MARMES ROCKSHELTER

Tens of millions of years ago, the elements of nature created a shallow cave in the basalt along the west bank of the Palouse River, near its junction with the Snake River. Excavating the geologic anomaly in the mid-1960s, Washington State University anthropologist Roald Fryxell and a team of students found human and elk remains, as well as primitive tools and weapons made out of stone and bone, dating back to the end of the last ice age, some 10,000 years ago. At the time, the uncovered human remains were significantly older than any other skeletal remains found in the Western Hemisphere. More recent discoveries of human remains in Idaho and California predate "Marmes Man," but Fryxell's discoveries at what became known as the Marmes Rockshelter remain some of the most significant in the history of American archaeology. Sadly, the site was submerged in 1969. A levee that had been built to protect the cave from flooding caused by a new dam failed, rendering the famous dig site indefinitely inaccessible.

When you've had enough of the splendid view from Fryxell's Overlook, loop back up through the picnic area behind you on your way back to the parking lot. Most visitors leave it at that, which amounts to about a half mile of walking, all told.

If you are craving more, you can extend your visit and add another 2000–2500 steps (1–1.25 miles) to your daily pedometer tally by walking north from the parking area on a gravel path marked by a series of log stumps. Continue on for another third of a mile alongside some forlorn train tracks. Turn right (south) on the second dirt path, descending into a small side canyon with views directly across to Squaw Falls. This is yet another place you can turn around.

But true thrill seekers can keep going even farther, although the trail starts to get unstable as it makes its way to its terminus at

Castle Rock, the rocky headland that forms the top of Palouse Falls' big 186-foot drop. If you make it this far, congratulations! Now it's definitely time to turn around and head back to the parking area. Watch your step, as the same hazards exist on the way back as you encountered on the way out.

If you're a camper, you can spend the night in the campground adjacent to the waterfall overlook, falling asleep to the soothing and constant sound of falling water. If you can't spend the night, close your eyes and listen to the waterfall one last time before driving away—the tranquility will prepare you for the return trip on that washboard dirt road.

▲ The view of Palouse Falls and the Palouse River Canyon from Fryxell's Overlook.

LIST OF SPECIES

Plants

Alpine buckwheat + *Eriogonum pyrolifolium*

Alpine speedwell + *Veronica wormskjoldii*

American brooklime + *Veronica americana*

American dunegrass + *Leymus mollis*

American trailplant + *Adenocaulon bicolor*

Annual Indian paintbrush + *Castilleja exilis*

Antelope bitterbrush + *Purshia tridentata*

Applegate's Indian paintbrush + *Castilleja applegatei*

Arrowleaf balsamroot + *Balsamorhiza sagittata*

Austin's knotweed + *Polygonum austiniae*

Avalanche lily + *Erythronium montanum*

Bastardsage + *Eriogonum wrightii*

Beaked hazelnut + *Corylus cornuta*

Beaked spikerush + *Eleocharis rostellata*

Beard moss + *Ramalinaceae*

Beargrass + *Xerophyllum tenax*

Bicolor lupine + *Lupinus bicolor*

Big galleta + *Pleuraphis rigida*

Big sagebrush + *Artemisia tridentata*

Bigbract verbena + *Verbena bracteata*

Bigleaf maple + *Acer macrophyllum*

Bigseed biscuitroot + *Lomatium macrocarpum*

Bitterroot + *Lewisia rediviva*

Black cottonwood + *Populus trichocarpa*

Black hawthorn + *Crataegus douglasii*

Blazing star + *Mentzelia laevicaulis*

Bleeding heart + *Dicentra formosa*

Bloody crane's-bill + *Geranium sanguineum*

Blue bunchgrass + *Festuca idahoensis*

Blue field gilia + *Gilia capitata* ssp. *capitata*

Blue-eyed Mary + *Collinsia grandiflora*

Bluebunch wheatgrass + *Pseudoroegneria spicata*

Bonneville shootingstar + *Dodecatheon conjugens*

Bracken fern + *Pteridium aquilinum*

Bracket polypore + *Ganoderma basidiomycota*

Bracted lousewort + *Pedicularis bracteosa* var. *atrosanguinea*

Bride's bonnet + *Clintonia uniflora*

Brittle bladderfern + *Cystopteris fragilis*

Broadleaf cattail + *Typha latifolia*

Broadleaf lupine + *Lupinus latifolius*

Broadleaf stonecrop + *Sedum spathulifolium*

Broom snakeweed + *Gutierrezia sarothrae*

Brownplume wirelettuce + *Stephanomeria pauciflora*

Bulbous woodland-star + *Lithophragma glabrum*

Bull thistle + *Cirsium vulgare*

Butter-and-eggs + *Linaria vulgaris*

California fescue + *Festuca californica* var. *californica*

California spikenard + *Aralia californica*

Canada thistle + *Cirsium arvense*

Canadian horseweed + *Conyza canadensis*

Canadian milkvetch + *Astragalus canadensis*

Cascade aster + *Eucephalus ledophyllus*

Cascade barberry + *Mahonia nervosa*

Cat's ear + *Hypochoeris radicata*

Cheatgrass + *Bromus tectorum*

Cloudberry + *Rubus chamaemorus*

Coast larkspur + *Delphinium menziesii*

Coastal gumweed + *Grindelia maritima*

Common bistort + *Bistorta officinalis*

Common bugloss + *Anchusa officinalis*

Common camas + *Camassia quamash*

Common chokecherry + *Prunus virginiana*

Common columbine + *Aquilegia vulgaris*

Common elderberry + *Sambucus racemosa*

Common hawthorn + *Crataegus monogyna*

Common mullein + *Verbascum thapsus*

Common reed + *Phragmites australis*

Common snowberry + *Symphoricarpos albus*

Common St. John's wort + *Hypericum perforatum*

Common vetch + *Vicia sativa*

Common woolly sunflower + *Eriophyllum lanatum*

Common yarrow + *Achillea millefolium*

Coralroot orchid + *Corallorhiza mertensiana*

Cottonwood + *Populus deltoides*

Cous biscuitroot + *Lomatium cous*

Cow parsnip + *Heracleum lanatum*

Creeping barberry + *Mahonia repens*

Creeping thistle + *Cirsium arvense*

Cuddy Mountain onion + *Allium fibrillum*

Curl Leaf Mountain Mahogany + *Cercocarpus ledifolius*

Curly dock + *Rumex crispus*

Curlycup gumweed + *Grindelia squarrosa*

Cushion phlox + *Phlox pulvinata*

Cusick's Indian paintbrush + *Castilleja cusickii*

Darkthroat shootingstar + *Dodecatheon pulchellum*

Deer fern + *Blechnum spicant*

Deltoid balsamroot + *Balsamorhiza deltoidea*

Desert cryptantha + *Cryptantha angustifolia*

Desert Indian paintbrush + *Castilleja angustifolia*

Dewberry + *Rubus pubescens*

Douglas fir + *Pseudotsuga menziesii*

Douglas' buckwheat + *Eriogonum douglasii*

Douglas' aster + *Symphyotrichum subspicatum*

Douglas' monkeyflower + *Diplacus (Mimulus) douglasii*

Douglas' spirea + *Spiraea douglasii*

Dwarf evening-primrose + *Eremothera pygmaea*

Dwarf phacelia + *Phacelia tetramera*

Dwarf yellow fleabane + *Erigeron chrysopsidis*

Eelgrass + *Zostera marina*

Elephant's head + *Pedicularis groenlandica*

Elkweed + *Frasera speciosa*

Elm + *Ulmus* species

Engelmann spruce + *Picea engelmannii*

European sea rocket + *Cakile maritima*

Evergreen huckleberry + *Vaccinium ovatum*

False azalea + *Menziesia ferruginea*

False Solomon's seal + *Maianthemum racemosum*

Fawn lily + *Erythronium elegans*

Field sagewort + *Artemisia campestris* var. *scouleriana*

Flannel bush + *Fremontodendron*

Flett's fleabane + *Erigeron flettii*

Flett's violet + *Viola flettii*

Fool's Onion + *Brodiaea hyacinthina*

Gairdner's penstemon + *Penstemon gairdneri*

Garden valerian + *Valeriana officinalis*

Giant helleborine + *Epipactis gigantea*

Giant horsetail + *Equisetum telmateia*

Ginkgo + *Ginkgo*

Glacier lily + *Erythronium grandiflorum*

Globe penstemon + *Penstemon globosus*

Goatsbeard lichen + *Alectoria*

Goldencarpet buckwheat + *Eriogonum luteolum*

Grand fir + *Abies grandis*

Gray's lovage + *Ligusticum grayi*

Greasewood + *Sarcobatus vermiculatus*

Great Basin wild rye + *Leymus cinereus*

Green false hellebore/Indian hellebore + *Veratrum viride*

Green's mountain ash + *Sorbus scopulina*

Hairy clematis + *Clematis hirsutissima*

Hairy vetch + *Vicia villosa*

Harsh Indian Paintbrush + *Castilleja hispida*

Hall's violet + *Viola hallii*

Harvest brodiaea + *Brodiaea coronaria*

Heartleaf arnica + *Arnica cordifolia*

Hedgehog cactus + *Pediocactus simpsonii*

Henderson's rock spirea + *Petrophytum hendersonii*

Henderson's shooting star + *Dodecatheon hendersonii*

Hoary aster + *Dieteria canescens*

Hoary balsamroot + *Balsamorhiza incana*

Hoary cress + *Lepidium draba*

Hoary manzanita + *Arctostaphylos canescens*

Hood's phlox + *Phlox hoodii*

Hookedspur violet + *Viola adunca*

Hooker's indian pink + *Silene hookeri* ssp. *hookeri*

Hooker's willow + *Salix hookeriana*

Idaho fescue + *Festuca idahoensis*

Indian paintbrush + *Castilleja parviflora*

Indian ricegrass + *Oryzopsis hymenoides*

Inflated grasswidow + *Olsynium douglasii* var. *inflatum*

Jeffrey pine + *Pinus jeffreyi*

Juniper haircap moss + *Polytrichum juniperi*

Klamath fescue + *Festuca roemeri* var. *klamathensis*

Knobcone pine + *Pinus attenuata*

Koehler's rock cress + *Arabis koehleri* var. *stipitata*

Lady fern + *Athyrium filix-femina*

Lambstongue ragwort + *Senecio integerrimus*

Lance-leaf springbeauty + *Claytonia lanceolata* var. *pacifica*

Large-fruited desert parsley + *Lomatium macrocarpum*

Large-leaved lupine + *Lupinus polyphyllus*

Largeflower triteleia + *Triteleia grandiflora* var. *grandiflora*

Largehead clover + *Trifolium macrocephalum*

Lemmon's willow + *Salix lemmonii*

Lesser-bladder milkvetch + *Astragalus microcystis*

Licorice fern + *Polypodium glycyrrhiza*

Locoweed + *Oxytropis campestris*

Lodgepole pine +*Pinus contorta*

Longleaf phlox + *Phlox longifolia*

Low larkspur + *Delphinium bicolor*

Low pussytoes + *Antennaria dimorpha*

Madwort + *Asperugo procumbens*

Map lichen + *Rhizocarpon geographicum*

Maple + *Acer* species

McDonald's rockcress + *Arabis macdonaldiana*

Meadow deathcamas + *Zigadenus venenosus*

Meadow hawkweed + *Hieracium pratense*

Menzies' penstemon + *Penstemon davidsonii* var. *Menziesii*

Mock orange + *Philadelphus lewisii*

Morning glory + *Ipomoea* species

Moth mullein + *Verbascum blattaria*

Mountain hemlock + *Tsuga mertensiana*

Munro's globemallow + *Sphaeralcea munroana*

Naked broomrape + *Orobanche uniflora* var. *occidentalis*

Naked buckwheat + *Eriogonum nudum*

Narrowleaf mock goldenweed + *Nestotus stenophyllus*

Narrow-sepaled phacelia + *Phacelia hastata* var. *leptosepala*

Needle-and-thread grass + *Hesperostipa comata*

Netleaf hackberry + *Celtis reticulata*

Nineleaf biscuitroot + *Lomatium triternatum*

Noble fir + *Abies procera*

Nodding arnica + *Arnica parryi*

Nootka rose + *Rosa nutkana*

Ocean spray + *Holodiscus discolor*

Old man's whiskers + *Geum triflorum*

Old man's beard + *Usnea longissima*

Olympic aster + *Aster paucicapitatus*

Olympic Mountain synthyris + *Synthyris pinnatifida* var. *lanuginosa*

Olympic Mountain groundsel + *Senecio neowebsteri*

Oregon ash + *Fraxinus latifolia*

Oregon boxleaf + *Paxistima myrsinites*

Oregon grape + *Mahonia aquifolium*

Oregon oxalis + *Oxalis oregana*

Oregon white oak + *Quercus garryana*

Oval-leaf blueberry + *Vaccinium ovalifolium*

Pacific crabapple +*Malus fusca*

Pacific dogwood + *Cornus nuttallii*

Pacific madrone + *Arbutus menziesii*

Pacific ninebark + *Physocarpus malvaceus*

Pacific poison oak + *Toxicodendron diversilobum*

Pacific rhododendron + *Rhododendron macrophyllum*

Pacific yew + *Taxus brevifolia*

Palouse thistle + *Cirsium brevifolium*

Paper birch + *Betus papyrifera*

Parry's catchfly + *Silene parryi*

Parsley fern + *Cryptogramma cascadensis*

Parsnipflower buckwheat + *Eriogonum heracleoides* var. *angustifolium*

Pearly pussytoes + *Antennaria anaphaloides*

Pink alumroot + *Heuchera rubescens*

Pink honeysuckle + *Lonicera tatarica*

Pink mountain-heather + *Phyllodoce empetriformis*

Piper's bellflower + *Campanula piperi*

Ponderosa pine + *Pinus ponderosa*

Porcupine sedge + *Carex hystericina*

Port Orford cedar + *Chamaecyparis lawsoniana*

Prairie clover + *Dalea ornata*

Prairie star + *Lithophragma parviflorum*

Prickly lettuce + *Lactuca serriola*

Puget Sound gumweed + *Grindelia integrifolia*

Purple and white Chinese houses + *Collinsia heterophylla*

Purple loosestrife + *Lythrum salicaria*

Purple milkvetch + *Astragalus danicus*

Purple sage + *Salvia dorrii*

Quaking aspen + *Populus tremuloides*

Queen Anne's lace + *Daucus carota*

Rat-tail fescue + *Vulpia myuros* (var. *hirsuta*)

Red alder + *Alnus rubra*

Red fescue + *Festuca rubra*

Red flowering currant + *Ribes sanguineum*

Red osier dogwood + *Cornus sericea*

Reed canary grass + *Phalaris arundinacea*

Rigid sagebrush + *Artemisia rigida*

Rosy plectritis + *Plectritis congesta*

Round-leaved violet + *Viola orbiculata*

Rubber rabbitbrush + *Ericameria nauseosa*

Rush pussytoes + *Antennaria luzuloides*

Russian knapweed + *Rhaponticum repens*

Sagebrush buttercup + *Ranunculus glaberrimus*

Sagebrush mariposa lily + *Calochortus macrocarpus*

Sagebrush stickseed + *Hackelia diffusa*

Salal + *Gaultheria shallon*

Salmonberry + *Rubus spectabilis*

Sand dropseed + *Sporobolus cryptandrus*

Sand verbena + *Abronia*

Sandberg's bluegrass + *Poa sandbergii*

Saskatoon serviceberry + *Amelanchier alnifolia*

Saxifrage + *Saxifraga* species

Scarlet gilia + *Ipomopsis aggregata* ssp. *aggregata*

Scythe-leaf onion + *Allium falcifolium*

Serpentine fern + *Aspidotis densa*

Shaggy fleabane + *Erigeron pumilus*

Shasta red fir + *Abies magnifica*

Shooting star + *Dodecatheon* species

Short-lobe Indian paintbrush + *Castilleja brevilobata*

Showy phlox + *Phlox speciosa*

Showy sedge + *Carex spectabilis*

Shrubby cinquefoil + *Dasiphora fruticosa*

Sideoats grama + *Bouteloua curtipendula*

Siskiyou mat (Siskiyou ceanothus) + *Ceanothus pumilus*

Siskiyou iris + *Iris bracteata*

Sitka mountain ash + *Sorbus sitchensis*

Sitka spruce + *Picea sitchensis*

Sitka valerian + *Valeriana sitchensis*

Slender bog orchid + *Platanthera stricta*

Slender cryptantha + *Cryptantha gracilis*

Small fescue + *Vulpia microstachys*

Small-flowered bulrush + *Scirpus microcarpus*

Small-flowered paintbrush + *Castilleja parviflora*

Smooth cliffbrake + *Pellaea glabella*

Smooth sumac + *Rhus glabra*

Snow buckwheat + *Eriogonum nervulosum*

Snow queen + *Synthyris reniformis*

Spiny hopsage + *Grayia spinosa*

Spiny phlox + *Phlox hoodii*

Spreading wood fern + *Dryopteris expansa*

Spruce + *Picea* species

Sticky cinquefoil + *Potentilla glandulosa*

Sticky whiteleaf manzanita + *Arctostaphylos viscida*

Subalpine fir + *Abies lasiocarpa*

Sugar pine + *Pinus lambertiana*

Suksdorf's monkeyflower + *Mimulus suksdorfii*

Suksdorf's woodsorrel + *Oxalis suksdorfii*

Sulfur cinquefoil + *Potentilla recta*

Sulfur buckwheat +*Eriogonum umbellatum*

Sunflower mule-ears + *Wyethia helianthoides*

Tailcup lupine + *Lupinus caudatus*

Tall fescue + *Schedonorus arundinaceus*

Ternate buckwheat + *Eriogonum ternatum*

Thimbleberry + *Rubus parviflorus*

Thinleaf alder + *Alnus incana tenuifolia*

Thinleaf huckleberry + *Vaccinium membranaceum*

Threadleaf fleabane + *Erigeron filifolius*

Three-tip sagebrush + *Artemisia tripartita*

Thurber's needlegrass + *Achnatherum thurberianum*

Tiger lily + *Lilium columbianum*

Tisch's saxifrage + *Saxifraga tischii*

Tobacco root + *Valeriana edulis*

Tolm's onion + *Allium tolmiei*

Tolmie's saxifrage + *Micranthes tolmiei*

Tolmie's mariposa lily + *Calochortus tolmiei*

Twinberry honeysuckle + *Lonicera involucrata*

Twistedstalk + *Streptopus amplexifolius*

Two-eyed violet + *Viola ocellata*

Velvetleaf huckleberry + *Vaccinium myrtilloides*

Virginia strawberry + *Fragaria virginiana*

Waldo rockcress + *Arabis aculeolata*

Wallowa onion + *Allium tolmiei* var. *platyphyllum*

Western pearly everlasting + *Anaphalis margaritacea*

Western bracken fern + *Pteridium aquilinum*

Western columbine + *Aquilegia formosa*

Western crabapple + *Malus fusca*

Western goldenrod + *Euthamia occidentalis*

Western hemlock + *Tsuga heterophylla*

Western juniper + *Juniperus occidentalis*

Western larch + *Larix occidentalis*

Western red cedar + *Thuja plicata*

Western snowberry + *Symphoricarpos occidentalis*

Western starflower + *Trientalis latifolia*

Western swordfern + *Polystichum munitum*

Western trillium + *Trillium ovatum*

Western white pine + *Pinus monticola*

White fir + *Abies concolor*

White flower rein orchid + *Platanthera ephemerantha*

White-stemmed frasera + *Frasera albicaulis*

Wicker buckwheat + *Epilobium vimineum*

Wild buckwheat + *Fallopia convolvulus*

Winterfat + *Krascheninnikovia lanata*

Wood forget-me-not + *Myosotis sylvatica*

Woodsage + *Teucrium scorodonia*

Woodland strawberry + *Fragaria vesca*

Woods' rose + *Rosa woodsii*

Woolly sedge + *Carex pellita*

Yellow evening-primrose + *Oenothera flava*

Yellow fritillary + *Fritillaria pudica*

Yellow iris + *Iris pseudacorus*

Yellow rabbitbrush + *Chrysothamnus viscidiflorus*

Yellow salsify + *Tragopogon dubius*

Yellow willow + *Salix lutea*

Animals

Aggregating anemone + *Anthopleura elegantissima*

American badger + *Taxidea taxus*

American beaver + *Castor canadensis*

American black bear + *Ursus americanus*

American coot + *Fulica americana*

American dipper + *Cinclus mexicanus*

American kestrel + *Falco sparverius*

American pipit + *Anthus rubescens*

American red squirrel + *Tamiasciurus hudsonicus*

American robin + *Turdus migratorius*

American wigeon + *Mareca americana*

Anna's hummingbird + *Calypte anna*

Bald eagle + *Haliaeetus leucocephalus*

Barn swallow + *Hirundo rustica*

Barrow's goldeneye + *Bucephala islandica*

Belding's ground squirrel + *Urocitellus beldingi*

Belted kingfisher + *Megaceryle alcyon*

Bewick's wren + *Thryomanes bewickii*

Black bear + *Ursus americanus*

Black oystercatcher + *Haematopus bachmani*

Black swift + *Cypseloides niger*

Black-billed magpie + *Pica hudsonia*

Black-capped chickadee + *Poecile atricapillus*

Black-crowned night heron + *Nycticorax nycticorax*

Black-tailed jackrabbit + *Lepus californicus*

Blue dasher + *Pachydiplax longipennis*

Blue-winged teal + *Anas discors*

Bobcat + *Lynx rufus*

Boisduval's blue + *Aricia icarioides*

Brandt's cormorant + *Phalacrocorax penicillatus*

Brewer's sparrow + *Spizella breweri*

Brook stickleback + *Culaea inconstans*

Brook trout + *Salvelinus fontinalis*

Brown pelican + *Pelecanus occidentalis*

Brown trout + *Salmo trutta*

Bufflehead + *Bucephala albeola*

Bull trout + *Salvelinus confluentus*

Bullock's oriole + *Icterus bullockii*

Bushtit + *Psaltriparus minimus*

Bushy tailed woodrats + *Neotoma cinere*

Butter clam + *Saxidomus giganteus*

Caddisfly + *Trichoptera*

California mountain kingsnake + *Lampropeltis zonata*

California quail + *Callipepla californica*

California sea lion + *Zalophus californianus*

California sister + *Adelpha californica*

Canada goose + *Branta canadensis*

Canvasback + *Aythya valisineria*

Canyon wren + *Catherpes mexicanus*

Cardinal meadowhawk + *Sympetrum illotum*

Cascade golden-mantled ground squirrel + *Callospermophilus saturatus*

Cedar waxwing + *Bombycilla cedrorum*

Chinook salmon + *Oncorhynchus tshawytscha*

Chukar + *Alectoris chukar*

Chum salmon + *Oncorhynchus keta*

Cinnamon teal + *Anas cyanoptera*

Coho salmon + *Oncorhynchus kisutch*

Columbian black-tailed deer + *Odocoileus hemionus columbianus*

Columbian ground squirrel + *Urocitellus columbianus*

Columbian white-tailed deer + *Odocoileus virginianus leucurus*

Common garter snake + *Thamnophis sirtalis*

Common goldeneyes + *Bucephala clangula*

Common loon + *Gavia immer*

Common merganser + *Mergus merganser*

Common murre + *Uria aalge*

Common nighthawk + *Chordeiles minor*

Common poorwill + *Phalaenoptilus nuttallii*

Common slider + *Trachemys scripta*

Common wood nymph + *Cercyonis pegala*

Common yellowthroat + *Geothlypis trichas*

Cooper's hawk +*Accipiter cooperii*

Copepod + *Copepoda*

Cougar + *Puma concolor*

Coyote + *Canis latrans*

Crayfish + *Cambarus*

Crystal jellyfish + *Aequorea victoria*

Cutthroat trout + *Oncorhynchus clarkii*

Dall's porpoise + *Phocoenoides dalli*

Dark-eyed junco + *Junco hyemalis*

Darkling beetle + *Tenebrionidae*

Del Norte salamander + *Plethodon elongatus*

Douglas squirrel + *Tamiasciurus douglasii*

Dowitcher + *Limnodromus* species

Downy woodpecker + *Picoides pubescens*

Dungeness crab + *Metacarcinus magister*

Eastern cottontail rabbit + *Sylvilagus floridanus*

Eight-spotted skimmer + *Libellula forensis*

Peregrine falcon + *Falco peregrinus*

Ferruginous hawk + *Buteo regalis*

Fried egg jellyfish + *Phacellophora camtschatica*

Gadwall + *Mareca strepera*

Ghost shrimp + *Palaemonetes paludosus*

Gold-hunter's hairstreak + *Satyrium auretorum*

Golden eagle + *Aquila chrysaetos*

Golden hairstreak butterfly + *Habrodais grunus*

Golden kinglet + *Regulus satrapa*

Golden-crowned sparrow + *Zonotrichia atricapilla*

Goldeneye + *Bucephala clangula*

Goldfinch + *Spinus tristis*

Gray fox + *Urocyon cinereoargenteus*

Gray whale + *Eschrichtius robustus*

Gray-crowned rosy-finch + *Leucosticte tephrocotis*

Great blue heron + *Ardea herodias*

Great egret + *Ardea alba*

Great horned owl + *Bubo virginianus*

Great spangled fritillary + *Speyeria cybele*

Greater sage-grouse + *Centrocercus urophasianus*

Greater yellowlegs + *Tringa melanoleuca*

Greater scaup + *Aythya myrila*

Green darner + *Anax junius*

Green heron + *Butorides virescens*

Green-winged teal + *Anas carolinensis*

Grizzly bear + *Ursus arctos*

Ground squirrel + *Marmotini*

Harbor porpoise + *Phocoena phocoena*

Harbor seal + *Phoca vitulina*

Harlequin duck + *Histrionicus histrionicus*

Heart cockle + *Corculum cardissa*

Hoary marmot + *Marmota caligata*

Hooded merganser + *Lophodytes cucullatus*

Horned grebe + *Podiceps auritus*

Horned lark + *Eremophila alpestris*

Horse clam + *Tresus capax*

House finch + *Haemorhous mexicanus*

Humpback whale + *Megaptera novaeangliae*

Ice worm + *Mesenchytraeus solifugus*

Killdeer + *Charadrius vociferus*

Ladybug + *Coccinellidae*

Lahontan cutthroat trout + *Oncorhynchus clarkii henshawi*

Lapland longspur + *Calcarius lapponicus*

Lark sparrow + *Chondestes grammacus*

Lazuli bunting + *Passerina amoena*

Least chipmunk + *Tamias minimus*

Least sandpiper + *Calidris minutilla*

Lesser scaup + *Aythya affinis*

Lesser yellowlegs + *Tringa flavipes*

Lilac-bordered copper + *Lycaena nivalis*

Lion's mane jellyfish + *Cyanea capillata*

Loggerhead shrike + *Lanius ludovicianus*

Long-billed curlew + *Numenius americanus*

Long-eared myotis bat + *Myotis evotis*

Long-tailed weasel + *Mustela frenata*

Lorquin's admiral + *Limenitis lorquini*

Mallard + *Anas platyrhynchos*

Marbled murrelet + *Brachyramphus marmoratus*

Mayfly + *Ephemeroptera*

Merriam's ground squirrel + *Spermophilus canus*

Milbert's tortoiseshell + *Aglais milberti*

Monarch + *Danaus plexippus*

Moon jellyfish + *Aurelia labiata*

Moose + *Alces alces*

Mormon metalmark + *Apodemia mormo*

Mountain bluebird + *Sialia currucoides*

Mountain cottontail + *Sylvilagus nuttallii*

Mountain whitefish + *Prosopium williamsoni*

Mourning cloak + *Nymphalis antiopa*

Mule deer + *Odocoileus hemionus*

Muskrat + *Ondatra zibethicus*

Mute swan + *Cygnus olor*

North American porcupine + *Erethizon dorsatum*

North American river otter + *Lontra canadensis*

Northern alligator lizard + *Elgaria coerulea*

Northern flicker + *Colaptes auratus*

Northern flying squirrel + *Glaucomys sabrinus*

Northern goshawk + *Accipiter gentilis*

Northern harrier + *Circus cyaneus*

Northern leopard frog + *Lithobates pipiens*

Northern Pacific rattlesnake + *Crotalus oreganus*

Northern pikeminnow + *Ptychocheilus oregonensis*

Northern pintail + *Anas acuta*

Northern pygmy owl + *Glaucidium californicum*

Northern river otter + *Lontra canadensis*

Northern shoveler + *Spatula clypeata*

Northern spotted owl + *Strix occidentalis caurina*

Northwest garter snake + *Thamnophis sirtalis*

Olive scud + *Gammarus lacustris*

Olive-sided flycatcher + *Contopus cooperi*

Olympia oyster + *Ostrea lurida*

Olympic gull + *Larus glaucescens × occidentalis*

Olympic marmot + *Marmota olympus*

Orange-crowned warbler + *Vermivora celata*

Orca whale + *Orcinus orca*

Orchard mason bee + *Osmia lignaria*

Oregon spotted frog + *Rana pretiosa*

Osprey + *Pandion haliaetus*

Pacific chorus frog + *Pseudacris regilla*

Pacific fisher + *Pekania pennanti*

Pacific geoduck + *Panopea abrupta*

Pacific giant salamander + *Decamptodon tenebrosus*

Pacific loon + *Gavia pacifica*

Pacific oyster + *Crassostrea gigas*

Pacific tree frog + *Pseudacris regilla*

Painted lady + *Vanessa cardui*

Peregrine falcon + *Falco peregrinus*

Pied-billed grebe + *Podilymbus podiceps*

Pigeon guillemot + *Cepphus columba*

Pika + *Ochotona princeps*

Pileated woodpecker + *Dryocopus pileatus*

Pine grosbeak + *Pinicola enucleator*

Pink salmon + *Oncorhynchus gorbuscha*

Prairie falcon + *Falco mexicanus*

Pronghorn antelope + *Antilocapra americana*

Propertius duskywing + *Erynnis propertius*

Pseudoscorpion + order Pseudoscorpionida

Pumpkinseed + *Lepomis gibbosus*

Pygmy rabbit + *Brachylagus idahoensis*

Raccoon + *Procyon lotor*

Rainbow trout + *Oncorhynchus mykiss*

Razor clam + *Siilqua patula*

Red crossbill + *Loxia curvirostra*

Red-breasted merganser + *Mergus serrator*

Red-necked grebe + *Podiceps grisegena*

Red-necked phalarope + *Phalaropus lobatus*

Red-tailed hawk + *Buteo jamaicensis*

Red-throated loon + *Gavia stellata*

Red-winged blackbird + *Agelaius phoeniceus*

Redband trout + *Oncorhynchus mykiss gairdnerii*

Redhead + *Aythya americana*

Redside shiner + *Richardsonius balteatus*

Ring-billed gull + *Larus delawarensis*

Ring-necked duck + *Aythya collaris*

Rock wren + *Salpinctes obsoletus*

Rocky Mountain elk + *Cervus canadensis nelsoni*

Roosevelt elk + *Cervus canadensis roosevelti*

Roth forest snail + *Anguispira picta*

Rough-legged hawk + *Buteo lagopus*

Ruby-crowned kinglet + *Regulus calendula*

Rufous hummingbird + *Selasphorus rufus*

Sage thrasher + *Oreoscoptes montanus*

Sagebrush checkerspot + *Chlosyne acastus*

Sagebrush lizard + *Sceloporus graciosus*

Sandhill crane + *Grus canadensis*

Savannah sparrow + *Passerculus sandwichensis*

Sharp-shinned hawk + *Accipiter striatus*

Sharp-tailed grouse + *Tympanuchus phasianellus*

Sheridan's green hairstreak + *Callophrys sheridanii*

Shiner perch + *Cymatogaster aggregata*

Snow goose + *Chen caerulescens*

Sockeye salmon + *Oncorhynchus nerka*

Softshell clam + *Mya arenaria*

Song sparrow + *Melospiza melodia*

Sooty grouse + *Dendragapus fuliginosus*

Speckled dace + *Rhinichthys osculus*

Spotted towhee + *Pipilo maculatus*

Spring azure + *Celastrina ladon*

Steelhead trout + *Oncorhynchus mykiss*

Steller sea lion + *Eumetopias jubatus*

Steller's jay + *Cyanocitta stelleri*

Stonefly + *Plecoptera*

Striped sunstar + *Solaster stimpsoni*

Sunflower sea star + *Pycnopodia helianthoides*

Swainson's hawk + *Buteo swainsoni*

Tailed frog + *Ascaphus truei*

Tiger trout + *Salmo trutta* × *Salvelinus fontinalis*

Townsend big-eared bat + *Corynorhinus townsendii*

Townsend's chipmunk + *Tamias townsendii*

Tree swallow + *Tachycineta bicolor*

Trumpeter swan + *Cygnus buccinator*

Tundra swan + *Cygnus columbianus*

Turkey vulture + *Cathartes aura*

Upland sandpiper + *Bartramia longicauda*

Vaux's swift + *Chaetura vauxi*

Vesper sparrow + *Pooecetes gramineus*

Violet-green swallow + *Tachycineta thalassina*

Virginia opossum + *Didelphis virginiana*

Western bluebird + *Sialia mexicana*

Western fence lizard + *Sceloporus occidentalis*

Western gray squirrel + *Sciurus griseus*

Western grebe + *Aechmorphorus occidentalis*

Western gull + *Larus occidentalis*

Western meadowlark + *Sturnella neglecta*

Western pine elfin + *Callophrys eryphon*

Western pondhawk + *Erythemis collocata*

Western tiger swallowtail + *Papilio rutulus*

Western toad + *Anaxyrus boreas*

White pelican + *Pelecanus erythrorhynchos*

White-headed woodpecker + *Picoides albolarvatus*

White-tailed ptarmigan + *Lagopus leucura*

White-throated swift + *Aeronautes saxatalis*

Willow flycatcher + *Empidonax traillii*

Wood duck + *Aix sponsa*

Yellow-bellied marmot + *Marmota flaviventris*

Yellow-breasted chat + *Icteria virens*

Yellow-headed blackbird + *Xanthocephalus xanthocephalus*

Yellow-pine chipmunk + *Tamias amoenus*

Yellow-rumped warbler + *Setophaga coronata*

Yuma bat + *Myotis yumanensis*

SELECTED REFERENCES

Oregon

DEAN CREEK ELK VIEWING AREA

Oregon Wild. "Roosevelt Elk." https://oregonwild.org/wildlife/roosevelt-elk

ROUGH AND READY BOTANICAL WAYSIDE

Oregon Wild. "Flowering Plants of the Rough & Ready Creek Watershed." https://oregonwild.org/sites/default/files/featured-imgs/rough_and_ready_plant_list_2015_2_column.pdf

OREGON CAVES, CLIFF NATURE TRAIL

Bat Conservation International. "Climate Change and Bats." https://www.batcon.org/article/climate-change-and-bats/#:˜:text=Increased%20variation%20in%20climatic%20extremes,birth%20and%20survival%20of%20pups

ROGUE RIVER NATURAL BRIDGE

Meengs, Chad C., and Robert T. Lackey. "Estimating the Size of Historical Oregon Salmon Runs." *Reviews in Fisheries Science* 13, no. 1: 51–66. http://osu-wams-blogs-uploads.s3.amazonaws.com/blogs.dir/2961/files/2017/07/6.-Estimating-the-Size-of-Historical-Oregon-Salmon-Runs.pdf

SALT CREEK FALLS

Northwest Waterfall Survey. Tallest Waterfalls in Oregon. https://www.waterfallsnorthwest.com/Oregon/tallest

ISLANDS IN TIME TRAIL

Malaby, Sarah. U.S. Department of Agriculture, U.S. Forest Service. "Plant of the Week: Rubber Rabbitbush." https://www.fs.fed.us/wildflowers/plant-of-the-week/ericameria_nauseosa.shtml

ZUMWALT PRAIRIE PRESERVE

Averett, Joshua P., Lesley R. Morris, Bridgett J. Naylor, Robert V. Taylor, Bryan A. Endress. "Vegetation Change Over Seven Years in the Largest Protected Pacific Northwest Bunchgrass Prairie Remnant." https://journals.plos.org/plosone/article?id=10.1371/journal.pone.0227337#

The Nature Conservancy. "What's in Bloom? A Guide to Wildflower Watching on the Zumwalt Prairie Preserve." https://www.conservation-gateway.org/ConservationByGeography/NorthAmerica/UnitedStates/oregon/Documents/2014-Zumwalt-WildflowerWatching.pdf

Washington

KALALOCH BEACH 4

Tucker, Dave. Geology Underfoot In Western Washington. Missoula, MT: Mountain Press, 2015. https://nwgeology.wordpress.com/the-fieldtrips/beach-4-olympic-coast-folded-rocks-overturned-turbidites-beds-an-angular-unconformity-seastacks-and-a-great-beach-walk/

QUINAULT RAIN FOREST

Dietrich, Willian. *Natural Grace.* Seattle: University of Washington Press, 2003.

McNulty, Tim. *Olympic National Park: A Natural History*, 4th ed. Seattle: University of Washington Press, 2018.

TIDELAND ECOLOGY TRAIL

Harris, Jill. "Aquatic Invasive Species Profile: Pacific oyster, *Crassostrea gigas.*" https://depts.washington.edu/oldenlab/wordpress/wp-content/uploads/2013/02/Crassostrea-gigas_Harris.pdf

Peter-Contesse, Tristan, and Betsy Peabody. Reestablishing Olympia Oyster Populations in Puget Sound, Washington. Seattle: Washington Sea Grant Program, 2005. https://wsg.washington.edu/wordpress/wp-content/uploads/Reestablishing-Olympia-Oyster.pdf

TOUCH OF NATURE INTERPRETIVE TRAIL

Washington Department of Fish and Wildlife. "Penrose Point State Park." https://wdfw.wa.gov/places-to-go/shellfish-beaches/280680

NISQUALLY VISTA TRAIL

Northwest Conifer Connections. "Focus on Subalpine Fir." http://nwconifers.blogspot.com/2018/01/focus-on-subalpine-fir.html

Walsh, Megan. U.S. National Park Service. "Climatic and Human Influences on the Fire and Vegetation History of Subalpine Meadows—Mount Rainier National Park." https://www.nps.gov/articles/mora-influences-subalpine-meadows.htm

The Nature Conservancy. Washington Nature. "Critical Mass: Washington's Shrinking Glaciers." https://www.washingtonnature.org/fieldnotes/critical-mass-washingtons-shrinking-glaciers

TRADITIONAL KNOWLEDGE TRAIL

Russell, Samantha. "The Stinging Truth About Nettles: They're Good." http://grownorthwest.com/2011/05/the-stinging-truth-about-nettles-they%E2%80%99re-good/

LAYSER CAVE

U.S. Forest Service. National Lichens & Air Quality Database and Clearinghouse. http://gis.nacse.org/lichenair/

Emerson, Amy. "Digging Up the Past: East Lewis County Man Preserves Ancient Heritage of Gifford Pinchot National Forest." https://www.chronline.com/stories/digging-up-the-past-east-lewis-county-man-preserves-ancient-heritage-of-gifford-pinchot-national,252254

DECEPTION FALLS NATURE TRAIL

U.S. Forest Service. High Elevation White Pines. https://www.fs.fed.us/rm/highelevationwhitepines/Threats/blister-rust-threat.htm

U.S. Department of Agriculture. U.S. Forest Service Rocky Mountain Research Station. "Return of the King: Western White Pine Conservation and Restoration in a Changing Climate." https://www.fs.usda.gov/rmrs/return-king-western-white-pine-conservation-and-restoration-changing-climate

GINKGO PETRIFIED FOREST

Feldkamp, Lisa. "Attacking Invasive Cheatgrass at Its Root." https://blog.nature.org/science/2016/09/07/attacking-invasive-cheatgrass-root-soil-microbes-biocontrol-sage/

Ginkgoales: Fossil Record. https://ucmp.berkeley.edu/seedplants/ginkgoales/ginkgofr.html#:~:text=Approximately%20seven%20million%20years%20ago,about%202.5%20million%20years%20ago

DRY FALLS

Washington Native Plant Society. "Plant Assemblages of the Shrub-Steppe." https://www.wnps.org/ecosystems/shrub-steppe

Visalli, Dana. "Rare Plant Inventory and Community Vegetation Survey Sun Lakes State Park." http://www.pacificbio.org/publications/vegetation/state_parks/wa_east/Sun_Lakes_Report_2004.pdf

Mormon Metalmark Butterfly. "Eastern Washington." http://www.bentler.us/eastern-washington/animals/insects/butterflies/mormon-metalmark-butterfly.aspx

ACKNOWLEDGMENTS

First and foremost I would like to thank Stacee Lawrence, senior acquisitions editor at Timber Press, for shepherding this wonderful project. Her guidance allowed me to expand on the template so expertly crafted by Tom Wessels, author of the predecessor New England edition, and turn it into my own conceptual oeuvre. I love the places it's taken me—both physically and metaphysically—and now you are along for the ride. Thanks for joining me!

I'd also like to thank Timber project editor Julie Talbot, who line edited my copy with exacting precision, helping me hone detailed descriptions and clarify overarching points into what I regard as a fun and informative read. She also made sure the image selects were the best choices to illustrate the different chapters in the book.

Thanks also go to Sarah Milhollin, Timber's photo editor, for talking me through returning to fundamentals in my photography so I could provide the tack-sharp pictures needed to illustrate the book. Her early guidance has led to a renewed passion for photography that will no doubt serve me well in years to come. Kevin McConnell, another Timber photo editor, was also instrumental in sourcing the photos of plants and animals that I wasn't able to take myself.

Further shout-outs go to *50 Hikes With Kids* series author Wendy Gorton for sharing her knowledge on the Zumwalt Prairie, and to Betsy Peabody of Puget Sound Restoration Fund for setting me straight on the difference between Olympia and Pacific oysters and providing some oversight on my descriptions of oyster ecology.

Big thanks also are in order to my wife and kids for putting up with first the travel away from home and then the sequestering needed to research and write this manuscript. The creation of this book was a labor of love indeed, and I couldn't have thrown myself into it without their support.

The bulk of the work was completed during 2020 when the world was locked down during the ascendance of COVID-19. This unique situation made the job harder in some ways—sites closed to the public, the ability to travel restricted, and so on. But it also pre-sented opportunities, including less-crowded roads, trails, and camp-grounds, and more time at home to ruminate at the computer—so I ran with them. In the end, the ability to focus on the book provided a great escape from the pandemic (and political) problems facing down the country in 2020.

In retrospect, I couldn't have imagined a better way to while away the pandemic and unrest than by focusing on the most timeless topic of all, nature. I learned a lot about our amazing world in the process, and I hope you will learn something, too, from the chapters herein.

PHOTOGRAPHY CREDITS

All photographs are by the author, except for the following:

Library of Congress / *A Giant Fir tree, with lumberjacks, one lying in cut in tree, and other persons in front of tree*, ca. 1902. Photograph. LC-USZ62-51851, page 179
Steve Matson, page 38 (bottom)
David R. McAdoo, page 73 (top)
Richard Ramsden, page 187 (bottom)
University of Washington Libraries, Special Collections, Francois Matthes, photographer, WAS3111, page 226 (top)

ALAMY STOCK PHOTO

agefotostock, page 87 (middle)
All Canada Photos, page 299
Arterra Picture Library, page 91
Botanic World, page 87 (right)
Rick & Nora Bowers, page 96
Dennis Frates, pages 142, 144
Valerie Garner, page 298
Gunter Marx, page 118 (top)
Lee Rentz, page 187 (middle)
Penny Rogers, page 87 (left)
Witold Skrypczak, page 226 (bottom)
UtCon Collection, page 187 (top)
Leon Werdinger, page 145
Westend61 GmbH, page 90

DREAMSTIME.COM

Dana Kenneth Johnson, page 102
Pnwnature, page 17

ISTOCK PHOTO

alexmak72427, page 303 (top right)
AL-Travelpicture, page 278 (top)
BirdImages, page 61
Alexander Denisenko, page 204 (bottom left)
estivillml, page 130
kahj19, page 128
Elmar Langle, page 177 (top)
Mooneydriver, page 278 (bottom)
Tomas Nevesely, page 13
NNehring, page 56
rdparis22, page 242 (bottom)

SHUTTERSTOCK

Karl Bartik, page 74
Ryan M. Bolton, page 317
Jennifer Bosvert, page 149 (top)
Cascade Creatives, page 239
Michael Chatt, page 137 (middle)
James Dalrymple, page 88
Danita Delimont, page 323
Georgia Evans, page 73 (bottom)
Frank Fichtmueller, page 199 (right)
Mark A Lee, page 27
MTKhaled mahmud, page 22 (right)
meunierd, page 147 (right)

Vladimir Kogan Michael, page 148

Robert Mutch, page 86 (right)

portgrimes, page 257

Tom Reichner, page 29

RosieRocket, page 244 (top)

zschnepf, page 114

Sundry Photography, page 147 (left)

WIKIMEDIA COMMONS

Steve Redman (MORA), page 267 (top)

Scott Rheam, U.S. Fish and Wildlife
     Service, page 297 (right)

Yellowstone National Park, page 146 (left)

**Used under a CC0 1.0 Universal
Public Domain Dedication:**

Patrick Alexander, page 287 (bottom)

Bernard Spragg, NZ, page 270 (right)

**Used under a CCA-SA
2.0 Generic license:**

Judy Gallagher, page 22 (left)

Matt Lavin, page 146 (right)

Melissa McMasters, page 16

Andy Morffew, pages 33, 217

pseudacris_regilla1, page 234

Rock wren, page 111

Björn S., page 86 (left)

Tom Thai, page 210

Used under a CCA-SA 3.0 license:

Olaf Oliviero Riemer, page 149 (bottom)

**Used under a CCA-SA 4.0
International license:**

VJAnderson, page 109

Gaia Leo, page 248 (top)

Krzysztof Golik, page 46 (top)

THISISINDIANCOUNTRY, page 255

**Used under a GNU Free
Documentation license:**

Walter Siegmund, page 44

INDEX

Acarospora, 314

acorn barnacle, 158

Alaska cedar, 185, 222, 247

alder, 138, 256

algae, 82, 126, 205, 297

alluvial fan, 37, 42

alpine aster, 274

alpine buckwheat, 225

alpine glacier, 165, 224, 225–227

alpine meadow, 146, 182, 191, 273

alpine speedwell, 225, 274

American badger, 138, 297–298, 306, 315

American beachgrass, 12, 23, 24

American beaver, 234–235, 306

American black bear, 21

American brooklime, 230

American bushtit, 118

American coot, 32, 232, 305

American dipper, 165, 271–272

American dunegrass, 193, 195

American ginseng, 174–175

American goldfinch, 198, 262

American Indians, 47, 106, 241, 254, 272, 314–315

American kestrel, 16, 138, 305

American mink, 263

American pika, 110, 111

American pipit, 275

American red squirrel, 305

American robin, 197, 232

American searocket, 12

American stinging nettles, 244–245

American trailplant, 72, 247

American white pelican, 149

American wigeon, 148, 232, 262, 305

AmeriCorps, 85

anadromous trout, 174

angular unconformity, 154

Anna's hummingbird, 22, 87, 118, 197, 232

annual Indian paintbrush, 296

antelope, 125, 275

antelope bitterbrush, 125, 295, 324

antibiotics, 127

Antiquities Act, 56

ant, 67, 87, 96, 118, 129, 138

Applegate Group, 60

Applegate's Indian paintbrush, 136

arctic sweet coltsfoot, 154

argillite, 79–80

arrowleaf balsamroot, 117, 146, 296, 304

Asterisk Pass, 119, 120

Austin Pass Picnic Area, 273

Austin's knotweed, 297

avalanche lily, 274

bacteria, 170, 172

Bagley Glacier, 274

bald eagle, 16, 22, 32, 73, 118, 118–119, 148, 160, 165, 175–176, 216–217, 257–259

ballhead waterleaf, 146

banana slug, 154, 165

bark beetle, 170

barley, 311

barnacles, 158, 160

Barnes Butte, 113

barn swallow, 15–16, 197

barred owl, 73

Barrow's goldeneye, 298

basalt, 11, 13, 69, 71, 73–76, 85, 90, 92, 95, 96, 101–102, 106–107, 109, 111, 113, 123–124, 284–285, 290–295, 298, 307, 308, 311–313, 313, 318, 323, 325

basin wildrye, 315

bastardsage, 287

bat, 60–61, 68, 306
beach morning glory, 12
beadruby, 154
beaked hazelnut, 72, 213, 216, 242
beaked spikerush, 296
bears, 41, 73, 160, 165, 174, 203, 269, 284
bearberry, 21
beard moss, 265, 272
beargrass, 94
beaver, 33, 284, 315
Beck, George, 283, 284, 285
bees, 40, 257
beetles, 16, 21, 22, 60, 62, 87, 118, 129, 138, 170, 233, 268, 270, 300
Belding's ground squirrel, 138, 148
belted kingfisher, 22, 196, 232
Bering Land Bridge, 124
Bewick's wren, 87, 232
bicolor lupine, 117
bigbract verbena, 302, 303
big galleta, 287
bigleaf maple, 53, 71, 173, 175, 202, 205, 212, 230, 267
Big Meadow Trail, 190
big sagebrush, 125–126, 134, 287, 295, 324
bigseed biscuitroot, 146
Billy Frank Jr. Nisqually National Wildlife Refuge, 252–263
Billy Frank Jr. Tell Your Story Act, 255
birds, 15–16, 22–25, 32, 41, 46, 64, 73, 87, 90, 91, 96–98, 110, 117–119, 125, 127–129, 138, 147–149, 160–161, 165, 175–177, 193, 196–198, 199, 203, 213, 216, 232–233, 248, 253–254, 257, 269, 275, 298–299, 304–305, 315
birdsfoot trefoil, 12
bitterbrush, 125
bitterroot, 296, 304
black bear, 41, 73, 160, 165, 174, 270, 279, 315
blackberry, 247
black-billed magpie, 138

black-capped chickadee, 232
black cottonwood, 85, 117, 230, 296, 306
black-crowned night heron, 298
black hawthorn, 314–315
black locust, 247
black oak, 247
black oystercatcher, 16, 161, 196
black scoter, 16
black swift, 96–98, 275
black-tailed deer, 109
black-tailed jackrabbit, 297, 298, 315
black-throated gray warbler, 32
black turnstone, 16, 161
blazing star, 137
bleeding heart, 243, 274
bloody crane's-bill, 230
blowdowns, 170–171
Blue Basin, 131–141
Blue Basin Trail, 131
bluebell, 146
blue bunchgrass, 193, 195
bluebunch wheatgrass, 295, 315
blue camas, 45, 47
blue dasher dragonfly, 231
blue-eyed Mary, 86, 87
Blue Glacier, 183
blue-winged teal, 148, 305
boarding, 20
boardwalks, 49–50
bobcat, 21, 29, 73, 165, 297, 315
Bogachiel River, 163
bog blueberry, 21
Boisduval's blue butterfly, 300
Bolander's onion, 53
Boldt, George H., 254
Bonaparte's gull, 160
Bonneville shootingstar, 146
boring clam, 155
boxelder, 324
bracken fern, 47, 154, 200, 243, 245, 247, 275
bracket polypore fungus, 272
bracted lousewort, 187
Brandt's cormorant, 16, 198

Brewer's oak, 50
Brewer's sparrow, 298
bride's bonnet, 269
bristlecone pine, 107
brittle bladder fern, 65
brittle star, 160
broadleaf cattail, 28, 30, 260, 302, 306, 307
broadleaf lupine, 187, 224–225
broadleaf stonecrop, 49, 65
brook stickleback, 306
brook trout, 73
broom snakeweed, 134–135
brown pelican, 161, 217
brownplume wirelettuce, 287
brown trout, 73, 299
buckwheat, 39
bufflehead, 148, 232
bulbous woodland-star, 146
bull kelp, 156–157
Bullock's oriole, 149, 232, 298
bull thistle, 235, 302
bull trout, 184
bunchgrass, 143, 146, 147, 148, 297, 313
bushtit, 232
butter-and-eggs, 304
butter clam, 218
buttercup, 53
butterflies, 40, 118, 299–300

cackling geese, 262
caddisfly, 41, 73, 119
California blackberry, 247
California black oak, 53
California coffeeberry, 50
California fescue, 39
California laurel, 46
California mistmaiden, 49
California mountain kingsnake, 68
California quail, 149, 233, 298
California sea lion, 199, 263
California sister butterfly, 40
camas, 45, 85–86, 304
Camassia Natural Area, 84–91

camphor, 45–46
Canada geese, 32, 148, 262, 305
Canada goldenrod, 304
Canada thistle, 190, 297
Canadian argillite, 82
Canadian horseweed, 302
Canadian milkvetch, 146, 216
canola, 311
canvasback duck, 148, 232, 305
canyon desert-parsley, 49
canyon live oak, 49
canyon wren, 118, 298
capelin, 15
carbonization, 124
cardinal meadowhawk dragonfly, 231
Carr Inlet, 212, 213, 219
Cascade aster, 225
Cascade barberry, 46, 65, 203, 204
Cascade bilberry, 273, 274, 279
Cascade golden-mantled ground squirrel, 109–110
Cascades, 36–37, 39, 46, 62, 90, 92, 94–95, 97, 146, 222, 240, 267, 270, 284, 287
Cascades Volcano Observatory, 103
Cascadia subduction plate, 15
cascara, 243
Caspian tern, 16
Castle Rock, 326
cat's ear, 49
cattail, 33
cat-tail moss, 172
cattle, 144
Cave Creek, 55–56
cave cricket, 62
caves, 55–62
cedar elm, 79
cedar waxwing, 32, 64, 87, 117, 232
Central Washington University, 283
Chalet, 62
chalk, 113
Channeled Scablands, 290, 295, 301, 303, 319
Chateau, 55

cheatgrass, 129, 137, 287–288, 297
checkerbloom, 53
chestnut-backed chickadee, 22
chicken mushroom, 179
chickpea, 311
chickweed monkeyflower, 49
Chinook salmon, 41, 73, 73–74, 184, 210
chipmunk, 109, 110, 269
chiton, 160
chocolate lily, 47
chokecherry, 324
chukar, 149, 294, 298, 316
chum salmon, 184
cinnamon teal, 305
Cirque Rim, 182
Cirque Rim Trail, 184, 191
Civilian Conservation Corps, 92–94
Civilian Conservation Corps (CCC), 285,
    286
clams, 157, 196, 218
clam digging, 157
Clark Fork River, 80, 312
Clarno Arch, 125, 129–130
Clarno Arch Trail, 129–130
Clarno Palisades, 122–130
Clearwater River, 71
Cliff Nature Trail, 54–68
cliff swallow, 32
climate change, 47, 60, 74, 98, 144, 183,
    218, 222, 223, 227, 234, 248, 309
cloudberry, 221, 222
Coal Creek, 244
coastal cutthroat trout, 174
coastal ecosystems, 11–25, 21, 192–211
coastal gumweed, 195
coastal marten, 22
coastal storms, 170–171
coast larkspur, 39
Coast Range, 37, 62
Cobble Beach, 13
cod, 198, 199
Coeur d'Alene Tribe, 307
coho salmon, 73, 73–74, 184, 210

Columbian black-tailed deer, 21, 41, 65,
    67, 98, 185, 225, 263
Columbian ground squirrel, 305, 315
Columbian sharp-tailed grouse, 149
Columbian white-tailed deer, 138, 306, 315
Columbia Plateau, 147, 284, 287, 290,
    297, 301, 306, 324
Columbia River, 80, 283, 285, 291, 294
Columbia River Gorge, 78, 80, 94, 284,
    319
columnar basalt, 92, 95, 96
common bistort, 296
common bugloss, 147
common chokecherry, 315
common columbine, 230
common dragon moss, 49
common elderberry, 315
common goldeneye, 232
common guillemots, 15
common hawthorn, 230, 231
common loon, 198
common merganser, 232
common mullein, 291, 294, 307
common murres, 15
common nighthawk, 138
common selfheal, 53
common slider turtle, 234
common snowberry, 230, 248, 253, 302,
    315
common storksbill, 302
common vetch, 72
common wood nymph butterfly, 300
common woodrush, 53
common woolly sunflower, 147
common yarrow, 53, 137, 193–194, 308,
    311, 315, 324
common yellowthroat, 232
Communications Hill, 17
coniferous forest ecosystem, 69–76
conifers, 40, 45, 46–47, 47, 166–167, 175,
    182, 185, 200–201, 221, 274–275,
    284
Cooper's hawk, 148
coralroot orchid, 269–270

Cordilleran Ice Sheet, 205, 312
cormorant, 198
cottonwood, 284
cougar, 21, 29, 41, 138, 165, 306, 315
cous biscuitroot, 146
Cowlitz Tribe, 248
cow parsnip, 315
coyote, 21, 29, 36, 41, 138, 165, 235, 298, 306, 315
crab, 158
Crater Lake, 71, 74, 76
crayfish, 73, 173
creeping barberry, 36, 146
creeping thistle, 302
creodont, 123
crested wheatgrass, 129
cricket, 16
Crooked River, 113–121
Crooked River Caldera, 112–113
crows, 216
cryptobiotic soil crust, 297
Cuddy Mountain onion, 147
curl-leaf mountain mahogany, 117
curlycup gumweed, 315
cushion phlox, 146
Cusick's Indian paintbrush, 147
cutthroat trout, 41, 73, 299
cyanobacteria, 82

dabblers, 305
Dall's porpoise, 199
dams, 42, 73, 74, 80–81, 90, 282, 291, 312, 319, 325
dark-eyed junco, 64, 117, 197
darkling beetle, 300
darkthroat shootingstar, 146
Davidson, Elijah, 56
DDT, 216–217
Dean Creek Elk Viewing Area, 27–33
Deception Falls Nature Trail, 264–272
Deception Pass, 193, 195, 198, 199, 201
deciduous shrubs, 256–257
deciduous trees, 40, 45, 185, 212, 230, 284
deer, 47, 106, 203, 213, 249, 284

deer mice, 173
Del Norte salamander, 68
deltoid balsamroot, 39
desert cryptantha, 296
desert Indian paintbrush, 117
devil's club, 174–175, 179, 243, 270
dewberry, 221–222, 243, 247
Diamond Peak, 97–98
Diamond Peak Wilderness, 97–98
Dihedrals, 118
dike, 308
distillation, 124
divers, 305
dogs, 284
dogwood, 256
Douglas, David, 240
Douglas aster, 230
Douglas buckwheat, 146
Douglas fir, 17, 34, 42, 46–48, 62–64, 67, 71, 94, 153, 163, 165, 166–167, 168, 169, 180, 185, 195–196, 197, 200, 202, 205, 212, 222, 230, 240–241, 244, 247, 248, 255, 256, 265, 284, 286–287, 315
Douglas monkeyflower, 39
Douglas spirea, 315
Douglas squirrel, 67, 72, 173
dowitcher, 233
downy woodpecker, 232, 305
dragonfly, 231–232
driftwood, 155–156, 157, 194, 205
Dry Falls, 290–300
Dry Falls Visitor Center, 290
ducks, 23, 32, 198, 213, 232, 304, 309
Ducks Unlimited, 309
dull Oregon grape, 243–244, 247
dunes ecosystem, 18–25, 192–201
dunlin, 22
dusky grouse, 149
dwarf evening primrose, 296–297
dwarf hesperochiron, 146
dwarf phacelia, 297
dwarf ponderosa pine, 109
dwarf yellow fleabane, 146

Eagle Scouts, 212
eared grebe, 149
earthquakes, 14–15
eastern cottontail rabbit, 235, 263, 315
eastern gray squirrel, 90
eelgrass, 210
eggyolk lichen, 126–127
Eight Dollar Mountain, 65
eight-spotted skimmer dragonfly, 231
elephant, 124
elephant's head, 274
Eleven Point River, 71
elk, 27–32, 47, 106, 143, 144, 213, 249, 325
elkweed, 147
elm, 284, 288
endangered species,18, 23–25, 39, 98,
    127–128, 161, 174, 176–177, 216–217,
    296–297
Endangered Species Act, 22, 176, 177
Endangered Species List, 217
endemic species, 21, 40, 61–62, 182,
    186–187, 190, 194
Engelmann spruce, 315
English holly, 190
English ivy, 85, 91, 190
epiphytes, 48, 71, 153, 163, 172–173, 175,
    212, 242, 265
Ericameria nauseosa, 134
erratic rocks, 67, 77–83, 94, 165, 267,
    294, 295
Erratic Rock State Natural Site, 77–83
estuarine ecosystem, 158–160, 196,
    252–263
eurhynchium moss, 49
European beachgrass, 23
European searocket, 194
evening grosbeak, 111, 177
evergreen huckleberry, 20, 21, 45–46, 72,
    203, 204, 212–213, 215
everlasting pea plant, 79

falcon, 259
false azalea, 274
false Solomon's seal, 86, 87

fawn lily, 45, 86, 87
Feather River, 71
fern, 32, 64–65
ferruginous hawk, 148, 316
fescue, 39
Fiddler Mountain, 65
field sagewort, 193, 195, 198
Findley Buttes, 143
Fire and Ice Trail, 273–281
fire management, 129, 308
fires, 45, 47, 50, 137, 166, 169, 171,
    223–224, 242, 288
fireweed, 187, 274
fish hawk, 90
fishing, 161, 162, 254–255
fjord, 205
flannel bush, 287
Flett's fleabane, 187
Flett's violet, 187
flounder, 199
fool's onion, 86
"forage" fish, 15
forest edge ecosystem, 53
fork moss, 49
fossils, 124, 138–139, 141
Four Corners, 130
fragrant sumac, 324
freshwater shrimp, 119
fried egg jellyfish, 210, 211
frogs, 173, 260, 298
Frog Pond Trail, 230, 235
Fryxell, Roald, 324, 325
Fryxell's Overlook, 324–325, 326
fungi, 82, 126, 169–170, 172–173, 177, 179,
    267
fungicide, 168

gadwall, 148, 232, 305
Gairdner's penstemon, 296
garden valerian, 221
Garry oak, 40, 46, 230
geese, 23, 32, 213, 304
Geologic Time Trail, 123, 129
ghost shrimp, 210

giant green anemone, 13, 158
giant helleborine, 296
giardia, 53, 76, 268
Gifford Pinchot National Forest, 246
Ginkgo Petrified Forest State Park, 282–289
ginko, 283, 284, 288–289
glacial erratic rocks, 67, 77–83, 94, 95, 165, 267, 294, 295
glaciation, 60, 310
glacier lily, 274
glaciers, 67, 78, 96, 97, 100, 124, 165, 182–184, 205, 220, 221, 224, 225–227, 240, 255, 267, 273, 274, 281, 291
glaucous-winged gull, 160
globe penstemon, 147
Gold Beach, 71
goldencarpet buckwheat, 39
golden-crowned kinglet, 87
golden-crowned sparrow, 32, 233
golden eagle, 111, 129, 148, 275, 298
goldeneye, 305
golden hairstreak, 40
goldfinch, 298
gold-hunter's hairstreak, 40
gooseneck barnacle, 158
Grand Coulee, 291, 294
grand fir, 315
grapevine cultivation, 82
grasses, 12, 32
grasshopper, 16, 129
grassland ecosystem, 311–316
Gray Butte, 113
gray-crowned rosy-finch, 275, 298
gray fox, 36, 41, 117
gray partridge, 149
gray rabbitbrush, 106
Gray's lovage, 225
gray whale, 16–17, 161, 200
greasewood, 295
Great Basin spadefoot toad, 129
Great Basin wild rye, 117, 296
great blanketflower, 304

great blue heron, 33, 138, 149, 197, 233, 260–261, 298
great egret, 33, 298
greater sage-grouse, 117, 127–128, 288, 298
greater scaup, 232
greater yellowleg, 233
great horned owl, 22, 138, 259, 305
great spangled fritillary butterfly, 300
grebe, 149
Green Alkali Lake, 293, 294, 299
green darner dragonfly, 231
Greene's mountain ash, 72, 94
green false hellebore, 221, 247
green heron, 233
green-winged teal, 262, 305
grizzly bear, 279
Grizzly Mountain, 113
ground squirrel, 298
grouse, 127–128, 250
gulls, 160, 196, 198

habitat loss, 23, 32, 33, 90, 98, 128, 129
haircap moss, 49
hairy clematis, 146
hairy goatsbeard lichen, 185–186
hairy hermit crab, 160
hairy manzanita, 20–21
hairy vetch, 303, 304
hairy woodpecker, 305
Hall's violet, 38, 39, 53
harbor porpoise, 199
harbor seal, 14, 199, 263
hare, 110, 279
harlequin duck, 232
harvest brodiaea, 39, 86
haustoria, 136
hawthorn, 138
heartleaf arnica, 221, 247
heath, 55
Heather Meadows Visitors Center, 273
hedgehog cactus, 137
Heermann's gull, 160
hemlock, 284

Henderson's angelica, 12
Henderson's rock spirea, 187
Henry M. Jackson Visitor Center, 221
herbicides, 129, 288
heron, 22
herring, 198, 199
herring gull, 160
high-elevation forest, 221
High Ridge Trail, 191
High Ridge Trails, 182
Himalayan blackberry, 190, 217–218, 233, 247
hoary aster, 137
hoary balsamroot, 146
hoary cress, 297
hoary manzanita, 40, 41, 42
hoary marmot, 278–279
Hoh River, 163
holly, 64
Hood Canal, 203, 204, 205, 210
hooded merganser, 305
hoodoos, 135
Hood's Channel, 205
Hood's phlox, 117
hookedspur violet, 146
Hooker's Indian pink, 39
Hooker's willow, 230
horned grebe, 149, 232
horned lark, 147–148, 275
Horned Lark Trail, 143–144, 147, 148
horse, 123, 124, 284
horse chestnut, 284, 288
horse clam, 218
horsetail, 243
house finch, 233
huckleberry, 250
human remains, 325
Humboldt marten, 22
Hume Road, 311
hummingbird, 41
humpback whale, 161, 200
humus, 175
hunting, 32, 47, 223, 254, 263, 309
Hurricane Ridge, 181–191

Hurricane Ridge Road, 182, 190
hydrangea, 138

ice dam, 80–81, 90, 291, 312, 319
Ice Pond, 306–307
ice worm, 183
Idaho fescue, 39, 295, 315, 324
igneous rock, 101–102
Illinois River Valley, 65
Illinois Valley Garden Club, 34
incense cedar, 50, 53, 71
Indian hellebore, 86
Indian paintbrush, 136, 187, 225
Indian ricegrass, 295
Indigenous people, 45, 86, 117, 168, 202, 208, 223, 239, 240, 243, 250, 254–255, 307
inflated grasswidow, 146
Inland Northwest Land, 309
insects, 22, 23, 40, 42, 60–62, 67, 73, 87, 96, 110, 118, 169, 170, 196, 231–232, 233, 257
Intermountain West, 315
intertidal zone, 160, 218
invasive plants, 12, 23–24, 64, 129, 137, 147, 190, 287–288, 297, 304, 309
iron, 81, 117
Islands in Time Trail, 131–141

jay, 242
Jeffrey pine, 20, 34, 43, 50, 53
jellyfish, 210–211
John Day Fossil Beds National Monument, 123, 131–141
John Day River, 131–134
Juan de Fuca Plate, 36, 154
junegrass, 315
juniper, 196
juniper haircap moss, 269

Kalaloch Beach 4, 152–162
Kalaloch Creek, 153
Kalmiopsis Wilderness, 42
killdeer, 32, 232

Klamath Mountains, 39, 62
Klamath rockcress, 50
knobcone pine, 64
Koehler's rockcress, 39
kolks, 294

ladybug, 314
lady fern, 65, 177
lahars, 123, 284
Lahontan cutthroat trout, 299
Lake Missoula, 90, 291, 312
Lake Quinault, 165, 168, 171
Lake Washington, 228, 232, 238
lambstongue ragwort, 146
lanceleaf springbeauty, 146, 187
land snail, 67
Lapland longspur, 275
largeflower triteleia, 147
largehead clover, 146
large-leaved lupine, 230, 304
lark sparrow, 298
Lava Butte, 101, 106, 111
lava flows, 100–111
Lava Ness Monster, 106–107
lava tubes, 69, 74–75
Layser Cave, 246–251
lazuli bunting, 298
least chipmunk, 305
least sandpiper, 22, 233
"leave no trace" guidelines, 116
Lecidella, 81
Lemmon's needlegrass, 39
Lemmon's willow, 315
Lenore Canyon, 290, 291, 293, 294–295
lentil, 311
leopard lizard, 138
lesser-bladder milkvetch, 187
lesser scaup, 148, 232
lesser yellowleg, 233
Lewis mockorange, 324
lichen, 65, 71, 81–82, 87, 126–127, 137, 169,
    172, 185, 248–249, 297, 307, 314
licorice fern, 49, 172
lilac-bordered copper butterfly, 300

"lilac of the lava flow", 106
limpet, 157, 160
Limpy Creek Botanical Trail, 44–53
lion's mane jellyfish, 211
lithification, 80
lithosols, 295, 296
littleneck clam, 218
little willow flycatcher, 68
liverwort, 172
lobaria lichen, 248
locoweed, 296
lodgepole pine, 71, 185, 200, 201, 315
loess, 294, 295, 313
loggerhead shrike, 298, 316
logging industry, 73, 177, 179, 200
long-billed curlew, 22, 316
longleaf phlox, 296
long-tailed weasel, 109, 235, 263, 306
loon, 198
Lorquin's admiral butterfly, 300
low larkspur, 296
low pussytoes, 146
lungwort, 49
lupine, 224–225, 256
Lyons Ferry State Park, 319

madwort, 297
magnolia, 123
Magnuson Park Wetlands, 228–238
maidenhair fern, 65, 177
mallard, 32, 232, 262, 305
Manila clam, 218
mantle rock, 37
manzanita, 20–21, 39, 39–40, 49
maple, 138, 173, 284, 286–287
map lichen, 94, 95
marbled murrelet, 161, 165, 176–177, 197
mariposa lily, 53, 296
Marmes Man, 325
Marmes Rockshelter, 324, 325
marmot, 110
marten, 22
martin, 165
Mass, Cliff, 171

mayflies, 41, 73, 119
McAllister Creek, 263
McDonald's rockcress, 39
McNulty, Tim, 172
meadow deathcamas, 147
meadow hawkweed, 147
medicinal plants, 46, 117, 127, 174–175, 201, 241, 244–245, 314–315
Medusahead rye, 137
Menzies' penstemon, 225
Merriam's ground squirrel, 118
mew gull, 160
mice, 259, 298
Middle Fork Willamette River, 98
Middle Pine Lake, 302, 306, 307
mining, 42–43
mink, 165, 263
Missoula Floods, 78, 80, 82, 90, 312–313, 318, 319
Missouri goldenrod, 314, 315
mixed forest ecosystem, 45–48
mock orange, 117, 296
monarch butterfly, 118
moon jellyfish, 211
Moores Ridge, 42
moose, 28, 306
mormon metalmark butterfly, 299
morning glory, 117
Morning Glory Wall, 116
moss, 65, 67, 96, 169, 172–173, 179, 297
moth mullein, 39
Mount Adams, 250
mountain bluebird, 275
mountain chickadee, 111
mountain cottontail, 118
mountain goat, 275–278
mountain hemlock, 185, 222, 274–275
mountain quail, 41, 149
mountain sheep, 250
mountain spray, 106
Mount Baker, 273, 274–275, 279
Mount Elijah, 56, 60
Mount Herman, 274
Mount Hood, 79, 90, 94

Mount Mazama, 74
Mount Olympus, 165
Mount Rainier, 219, 220, 221, 222, 223, 225, 255
Mount Rainier National Park, 221, 224, 227, 246
Mount Saint Helens, 248
Mount Shuksan, 276–277, 281
mourning cloak butterfly, 300
mouse-deer, 138
Muir, John, 271
mulberry, 138
mule deer, 117, 129, 138, 144, 288, 298, 315
Multnomah Falls, 94
Munro's globemallow, 136
muskrat, 33, 235, 298, 315
mussels, 158, 196
mute swan, 138
mycorrhizal fungi, 173
myrtle, 46
Myrtle Falls, 221

naked broomrape, 39
naked buckwheat, 39
narrowleaf mock goldenweed, 117
narrowleaf willow, 324
narrow-sepaled phacelia, 187
NASA, 102
National Cancer Institute, 201
National Oceanic and Atmospheric Administration (NOAA), 14, 228
National Register of Historic Places, 13
National Weather Service, 14
Natural Bridge Campground, 69
The Nature Conservancy (TNC), 85, 91, 143–144, 148
needle-and-thread grass, 295
netleaf hackberry, 134, 294, 324
Newberry National Volcanic Monument, 100–111
Newberry Volcano, 101, 103, 111
nickel, 43
nimravid, 138
nineleaf biscuitroot, 146, 304

Nisqually Estuary Boardwalk Trail, 263
Nisqually Estuary Trail, 259–260
Nisqually Glacier, 220
Nisqually Glacier Overlook, 225–227
Nisqually Reach, 263
Nisqually River, 253, 255
Nisqually Tribe 254–255
Nisqually Vista Trail, 220–227
nitrogen, 256–257
noble fir, 64
nodding arnica, 39
Nootka rose, 117, 195, 230, 259, 260
Norm Dicks Visitor Center, 255
North American tectonic plate, 154
northern alligator lizard, 234
northern flicker, 22, 118, 196, 232, 305
northern flying squirrel, 67, 72, 165, 173
northern goshawk, 68, 148
northern harrier, 16, 22, 261–262, 305, 316
northern leopard frog, 138
northern Pacific rattlesnake, 42, 298, 317
northern pintail, 148, 262, 305
northern pocket gopher, 138
northern pygmy owl, 305
northern shoveler, 148, 305
northern spotted owl, 67, 73, 177
northwestern garter snake, 234
Northwest Forest Plan, 177
nothern harrier, 148

oak, 40, 284
Obama, Barack, 43, 255
obsidian, 102, 251
ocean spray, 72, 200, 247
ochre sea star, 13, 158–160
O.H. Hinsdale Interpretive Center, 28
Okanogan Valley, 291
old-growth forest, 60, 67, 73, 165–166,
    168, 171, 173, 176–179, 265
old man's beard lichen, 48, 172, 200,
    201, 248
old man's whiskers, 146
Oldsville Road, 78
olive scud, 119

olive-sided flycatcher, 22, 68
Olympia oyster, 205–210, 218
Olympic aster, 187
Olympic gull, 196
Olympic marmot, 186
Olympic Mountain groundsel, 187
Olympic Mountain synthyris, 187
Olympic National Forest, 163
Olympic National Park, 182, 184
Olympic Peninsula, 153, 155, 163, 168, 172,
    182, 186, 191
Olys, 205–210
orange-crowned warbler, 197
orca, 161, 200
orchard mason bee, 118
Oregon
    Camassia Natural Area, 84–91
    Clarno Palisades, 122–130
    Cliff Nature Trail, 54–68
    Dean Creek Elk Viewing Area, 27–33
    Erratic Rock State Natural Site, 77–83
    Limpy Creek Botanical Trail, 44–53
    Oregon Caves National Monument and
        Preserve, 54–68
    Rimrock Trail, 112–121
    Rogue River Natural Bridge, 69–76
    Rough and Ready Botanical Wayside,
        34–43
    Salt Creek Falls, 92–99
    Tahkenitch Dunes, 18–25
    Trail of the Molten Land, 100–111
    Yaquina Head Outstanding Natural
        Area, 10–17
Oregon ash, 85, 213
Oregon boxleaf, 72
Oregon Caves National Monument and
    Preserve, 54–68
Oregon crabapple, 213
Oregon Department of Fish and Wildlife,
    27
Oregon Dunes National Recreation Area,
    18
Oregon grape, 64, 117
oregon lungwort, 172

Oregon myrtle, 46
Oregon oxalis, 72, 177
Oregon spikemoss, 172
Oregon Trail, 143
Oregon white oak, 40, 46–47, 50, 87, 230
oreodont, 138
osprey, 22, 32, 73, 90, 91, 148, 165, 176
oval-leaf blueberry, 269
overturned turbidites, 154
oxeye daisy, 230
oyster, 196, 205–210

Pacific blackberry, 247, 248
Pacific chorus frog, 87, 233–234
Pacific dogwood, 64, 71, 94, 247
Pacific fisher, 73
Pacific Flyway, 15, 22, 197, 253
Pacific geoduck, 218
Pacific loon, 198
Pacific madrone, 47–48, 54, 55, 64, 71, 87,
    200, 203–204, 205, 216
Pacific ninebark, 230, 257
Pacific Northwest Seismic Network, 103
Pacific oyster, 205–208, 218
Pacific poison oak, 313, 315
Pacific razor clam, 157
Pacific reedgrass, 28, 30, 153
Pacific rhododendron, 18, 72, 101
Pacific silver fir, 222
Pacific tree frog, 233–234
Pacific wax myrtle, 12
Pacific yew, 185, 200–201
padded realm, 172
Painted Hills Unit, 135
painted ladies, 118, 300
pallid-winged grasshopper, 109
palm, 123
Palouse Falls, 317–326
Palouse thistle, 315
Palus Tribe, 307
Panamanian land bridge, 124
paper birch, 238
Parry's catchfly, 225
parsley fern, 65

parsnip-flower buckwheat, 146
pea, 138
Peabody, Betsy, 209
pearly pussytoes, 147
Pearsoll Peak, 65
pelagic cormorant, 16
pemmican, 106
Penrose Point, 218, 219
Penrose State Park, 212–219
peregrine falcon, 16, 216–217, 262, 298,
    305
pesticides, 129
petrified logs, 283–289
piddock clam, 155, 158
pied-billed grebe, 149, 232, 252, 262
pigeon guillemot, 16, 198
pika, 110, 111, 278, 279
pileated woodpecker, 41–42, 67, 165, 305
Pine Creek, 144, 147, 148
pine grosbeak, 275
Pine Lakes Loop Trail, 301–309
pinemat manzanita, 94
pine siskin, 22
pink alumroot, 315, 324
pink honeysuckle, 203, 204
pink mountain-heather, 274
pink salmon, 184
Piper's bellflower, 187
pitch, 169, 241
plover, 23–25
poet's narcissus, 304
poison ivy, 315
poison oak, 85, 86
polar cod, 15
pollinators, 40–41, 134, 244, 256, 257,
    270, 301, 304
ponderosa pine, 48, 49, 53, 64, 71,
    106–109, 117, 118, 307, 315
porcupine, 315
porcupine sedge, 296
Port Orford cedar, 20, 55, 64
Powell Butte, 113
prairie clover, 137
prairie falcon, 298

prairie goldenrod, 324
prairie star, 304
prescribed burns, 47
prickleback, 160
prickly lettuce, 287
Prineville Reservoir, 113
Priority Species, 306
pronghorn antelope, 129, 138
Propertius duskywing, 40
pseudoscorpion, 62
Ptarmigan Ridge, 275
puffin, 15
Puget Sound, 205, 212, 219, 253, 254, 255, 263
Puget Sound gumweed, 194
pumpkinseed, 306
purple and white Chinese houses, 39
purple loosestrife, 297
purple martin, 32
purple milkvetch, 296
purple sage, 137
purple sea urchin, 13
pygmy nuthatch, 111
pygmy rabbit, 129, 288

quail, 149
quaking aspen, 86, 89, 144, 303, 306, 315
Quarry Cove, 11–12
Queen Anne's lace, 79, 230–231
Queets River, 163
Quinault Loop Trail, 180
Quinault Rain Forest Nature Trail, 163–180
Quinault River, 163, 165
Quinault River Valley, 166–167
Quinault Valley glacier, 165

rabbit, 110, 213, 250, 259, 279, 298, 316
raccoon, 21, 117, 160, 165, 174, 235, 259, 269, 315
rainbow trout, 73, 299
raptors, 32, 118–119, 148, 165, 257–259, 261–262, 305–306, 316
rare plants, 39, 149

rat-tail fescue, 39
rattlesnake, 121, 123, 131
raven, 216
red alder, 53, 213, 230, 241–242, 247, 265
red-backed vole, 165, 173
red-belted polypore, 179
red-breasted merganser, 198
red-breasted nuthatch, 111
red crossbill, 22, 111, 197
red elderberry, 154
red fescue, 21, 195
red-flowering currant, 200
redhead duck, 148, 232, 305
red huckleberry, 247
Red Mountain, 42
red-naped sapsucker, 305
red-necked grebe, 232
red-necked phalaropes, 305
red-osier dogwood, 230, 256, 296, 304
red rock crab, 160
red rock rainforest, 36
redside shiner, 306
red-tailed hawk, 16, 111, 138, 148, 262, 305, 316
redtail surfperch, 161, 162
red-throated loon, 198, 199
red tree vole, 72
red-winged blackbird, 32–33, 149, 232, 298
redwood, 130
Redwood Highway, 34
reed canary grass, 306
Reflection Lakes, 221
reptiles, 233, 234
rhinoceros, 138
rhododendron, 94
rhodora, 247
rigid sagebrush, 295
Rimrock Trail, 112–121
ring-necked duck, 148, 305
ring-necked pheasant, 149
Rio Grande River, 71
Riparian Forest Overlook, 255
river otter, 73, 165, 173–174, 235, 263, 306

rock climbing, 113, 116
rockfish, 199
rock outcrop ecosystem, 48–49
rockweed, 156
rock wren, 111, 316
Rocky Mountain elk, 28, 109, 117, 129, 138, 298, 306
Rocky Mountain juniper, 125, 126
rodents, 33, 40, 72–73, 109–110, 138, 148, 173, 213, 233, 279, 316, 323
Rogue River, 69–76
Rogue River Natural Bridge, 69–76
Rogue River–Siskiyou National Forest, 45
Roosevelt, Franklin, 285
Roosevelt elk, 27–32, 41, 98, 144, 165, 225, 270
Rope-de-Dope Trail, 121
rosy plectritis, 85, 86
Roth forest snail, 67
Rough and Ready Botanical Wayside, 34–43
Rough and Ready Creek, 34, 36
rough-legged hawk, 148
roundleaf alumroot, 147
round-leaved violet, 274
rubber rabbitbrush, 106, 134
ruby-crowned kinglet, 87
ruddy duck, 148
ruffed grouse, 149, 165
rufous hummingbird, 138, 197
rush pussytoes, 147
Russian knapweed, 137, 297

saber-toothed cat, 284
sagebrush, 117, 121, 123, 124–125, 129
sagebrush buttercup, 146, 304
sagebrush checkerspot butterfly, 300
sagebrush lizard, 129, 138, 298
sagebrush mariposa lily, 117
sagebrush stickseed, 296
sage-steppe ecosystem, 124–130
sage thrasher, 129, 298
Saint Croix River, 71

salal, 12, 17, 72, 153, 177, 200, 202, 213, 243, 247
Salal Hill, 16, 17
salamander, 174
salmon, 73, 73–74, 174, 184, 199, 250, 255, 262
salmonberry, 177, 203, 242–243, 270
Salmon River, 71
Salt Creek Canyon, 92, 96
Salt Creek Falls, 92–99
Salt Creek Sno-Park, 92
saltwater ecosystem, 160
Sandberg bluegrass, 295, 315
sandeel, 15
sanderling, 22
sandhill crane, 137, 138
sand lance, 15
Sand Point, 228–238
sandstone, 154–155, 156, 158
sand verbena, 21, 195
Saskatoon serviceberry, 287, 304, 315, 324
savanna ecosystem, 87–90, 124, 143
Savannah sparrow, 197, 316
saxifrage, 296
saxitoxin, 157
scarlet gilia, 147
Scotch broom, 23
scythe-leaf onion, 39
seagull, 156, 160
Seal Rock Campground, 202
sea otter, 161
seashore bluegrass, 21
sea snail, 160
sea stacks, 158
sea star, 158–160
Sea Star Wasting Syndrome, 160
Seats Dam, 42
sedges, 12
seep monkeyflower, 324
semitropical rain forest ecosystem, 123
serpentine ecosystem, 49–53
serpentine fern, 65
serpentine soils, 37
shaggy fleabane, 146

shale, 80, 154
sharp-shinned hawk, 148
sharp-tailed grouse, 316
Shasta red fir, 71
Sheep Rock Unit, 131–141
shellfish harvesting, 157
shellfish poisoning, 157
Sheridan's green hairstreak butterfly, 300
shield volcano, 97
shooting star, 53, 296
shorebirds, 15–16, 18, 23–25, 193, 198
shore pine, 12, 20
shortbeaked agoseris, 225
short-eared owl, 316
short-lobe Indian paintbrush, 53
showy milkweed, 304
showy phlox, 39
showy sedge, 187
shrimp, 119, 198, 210
shrub steppe ecosystem, 324
sickle-top lousewort, 187–190
sideoats grama, 315, 324
silica, 37, 49, 79, 80, 81, 102, 268, 285
silver bur ragweed, 194
silver fir, 94, 185
silverweed cinquefoil, 12
Siskiyou chipmunk, 40
Siskiyou iris, 39
Siskiyou manzanita, 40
Siskiyou mat, 39, 53
Siskiyou Range, 34, 39, 40, 42, 45, 56,
        62, 65
Sitka mountain ash, 222, 275
Sitka spruce, 17, 20, 153, 165, 167–168,
        185, 193, 198, 200, 222, 229, 230,
        247, 267
Sitka valerian, 274
Sitka willow, 12
Siuslaw hairy necked tiger beetle, 21, 22
skunk cabbage, 21, 153–154, 243,
        270–271
sledding, 20
slender bog orchid, 274
slender cryptantha, 296

slough sedge, 21
small fescue, 39
small-flowered bulrush, 296
small-flowered paintbrush, 274
smallflower melic, 12
Smith Rock, 112–116, 119–121
smooth cliffbrake, 297
smooth sumac, 315
snags, 170–171
snail, 160, 233
Snake River, 319
sneaker waves, 11, 25
Snoopy, 119, 120
Snoqualmie Casino, 240
Snoqualmie Tribe, 240
Snoqualmie Tribe Environmental and
        Natural Resources Department,
        240–244
snow buckwheat, 295, 299
snow geese, 148
snow queen, 72
snowshoeing, 221
sockeye salmon, 184
softshell clam, 218
song sparrow, 16, 232
sooty grouse, 36
sora rail, 149
South Yamhill River, 78
Spanish moss, 172
speckled dace, 306
speleothems, 56
spiders, 87, 118, 138, 233
spiny hopsage, 295
spiny phlox, 146
Spokan(e) Tribe, 307
spotted knapweed, 137
spotted towhee, 87, 117, 196, 232
sprat, 15
spreading wood fern, 265, 269
spring azure butterfly, 300
springboard, 179
spring queens, 45
springtail, 62
spruce, 284, 288

Squaw Falls, 318–319
Squaw Peak, 65
squirrel, 22, 110, 213, 216, 259, 269, 278–279
stalactites, 56
stalagmites, 56
steelhead salmon, 184
steelhead trout, 41, 210
Steller sea lion, 199
Steller's jay, 64, 216
Steptoe, Edward, 314
Steptoe Butte, 310–316
stereo olfaction, 29
Stevens, Isaac, 254
sticky cinquefoil, 147
sticky geranium, 304
sticky whiteleaf manzanita, 40
stinging nettles, 244–245
St. John's wort, 302
stonefly, 73
study plots, 91
sub-alpine fir, 94, 185, 221–224, 247
sub-alpine meadow, 220, 221–225
subtropical forest, 283
sugar pine, 64
Suksdorf's monkeyflower, 296
Suksdorf's woodsorrel, 72
sulfur buckwheat, 30, 39, 106, 117
sulfur cinquefoil, 147
summer run chum salmon, 210
sunburst lichen, 81
sunflower mule-ears, 146
Sun Lakes, 290
Sunrise Point, 191
surfbird, 16
Swainson's hawk, 148, 316
Swainson's thrush, 177, 243
swan, 304, 305
sweetbriar rose, 315
sweetgum, 284, 288
switchgrass, 304
sword fern, 64, 156
sycamore, 284

Table Mountain, 274
Taft, William Howard, 56
Tahkenitch Campground, 20
Tahkenitch Dunes, 18–25
tailcup lupine, 136
tailed frog, 68
tall fescue, 39
tanoak, 71
taxol, 201
tectonic uplift, 57–60
temperate grassland ecosystem, 142–149
temperate rain forest ecosystem, 17, 18, 20, 73, 156, 161, 163–180, 202, 216, 265
Terminal Lake, 281
ternate buckwheat, 39
terrestrial ecosystem, 160
Thayer's gull, 160
thimbleberry, 94, 177, 270
thinleaf alder, 296
thinleaf huckleberry, 221, 222, 247, 274, 279
threadleaf fleabane, 296
three-tip sagebrush, 117, 124–125, 134, 287, 295, 315
thrush, 165, 198
Tideland Ecology Trail, 202–211
tiger trout, 299
Tisch's saxifrage, 187
toadflax, 137
tobacco root, 147
Tolmie's mariposa lily, 39
Tolmie's saxifrage, 274
Tolm's onion, 147
tortoise, 124
Touch of Nature Interpretive Trail, 212–219
Townsend bigeared bat, 61
Townsend's chipmunk, 67, 72, 173
Traditional Knowledge Trail, 239–245
Trail of Fossils, 129
Trail of the Molten Land, 100–111
Trail of the Whispering Pines, 101
Trailside Museum, 285, 286
Trapeliaceae, 82

Treaty of Medicine Creek, 254–255
tree rings, 169
Trees of Stone Interpretive Trail, 283–287
tree swallow, 232
troglobite, 62
trout, 73, 119, 174, 299
truffles, 173
trumpeter swan, 138, 148, 197, 305
tsunamis, 14–15
tube worm, 160
tufted hairgrass, 21
tumbleweed, 319, 324
tundra swan, 148, 305
turkey vulture, 111, 148
Turnbull National Wildlife Refuge, 301–309
turtle, 173
Twin Barns Loop, 255, 259
twinberry honeysuckle, 230
twistedstalk, 269
Tye River, 265, 267, 271

ultramafic, 37, 49
Umatilla Rock, 290, 293, 294, 296
umbellulone, 46
ungulates, 144–146, 190
University of Washington, 103
upland sandpiper, 316
Upper Bagley Lake, 279, 280
urchin, 158, 160
U.S. Bureau of Land Management, 11, 27, 34, 42
U.S. Congress, 71
U.S. Fish and Wildlife Service, 23, 128
U.S. Forest Service, 42, 49, 74, 97, 100, 166, 248, 267
U.S. Geological Survey, 103
U.S. Highway 2, 265
U.S. Highway 38, 27, 28
U.S. Highway 58, 92, 97
U.S. Highway 97, 100
U.S. Highway 101, 20, 182, 202
U.S. Highway 199, 34
U.S. National Park Service, 54, 61, 171, 183, 225

Vancouver, George, 205
vanillaleaf, 67, 221, 243, 247
Vantage Road, 283
Vaux's swift, 275
velvetleaf huckleberry, 314, 315
vesper sparrow, 316
vine maple, 53, 71, 85, 94, 153, 173, 175, 242, 247
violet-green swallow, 16, 232
Virginia opossum, 235
Virginia strawberry, 146
viticulture, 82
volcanic ecosystem, 100–111
volcanism, 95–96, 113, 123–124, 265, 284, 312, 323
volcanoes, 36, 57, 97, 101, 103, 113, 123, 274
vole, 22, 259, 298
Vulcan Peak, 42

Waldo rockcress, 39, 50
Wallowa Mountains, 143, 144
Wallowa onion, 146
walnut, 284
Wanapum Dam, 282
wandering tattler, 161
warbler, 23
Washington
    Billy Frank Jr. Nisqually National Wildlife Refuge, 252–263
    Deception Falls Nature Trail, 264–272
    Dry Falls, 290–300
    Fire and Ice Trail, 273–281
    Ginkgo Petrified Forest State Park, 282–289
    Hurricane Ridge, 181–191
    Kalaloch Beach 4, 152–162
    Layser Cave, 246–251
    Magnuson Park Wetlands, 228–238
    Nisqually Vista Trail, 220–227
    Palouse Falls, 317–326
    Pine Lakes Loop Trail, 301–309
    Quinault Rain Forest Nature Trail, 163–180

Washington (continued)
    Steptoe Butte, 310–316
    Tideland Ecology Trail, 202–211
    Touch of Nature Interpretive Trail,
       212–219
    Traditional Knowledge Trail, 239–245
    West Beach Sand Dunes, 192–201
Washington Department of Fish and
    Wildlife, 218
Washington State Normal School, 283
Washington State Route 17, 291
Washington State Route 261, 318
Washington State University, 325
waterfalls, 53, 73, 92–99, 123, 130, 175,
    179, 264–272, 290–300, 317–326
waterfowl, 148, 232, 253, 262, 263, 302,
    304–305
water lily, 33
wax currant, 106
weasel, 22
wedgeleaf violet, 53
welded tuff, 113
West Beach Sand Dunes, 192–201
western azalea, 53
western blue flag, 304
western columbine, 72
western crabapple, 230
western fence lizard, 121
western goldenrod, 137
western gray squirrel, 87, 90, 263
western grebe, 16, 232
western gull, 16, 160
western hemlock, 71, 94, 153, 155, 165,
    166, 167–168, 179, 185, 213, 247,
    267, 315
western honey bee, 257
western juniper, 117, 118, 131, 134, 324
western larch, 315
western maidenhair fern, 72
western meadowlark, 16, 316
western pearly everlasting, 221, 247
western pine elfin butterfly, 300
western pondhawk dragonfly, 231

western red cedar, 17, 165, 167–168, 179,
    185, 204, 212, 213–216, 241–242,
    248, 256, 267, 315
western snowberry, 195
western snowy plover, 23–25
western starflower, 72, 243
western stoneseed, 147
western sword fern, 17, 72, 154, 169, 177,
    213, 243, 245, 247
western tanager, 177
western toad, 138
western trillium, 65, 86, 213, 243, 269
western white clematis, 324
western white pine, 64, 185
whale, 161, 200
wheat, 311, 312, 313
white-crown sparrow, 16
white cup lichen, 49
white fir, 64, 71, 247
white flower rein orchid, 72, 73
white-headed woodpecker, 305
white-nose syndrome, 61
white pelican, 305
white pine, 267
white pine blister rust, 267
white rhododendron, 187
white-stemmed frasera, 117
white-tailed ptarmigan, 275
white-throated swift, 118, 294
wholeleaf saxifrage, 146
wicker buckwheat, 39
Wild and Scenic Rivers Act, 71
wild buckwheat, 39, 287
wildflower blooms, 34, 45, 100, 117, 131,
    136–137, 143, 146, 182, 186–187, 221,
    224–225, 230–231, 269–270, 274,
    296, 304
wild ginger, 243
wild lily-of-the-valley, 243
wild onion, 53
wild rose, 126
wild turkey, 149
Willaby Creek, 165, 173, 175–176

Willamette National Forest, 98
Willamette Pass, 92, 97, 98
Willamette River, 90
Willamette Valley, 78–79, 81, 82, 83, 85, 86
willow flycatcher, 232
Wilson's snipe, 149
Winslow Pool, 301
winterfat, 287, 295
winter salmon, 263
winter wren, 165
wolf eel, 160
Wolf River, 71
wood duck, 148, 262, 305
wood forget-me-nots, 230
woodland strawberry, 146
woodpecker, 22, 242, 305
wood sage, 297
Woods' rose, 296, 302
woolly sedge, 296
wrentit, 22

Xanthoria elegans, 81
xeric plants, 103–106

Yakama Tribe, 248, 307
Yaquina Bay Lighthouse, 11, 12–13
Yaquina Head Outstanding Natural Area, 10–17
yellowbell, 136, 146
yellow-bellied marmot, 118, 138, 297, 323
yellow-breasted chat, 298
yellow chanterelle, 173
yellow daisy, 106
yellow evening-primrose, 146
yellow fritillary, 136, 304
yellow-headed blackbird, 298
yellow iris, 53, 230
yellow-pine chipmunk, 109, 110, 305
yellow rabbitbrush, 120, 121, 295, 296, 299, 324
yellow-rumped warbler, 196–197
yellow salsify, 302
yellow willow, 296

Zumwalt-Buckhorn Road, 143
Zumwalt Prairie Preserve, 142–149

RODDY SCHEER is a journalist, author, and photographer specializing in environmental issues, the outdoors, and travel. He has penned guidebooks to waterfalls in Washington and hikes in Southern California as well as hundreds of travel articles for magazines including *Northwest Travel, E-The Environmental Magazine, Seattle Magazine,* and others. He also produces the weekly environmental Q & A column EarthTalk, which is syndicated to more than 1000 different media outlets across North America. The three-time Society of Professional Journalists "Excellence in Journalism" winner lives in Seattle with his wife and two children.